THE JOB SEARCH NAVIGATOR

An Expert's Guide to Getting Hired, Surviving Layoffs, and Building Your Career

MATT DURFEE

AN AGATE IMPRINT

CHICAGO

Library of Congress Cataloging-in-Publication Data

Durfee, Matt.
The job search navigator : an expert's guide to getting hired, surviving layoffs, and building your career / Matt Durfee.
     pages cm
Includes index.
ISBN 978-1-57284-185-7 (pbk.) -- ISBN 1-57284-185-0 (pbk.) --
ISBN 978-1-57284-768-2 (ebook) -- ISBN 1-57284-768-9 (ebook)
1. Job hunting. 2. Career changes. 3. Career development. I. Title.
HF5382.7.D87 2016
650.14--dc23
                    2015033427

10 9 8 7 6 5 4 3 2 1   16 17 18 19 20

B2 is an imprint of Agate Publishing. Agate books are available in bulk at discount prices.
agatepublishing.com

PRAISE FOR MATT DURFEE
AND *THE JOB SEARCH NAVIGATOR*

"Matt's expertise in this space is unmatched. We live in a world where constant reinvention is the rule and *The Job Search Navigator* is essential reading for those who want to take control of their career trajectory."

> —**Scott Westerman**, executive director & associate vice president for alumni relations, Michigan State University

"What the world doesn't need is another academic, theoretical, and philosophical treatise on the job market—and that is exactly what *The Job Search Navigator* is not. Well-told personal stories, an authoritative and clear voice, and tested tactics make this book refreshing and tremendously useful. Eventually, you'll want to move up or you'll need to move on and *The Job Search Navigator* is both chart and compass for the journey."

> —**Bob Allen**, chief storytelling officer, IDEAS Media & Experience Design

"In *The Job Search Navigator*, Matt Durfee has succeeded mightily in creating a compelling, educational, and entertaining work that draws from his own deep experience on both sides of the employment desk. You will be both inspired and informed by this read."

> —**Thomas D. Christopoul**, former chairman of Jackson Hewitt Tax Service, partner and cofounder of 54 Madison Partners

"Unsurprisingly, Matt Durfee's book is absolutely spot on. He is a well-trained professional with real experiences on transition. No one is more capable of helping people reconnect. Read the book and this comes through clearly. His passion and knowledge of how to help people reconnect or find the next opportunity is unmatched. He is 'The Man' when it comes to career transitions."

> —**Dave Loeser**, sr. vice president of worldwide human resources, unisys

"Finding a job is hard to do . . . finding the right job even harder. *The Job Search Navigator* is the guide job seekers of all types can use to navigate the ever-changing employment process. Matt has provided a business plan with examples that are critical, on point, and actionable. His insights are refreshingly honest, deeply personal, and provide easy-to-follow steps that will make anyone's search more successful."

> —**Rick Walsh**, chairman & CEO, The Knob Hill Companies, chair emeritus at University of Central Florida

"This book rocks! Comprehensive, relevant, emotional, honest—the perfect set list for getting your career back to rock icon status."

> —**Jim Knight**, author of *Culture That Rocks: How to Revolutionize Your Company's Culture*

"A no-holds-barred view of career management in a turbulent world. *The Job Search Navigator* provides a reality-based perspective that should be of value to all who read and follow its insights."

> —**Len Schlesinger**, president emeritus at Babson College, Baker Foundation professor, Harvard Business School

"Matt Durfee's model for finding a new job provides just what job seekers need to move through each phase of the human change process. By providing expert insights, he makes it possible to get excited about and focused on future opportunities and to let go of the emotional constraints that confront change."

> —**Tim Galusha**, vice president of human resources, Matrix Absence Management

*To my daughter, Jacqueline Durfee, whom I love to the moon and back,
and to my mother and father, Midge and Jerry Durfee,
whom I love to heaven and back.*

CONTENTS

FOREWORD

William N. Cooke, PhD

*PROFESSOR AND DIRECTOR OF MICHIGAN STATE UNIVERSITY'S
SCHOOL OF HUMAN RESOURCES AND LABOR RELATIONS*

Today's global marketplace continues to become ever more competitive, unpredictable, and unforgiving. In this new economic world order, companies are struggling earnestly to sustain competitiveness by adapting in a variety of ways. These adaptations include adjusting to the digital age, pressing for greater efficiencies and productivity, eliminating unprofitable products and services, downsizing and closing operations, investing and outsourcing abroad, brokering mergers and acquisitions, dumping CEOs, and otherwise restructuring and shedding employees. Losing the competitive edge, even briefly, is too costly to company fortunes—costly, in particular, to hardworking and talented people spread throughout organizations, including in the treasured C-suites.

Even during periods of full employment, this volatility and the consequent displacement of employees has become the way of life in the marketplace. Indeed, even high performers can no longer expect lifetime employment within a single enterprise. The best personal strategy, therefore, is to prepare oneself to deal with the disruption inherent in the new economic order and to take advantage of opportunities hidden within it.

Do you have a plan for achieving your own long-term career aspirations in an unpredictable world? If you learn tomorrow or next year that you have been displaced, do you have an effective career transition plan that will take full advantage of the talents and skills you have to offer? Most of us do not, but we all need one if we hope to turn disruptions in our careers—and in the lives of our families—into opportunities for growth.

In *The Job Search Navigator*, Matt Durfee, a seasoned and expert navigator of these uncertain waters, shows us the way. Within its pages, you will find much more than a few standard guidelines on how to search for job opportunities, write a resume, conduct interviews, and negotiate job offers. These topics are addressed with detailed analysis, sage advice, and rare insight from Durfee's vast experiences as a job candidate, recruiter, and career-transition coach. He challenges readers to think strategically about their career aspirations and guides them to develop their own long-term career plans that will prepare them to continue pursuing these aspirations even in the wake of displacement.

In Chapter 1, Durfee addresses the emotional turmoil and stress that accompany an unexpected discharge and shares firsthand accounts of these experiences. He discusses the importance of understanding and accepting unanticipated change and of developing a healthy attitude toward it. This mindset can help readers to better their current career paths or pursue new ones, as well as achieve personal growth and happiness.

In Chapter 2, Durfee explains that a moment of transition is an especially good time to take a fresh look inward. At this critical juncture, the fundamental question is whether to stay on your current career path or find a new path that aligns better with your personal aspirations. To answer this all-important question, Durfee walks us through how to thoroughly research options and objectively assess our own skills and interests. He warns against the short-term impulse to simply secure a steady paycheck. In this chapter and throughout the book, testimonials from executives, recruiters, and associates bridge the gap between theory and reality.

In Chapter 3, Durfee asserts that the best resume wins. A resume is a powerful marketing tool that highlights your expertise, skills, and accomplishments. When employers winnow down a heap of resumes at breakneck speed, the ability to craft an excellent resume and cover letter is crucial if you want to be noticed. Durfee's template and nuanced advice will teach you how a well-constructed resume can open doors.

Getting your resume in the right hands is also essential to furthering your candidacy. This takes enlisting the support of others by tapping into your network of associates and friends. In Chapters 4 and 5, Durfee explains how to build a vast network, how to access the myriad avenues employers utilize to recruit talent, and how to maximize employers' interest in you as a prospective candidate.

Having landed an interview, how do you then increase the likelihood of getting the job offer? This is where discipline, practice, and commitment carry you through a challenging and often ambiguous process. Chapter 6 walks you through preparing and rehearsing for the upcoming interview. It teaches you how to answer hypothetical questions, which test your ability to think on your feet, as well as behavioral-based questions, which require you to discuss your past experiences in a way that provides evidence of the skills and competencies you possess. This chapter also discusses what interviewers are typically looking for so that you will be ready to communicate your qualifications and attributes in the clearest way possible.

Chapter 7 covers the interview itself: how to sell your technical and personal fit for the job, present yourself professionally, and stay positive and focused throughout what can be an exhausting process. Durfee also shares his secrets for responding to questions about compensation, appropriately inquiring about the job and work culture, and asking the right questions about the status of your candidacy and next steps in the selection process.

Having successfully navigated your way through the interview with Durfee's advice, you might soon be confronted with the decision to accept, reject, or negotiate an offer of employment. Since negotiations can be viewed as the art of the possible, in Chapter 8, Durfee provides behind-the-curtain insights into how to tactfully

sway hiring managers toward enhancing the salary, benefits, bonuses, and non-financial perks of an initial job offer.

Taking into account the broader picture of career transitions,
your job search isn't over when you are hired. Instead, you must
then take ownership of your own development as a new employee.
This requires making the most of your onboarding experience,
which Durfee lays out plainly in Chapter 9 in four steps: diagnose,
design, develop, and deliver. By laying out and adhering to your onboarding plan, you will be able to achieve the results you promised
in your job interview. Failure to do so may result in having to look
for another job sooner than you thought possible. In Chapter 10,
Durfee underscores the importance, in an increasingly turbulent
job market, of focusing on long-term aspirations and preparations
for a future that will likely involve more career transitions.

The Job Search Navigator by Matt Durfee is one of those rare
books we all need to read. It will change how you look at your career
and personal life, get you through any immediate career transition
you may be facing, and help you develop a long-term strategy for
career success and personal growth. It is an enjoyable read full of
real-life experiences and down-to-earth advice that no other author
has so effectively incorporated before.

THE RELUCTANT EXPERT

"If you're going through hell, keep going."
Sir Winston Churchill (1874–1965)
British Prime Minister

I never intended to be an expert in the job search process, yet here I am.

As with a lot of people who have acquired specialized skills in one field or another, I have found the process of developing an expertise isn't always easy or enjoyable. In fact, it can be downright maddening and, at times, terribly discouraging. Indeed, much of what I know is not just derived from recruiting talent or having myself landed great jobs. Rather, it comes from blowing countless interviews and from the *nine times* my bosses have told me my job was going away.

My long career in human resources, recruiting, and outplacement has provided me with unique and comprehensive perspectives on what it takes to find and land a job. Charged with recruiting and interviewing responsibilities for former employers such as PepsiCo, Nestlé, Marriott Corporation, Coca-Cola Enterprises, Hard Rock Cafe, Frito-Lay International, Centex Homes, Viewpost, and Bank One, I know firsthand why some job candidates get hired and why others do not. Like a bouncer at a chic New York City dance club,

I have been the gatekeeper with the rather omnipotent authority of deciding who gets in the door and who does not. At times, this put me in charge of the hiring process for tens of thousands of jobs around the globe, ranging from entry-level positions to company presidents. As the founder and current president of outplacement providers the Navigator Institute and Navigator Executive Advisors, I've coached thousands of unemployed clients on effective job search skills, which keeps me current on emerging trends in the selection process. If you are a recent college graduate anxious to put your education to work, rest assured this book is as applicable to you as it is to the sixty-five-year-old chief executive looking for one last corner office suite to occupy before retirement.

While increasingly challenging, complex, and sometimes daunting, looking for a new job does not need to be an exercise in futility. While it's true the competition for good jobs can be extremely fierce, at any given time there are also millions of open job postings, and every month tens of thousands of new jobs are being created in industries ranging from health care technology to discount retail. Even in the best economic times, however, it is not atypical for a single job posting to generate thousands of resumes. In order to catch the attention of recruiters and outperform the slew of other applicants, it is often the case that candidates must excel at *every aspect* of the job search process.

One of the pleasures of my work as a job search coach is witnessing my new clients' rapid transformation from overwhelmed and apprehensive to confident and inspired. I believe the reason for this metamorphosis is that I drive home the point that there is no singular step in the process that is too complex for them to master. Certainly there is much to learn about finding and landing a new job, but, like eating an elephant, it's doable when approached one bite at a time.

I think it is worth mentioning that a driving force behind writing this book was my own frustration earlier in my career, when I was out of work and unable to find a credible and effective guide for helping me secure employment. Without exception, the subject matter experts I encountered could only muster one-dimensional opinions as job givers—without much, if any, experience as *job seekers*. In comparison, it is entirely possible that I have hired, not hired, been hired, not been hired, fired, and been fired more than anyone on the planet! As droll as that may be, my clients benefit from my 360-degree perspective on career transitions, and I am certain that you will too.

Lessons Learned the Hard Way

From a personal standpoint, writing this book wasn't always pleasant. On some occasions, it was even a little painful. The reason, as you will soon discover, is I am very candid, open, and honest about what it takes to secure a new job in today's competitive employment market, which means I rely on many of my own job search failures to illustrate lessons that ultimately contributed to repeated success. While I would have preferred to only reference the many times as a job candidate when I did the right things and was extended an offer, that would have portrayed an incomplete and disingenuous picture of my experiences and what can be learned as you launch your own job search.

While I do share how to impress recruiters and hiring managers based on my own corporate career triumphs, much can also be learned from dissecting the reasons behind my countless interviewing missteps and the ensuing professional and personal fallout every time I was told that I no longer had a job. In an effort to ensure the adage that "those who fail to learn from history are doomed to repeat it" does not go unheeded, I freely share incidents when I inadvertently torpedoed my own candidacy and how, by avoiding the same mistakes, you can significantly reduce the ramp-up time until you become optimally proficient in your job search.

On a few occasions when my job was eliminated, I was offered positions elsewhere within the business or the parent company. As relocation was required every time this option was extended, sometimes I accepted the offer and moved to a different city, and other times I took a severance package—or "parting gift" as one of my bosses called it—and departed jobless. Either way, I still had to deal with the emotions of change and the realization that my livelihood was at the mercy of my corporate superiors. In addition to changing jobs out of necessity, I also did so to satisfy my own career ambitions in those instances when the opportunities presented were just too compelling to turn down.

THE FACTORIES OF FLINT

One reason I never expected to be an expert in the career transition field is I grew up in a town whose economy was dominated by General Motors during the company's heyday, and a job for life was largely an expectation—if not a presumed birthright. Indeed, three generations of family and friends went to work in one of the many factories and for most of them it was their first and only employer. As members of the United Automobile Workers union, they could expect to retire with full pensions and health benefits after thirty years of work. Many of my buddies and cousins went straight to work building trucks and automobiles after high school and were pretty much set financially for the rest of their lives at forty-eight years of age.

Even though there were occasional layoffs at the auto factories, few people expected them to be permanent, and for the most part, they were right. It wasn't the easiest or the most enjoyable work in the world, but given the pay, benefits, and perpetual employment, it was a pretty good deal. While I personally never warmed up to the idea of working in an auto factory, the thought of working for only one employer throughout my entire career did have considerable appeal to me beginning at an early age.

My parents, Midge and Jerry, had no interest in working in the factories either. For that matter, neither my mom nor my dad had any intention of punching a time clock or working for a weekly paycheck for anyone. Instead, they chose careers that gave them tremendous personal independence along with the irregular but often lucrative income that came with earning 100 percent of their pay from sales commissions. Partly because my parents sold boats and real estate and the family income of my youth was very sensitive to even the slightest economic tremors, I set my sights on a career that would offer me a stable bi-weekly paycheck, company-paid health benefits, a generous pension plan, and maybe even an engraved gold watch at some far-off retirement party.

A SPARTAN EXISTENCE

In pursuit of a career path different from those of my family and friends, I enrolled at Michigan State University, where I earned my bachelor's degree in political science and a master's degree in labor and industrial relations. Unfortunately, bad timing unceremoniously placed me in a position where a crushing recession meant my freshly printed degrees were now in little demand among the limited number of visiting employers who were still recruiting graduating students at the campus placement center. Despite the contracted economy, I was confident I would receive a job offer, if not offers, from the recruiters who were scheduling interviews. I was wrong.

I realize now that my initial optimism was due in part to having landed jobs for a great majority of the hourly positions I had applied for prior to entering graduate school. Deep down, I also think I just couldn't handle the very real possibility of being broke, jobless, and in so much debt at such an early age. As I'll share later in this book, my ineptness at interviewing cost me dearly, and instead of job offers, I departed college with a box full of rejection letters.

When I finally landed a job at Marriott's corporate headquarters in Bethesda, Maryland, four months after graduation (and with student loan payments looming on the near horizon), I was both thrilled and relieved. Up until that point, my experience in the job search process had been all about learning from failure. For me, the Marriott job offer was a deeply personal and professional triumph. It was something I had earned the hard way through the cumulative experiences of a lot of trial and error and the disappointment of countless missed opportunities.

THE CORPORATE RIDE

Despite my many job losses, I would not trade my career in corporate America for anything. While I may have had more than my fair share of setbacks, I also prospered in many ways. For instance, my various employers sent me to places around the globe that I could only dream of while growing up in my small town. At company expense, I traveled to Australia, Singapore, Rome, Venice, Florence, London, Paris, Barcelona, Madrid, Edinburgh, and Prague. I also had some extended assignments that sent me to the island of Kauai,

Hawaii, for eight months and, in another tour of paradise, to most of Mexico's premier resort towns for four months.

On one occasion in 1991, when I was working for Nestlé's Stouffer Hotels & Resorts Company (now Renaissance Hotels), I was escorted into the office of Bill Hulett, the company President, by Roger Green, my boss and the Senior Vice President of Human Resources. Having no clue as to the purpose of the meeting, I was astonished when they informed me I was being assigned to temporary duty with the U.S. State Department to represent the U.S. Council for International Business at the United Nations/International Labor Organization conference in Geneva, Switzerland. In the course of my assignment, I attended sessions and cocktail receptions with U.S. Secretary of Labor Elizabeth Dole and her successor, Lynn Morley Martin; Nelson Mandela; Lech Wałęsa, Solidarity leader and later President of Poland; and AFL-CIO President Lane Kirkland. Culminating with a speech I gave to the U.N. General Assembly in front of over one thousand representatives from more than one hundred countries, it was a surreal experience and a stark contrast to the auto factories back home.

Durfee's Laws

Throughout this book, you will see references to Durfee's Laws. Whether you need to craft a winning resume, learn how to ace an interview, develop effective networking skills, master the multifaceted power of LinkedIn, negotiate a job offer, or develop skills in any of the other critical subject matters, Durfee's Laws are nuggets of wisdom summarizing some of the most critical lessons of the job search process. Many of them are the direct results of the insider perspectives I acquired as a recruiter and outplacement career adviser—and some of them are the lessons I learned, often reluctantly, the hard way. In contrast to Murphy's law, which proclaims, "Whatever can go wrong will go wrong," Durfee's Laws profess, "Whatever can go right requires knowledge, practice, and discipline." In other words, if you are serious about increasing the odds of landing a new job, it's very much in your best interests to take the time necessary to learn and implement the contents of this book.

In addition to my own expertise, I interviewed a great number of highly respected human resources executives and search firm recruiters who also know what it takes for candidates to make it through the gauntlet of the hiring process. A consistent theme from these discussions is the seriousness these professionals assign to their staffing responsibilities. They have clear expectations of how candidates should convey their potential fit for their organizations, and they leave very little to chance. I suggest you consider their advice carefully but with the caveat that there is simply no one right way to get a job. I freely acknowledge that while our collective counsel is surprisingly universal for the overwhelming majority of professions and career levels, not everything will apply to every individual or every situation.

Beware, too: there is no shortage of unfounded and sometimes outright ridiculous information out there on how to conduct a job search. Sometimes it seems whenever I turn on the television or read an article, someone is claiming to be an authority on the topic. With minimal research, I have found many of these individuals lack substantive and practical experience. Rather, they are former public relations consultants, organizational development specialists, or even fashion experts whose careers are seemingly void of any meaningful recruiting or hiring responsibilities. Through self-promotion and an absence of due diligence on the part of the media, they nonetheless end up on morning talk shows or published on Internet job boards spouting simplistic and sometimes even harmful job search advice.

Ignorance Is Not Bliss

Among the many lessons I've learned about setting career goals is things don't always go according to plan. As a result, resiliency and the willingness to continually adapt and learn are essential attributes for anyone striving to stay ahead of obsolescence. That is why, rather than jumping straight into the technical aspects of a job search, the first chapter of this book is devoted to dealing with change and coping with the stress of a job loss, which, on the scale of traumatic events, ranks not too far behind divorce and the death of a loved one. By offering critical insights into managing the emotional roller coaster and the perpetual uncertainty that generally accompanies a job search, I am convinced you will be much better prepared to both endure and succeed.

Regardless of your current personal and professional circumstances, I encourage you to take the content of this book seriously. For reasons I find quite inexplicable, most people will devote more time and money to a couple of rounds of golf than they will to learning how to land a job that could change their lives. The stakes are simply too high and the forces of change too powerful to leave your job search to the whims of chance or the mercy of ignorance. As I regularly advise my clients, study the ensuing material as if you were preparing for a final exam. Landing a new job that brings you happiness and fulfills your career aspirations is entirely worth the effort.

"We know what we are, but know not what we may be."
WILLIAM SHAKESPEARE (1564–1616)
POET AND PLAYWRIGHT

CHAPTER 1

DEALING WITH JOB LOSS

"I'm not afraid of storms, for I'm learning to sail my ship."
Louisa May Alcott (1832–1888)
Novelist, Little Women

Numerous studies, client coaching sessions, and vast personal experience confirm that the loss of employment is one of life's most stressful events. Until relatively recently, there really was no reason to know this in the United States, particularly if you were working for a big corporation. In many cases, an implied social contract meant that as long as you did your job, you could expect a long and secure career with your employer.

While many factors such as technological advances, mergers, competition, globalization, and deregulation have significantly contributed to a much harsher and less secure work environment, old and established expectations die hard. However, regardless of actual preparedness and perceived fairness, individuals are increasingly being called upon to confront change in the form of job loss. Failure to embrace this reality can result in considerable disillusionment, emotional turmoil, financial loss, and personal hardship. With respect to the job search process, if you can't quickly shake off the past and focus on the future, it's unlikely you'll have much luck finding another job.

I once had a client of Navigator Executive Advisors whose job as a senior executive was eliminated due to a restructuring. The company he was working for significantly changed its strategic direction, and his role was simply no longer needed. We were charged with helping him develop his job search skills. As he had amassed nearly two thousand names in his contact files, I figured he would almost immediately launch an effective job search campaign. After several coaching sessions and no apparent progress with his job search, I asked what kind of feedback he was getting from his networking contacts. Somewhat sheepishly, he admitted he had not reached out to more than a handful of people. When pressed as to the reason why, his response was, "I feel like such a putz." My coaching approach instantly shifted from teaching him networking skills to helping him understand he had no reason to feel embarrassed about the elimination of his job (after all, his unemployment was entirely unrelated to his performance or conduct). Until he could come to terms with that, his extensive list of contacts was of no value.

While change is not always easy to embrace, this chapter is intended to help you understand it, manage it, and even prosper from it, both professionally and personally. Indeed, many individuals credit involuntary unemployment as the turning point to a more meaningful, fulfilling, and prosperous life. Rarely, however, can a successful transition be achieved without considerable resolve, resilience, focus, discipline, and a perpetually healthy attitude.

Understanding Job Loss

Irrespective of reason, the loss of employment typically generates a wide range of emotional reactions. As illustrated in the example above, the ability to recognize, understand, and effectively deal with these emotions can greatly determine the success of one's efforts to transition into another job or career.

In her 1969 book, *On Death and Dying*, psychiatrist Elisabeth Kübler-Ross identified five stages of grief.[1] While the loss of employment is nowhere near as traumatic as confronting one's mortality, most of my clients have described the same emotional reactions and stages. The five stages are identified below along with examples suited for the topic:

1. **Denial:** "Surely, they can't be serious about letting me go!"
2. **Anger:** "After all I've done, how dare they do this to me?"
3. **Bargaining:** "How about taking me back in a different department?"
4. **Depression:** "I doubt anyone will ever offer me a decent job."
5. **Acceptance:** "It's time to move on and focus on the next chapter of my career."

Do any of these sound familiar? They certainly do to me. I have experienced and battled all of them when my jobs were lost.

The Power of Attitude

During a seminar on facilitative leadership I once attended in Chicago, the instructor shared some research conducted after the Vietnam War. The purpose of the study was to understand the impact that attitude had on the American prisoners of war (POWs) who endured prolonged imprisonment under horrendous conditions and with no clear end in sight. The attitudinal categories evaluated included:

- **Pessimist:** Pessimists have little confidence things will work out and tend to always expect the worst.
- **Realist:** Realists are practical and have the tendency to look at, or accept, things as they really are.
- **Optimist:** Optimists casually dismiss the idea that things can go wrong and are predisposed to take a hopeful and encouraging view.

In the career transition workshops my firm conducts for our clients' displaced employees, we regularly ask the attendees which of these attitudinal categories they feel fared better both mentally and physically during captivity. Which answer do you think is correct? Take a moment to consider your response before reading on.

To almost no one's surprise, the study found pessimists were pretty much doomed from the start. They essentially gave up without putting much mental effort into surviving. However, while most workshop attendees answer optimist, the answer is actually realist.

While it is true that optimists fared better at first, they had difficulty sustaining their positive outlook. As their captivity dragged on with no apparent end, sometimes for several years, many of them eventually gave up too. Realists, however, had no illusions about their predicament. They understood the uncertainty of their situation and knew surviving their ordeal was going to be a difficult and challenging task requiring a sustained level of resilience. They had the confidence they would endure and consciously fought the tendency to get either too depressed about their captivity or too hopeful it would soon end.

While the job search is not as dramatic or life threatening, I believe you can learn from the experiences of the POWs. As most people don't know when they will get another job, the end is uncertain. Similarly, a pessimistic outlook will stymie the job search process (as will depression). Too much optimism, however, can often lead to discouragement and frustration should interview after interview fail to produce an acceptable offer of employment. A realistic approach provides some degree of emotional buffer that also helps you maintain a more sustainable focus on the task at hand (i.e., finding a job) and better prepares you to deal with the unpredictability and frequent disappointments of the job search process.

Navigating Through a Job Loss

How individuals cope with and react to the the stages of grief can vary greatly. While some individuals may experience each of the five stages consecutively and for equal periods of time, others may encounter them in a different order or at a different pace. In particular, some may experience prolonged anxiety or depression. Still others may seem to skip certain reactions altogether.

David Butterfield was one of my first clients and an inspiring example of someone who seemed to instantaneously start and remain at Stage 5 (Acceptance). When his job was eliminated due to a downsizing, he concentrated only on the task at hand and simply refused to look backward. Two weeks into his search for an industrial marketing management position, he landed another six-figure job without having to relocate. For others, it is not uncommon to make progress toward the Acceptance stage and, often due to a setback, regress back to the Depression stage. With David as an exception, most people find the job search process is like an emotional roller coaster where they have to contend with the ups and downs of the ride.

The important thing is to recognize emotional volatility is natural and usually unavoidable. While it is not always pleasant, you should make every effort to understand and acknowledge that these reactions are to be expected when looking for a new job. Furthermore, you should resist negative tendencies such as isolating yourself from friends and family, being overly self-critical, or harboring excessive hostility toward your former employer. The sooner you can accept the change, the sooner you can effectively begin to transition your career.

Of course, you do not have to accept change. You can continue to wish for what once was. You can also simply quit your job search and toss this book on a shelf to collect dust. People who have achieved financial independence often choose not to accept change because it is no longer worth it to continue to adapt and adjust to the changes confronting them. Those with great contacts, professional fame, or just plain luck can sit back and wait for job offers to come to them. But for most others, the alternative to accepting change has much more dire consequences.

When I worked for Pepsi and non-cola beverages like Snapple were taking an increasingly bigger bite out of beverage market share, we shared a story about a man who confronted and reacted to change as a way to inspire the workforce to take the threat more seriously. It was called the "burning platform," and it went something like this:

> *A man had just survived a devastating explosion and fire on the offshore oil rig where he worked. In the dark of night, confronted with flames all around him, he jumped 150 feet from the rig's platform into the dark ocean. Given that the jump could have instantly killed him, he was asked why he did it. The man simply replied, "Well, if I didn't jump, I was going to die for sure."*

How about you? Do you really need to change? What are the consequences if you don't? Do you risk personal or professional devastation? Finally, what are some of the positive things you hope to get out of making a change? If you are struggling to understand or cope with a job loss, please read on.

Career Level Pyramid

While many factors determine how long it will take for someone to find another job, career level is among the most significant. As the following pyramid illustrates, it will normally take a senior executive much longer to find another position than an hourly worker largely because there are simply fewer jobs at the tops of organizations. For example, an employer may have five thousand employees but only one president. That same employer may have five hundred managers but only twenty-five vice presidents. Plus, in industries such as foodservice, hotels, and theme parks, the turnover rate among hourly employees is significantly higher than in the management ranks. Consequently, these employers may always be looking to hire employees at the hourly level while rarely looking to replace someone at the management level.

The following Career Level Pyramid illustrates that the higher the level, the longer it normally takes to find a job. As you review it, identify your career level and other factors that may affect your job search. Given this information, how long do you expect it will take you to find a job commensurate with your level?

Other factors that can have a significant effect on your job search include the following:

Employer Factors

- **Industry trends:** Booming sector vs. declining sector
- **Pay level:** Union vs. non-union rate, high salary vs. low salary
- **Skill level:** Highly skilled vs. unskilled, high demand vs. low demand
- **Economic conditions:** Recession vs. growth economy
- **Geography:** Growing population vs. shrinking population
- **Employer reputation:** Respected employer vs. poor or unknown reputation

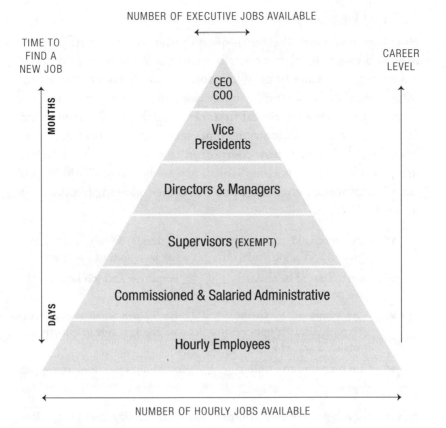

NUMBER OF EXECUTIVE JOBS AVAILABLE

TIME TO
FIND A
NEW JOB

MONTHS

CAREER
LEVEL

CEO
COO

Vice
Presidents

Directors & Managers

Supervisors (EXEMPT)

Commissioned & Salaried Administrative

DAYS

Hourly Employees

NUMBER OF HOURLY JOBS AVAILABLE

Employee Factors

- **Transferability:** The extent to which skills are transferable to other industries
- **Relocation preferences:** Willingness and ability to move for the job
- **Individual reputation:** Performance record, accomplishments, personality, style, trustworthiness, sponsorship, professional references, character
- **Individual effectiveness:** Networking skills, determination, urgency, attitude
- **Personal profile:** Age, race, religion, gender, education, local vs. outsider
- **Resume continuity:** The degree to which a resume reflects stability, achievement, and focus.

Setting Goals

Now that you have a better understanding of how mental readiness and career level can contribute to the effectiveness of your job search, it is time to establish some realistic goals. While it is often said that searching for a job is a full-time job in itself, circumstances such as personal finances, health, family needs, and other individual considerations represent valid exceptions to this rule. Provided you are now committed to finding a new job, what are you prepared to accomplish on a weekly basis? To help you with this process, I encourage you fill in the following blanks with measurable goals:

- ✔ I am prepared to contact _____ friends, family, colleagues, acquaintances, job leads, etc., per week in search of a new job.

- ✔ I am prepared to research _____ employer and job board websites per week.

- ✔ I am prepared to spend _____ hours per week researching alternative career options (e.g., career change, self-employment, contract work, etc.).

- ✔ I am prepared to commit _____ total hours per week to my job search.

As your search progresses, you may want to modify these goals depending on your level of activity and results.

You're More Than Your Job

One of the reasons I really liked being employed by well-known companies was the immediate reaction I would get from people when I told them where I worked. For example, people thought Hard Rock was cool and Marriott was prestigious. As a testament to consumer awareness of the Cola Wars, when I worked for Coca-Cola, people immediately felt compelled to blurt out their preferred brand as in, "I only drink Pepsi" or "I really like Coke." I heard the very same reactions when I later worked for Pepsi. Once unemployed, however, responding to such a simple question as, "What do you do?" can suddenly become a little awkward.

For example, have you ever noticed how rare it is for someone with a full-time job to answer that question with "I'm a mom" or "I coach my kid's Little League team" or "I'm a Salvation Army volunteer on weekends"? Why is that? In short, I believe we tend to allow so much of our self-identity to be defined by our job and our employer's brand status that we feel a little lost when our job goes away along with the accompanying labels.

Despite such ingrained cultural conditioning, you truly are more than your job—and thank goodness! Otherwise, you would surely turn into a virtual shadow the moment you walk out of your office for the final time, toting cardboard boxes filled with those once-meaningful framed certificates of achievement.

To help clients achieve a healthier perspective on their jobs, and the meaning of their lives in general, I encourage them to write down at least ten non-work-related accomplishments they are proud of or simply feel good about. To help point them in the right direction, I ask them to consider things like family, friends, charities, volunteer work, hobbies, church, associations, and political activities. Not only does this exercise serve to prop up a battered confidence but it also opens the door for exploring more fulfilling career options and life goals.

Before proceeding further, I encourage you to set this book aside right now and spend the next few minutes creating your own list.

Don't Blow Your Recess

Have you ever seen a little kid on Christmas morning who seems to be having nearly as much fun playing with the empty box as the expensive gift it once protected? Inevitably, the parents then find themselves shoving the beeping electronic toy into the little guy's hands in a self-serving effort to make sure he appreciates the right object. I often wonder if those same simple pleasures like playing with the box aren't still within us, dormant and buried beneath the crushing weight of work and consumerism. Once money gets tight, it seems people are forced to find the answer. Often, I believe, the best things in life are still simple and they're still free.

When my job with a national homebuilder was eliminated at the onset of the Great Recession that officially started in 2007, I started having lunch at school with my daughter, Jacqueline, who was in the first grade at the time. Prior to this, my office was thirty miles away, and a long midday commute simply wasn't feasible. Now that I was free from the daily regimen of work, it was quite easy to find the time to pick up lunch at her favorite fast food restaurant and meet her outside of her classroom. We'd then have our own little picnic in the schoolyard's outdoor break area. Even after I launched my firm and was putting in long hours, I made it a point to keep a standing lunch date with her every Wednesday. I really hope she will one day look back upon her childhood and remember our father-daughter lunches as special and meaningful moments. Had it not been for my temporary unemployment, however, Jacqueline and I would have never had the chance to make this memory.

Prior to the homebuilding industry job, I worked as the Vice President of Global Talent Management for an international logistics company that restructured after I had been there only twenty days. I vividly remember my boss walking into my office on the morning of the nineteenth day and exclaiming, "We're getting fired tomorrow." When I asked why, he mentioned something about a restructuring of the entire company, including the elimination of the global team of which we were both a part. So after spending the afternoon planning the future with my soon-to-be ex-boss at the private golf country club where my soon-to-be ex-employer had a corporate membership, we both went into work the next morning and collected our severance packages.

Serendipitously, what followed were some of the best times in my marriage. The reason is that despite experiencing most of the stages of grief referenced above, I supplemented my job search with daytime dates with my then-wife, Irma. We would play tennis on our neighborhood courts in the middle of the week (which was kind of cool because nobody was around to see her beating me) and then head off to Starbucks and run errands together. I also found time to help coach and umpire my stepson's Little League team. When I was offered a job with Centex Homes three months later, all of us were kind of sad that my recess from work was coming to an end.

I now encourage my clients to learn from such personal experiences. True, it's unsettling not knowing how long your recess from the working world will last, but that shouldn't keep you from at least trying to take some advantage of the predicament. If you have young children, chances are they would love more time to play with their mom and dad. One of the great things about playing is it doesn't have to mean spending big money on theme park admissions or the latest video games. It can simply mean going to the beach, playing catch, riding bikes, going into the city to visit museums, hiking in a state park, or whatever. Sometimes playing means just doing as much stuff together as possible before the recess bell rings. As with my lunch dates with Jacqueline and my tennis matches with Irma, your activities may result in some very happy memories. Whatever you do and regardless of your age, it would be a shame if you were so singularly focused on your job search that you didn't somehow prosper from it long after you've gone back to work.

Combating Stress

One of the most harmful and detrimental by-products of change is stress. In the context of a job loss, the stress level is often exacerbated by personal matters and individual circumstances. As for me, my jobs have been eliminated with such frequency that I've actually developed the routine of cleaning out the garage before starting a job search.

REMOVE THE CLUTTER

While I don't mean to minimize the anxiety and the stress accompanying a job loss, I do believe there is an opportunity to use the time off from work to clear out some of the mental and material clutter that contributes to stress in other areas of life. This brings me back to my garage. When I was a corporate executive, I tended to travel frequently and work long hours. When I got home, it was usually dark, and I didn't have the energy or desire to do much around the house. But every time my garage door opened upon my return from work, I would sigh and say, "I have to find the time to clean this thing; it's driving me nuts."

So one of the first things I would do when I was unemployed was to give it a good cleaning. While the physical part of it provided me with some exercise, I also felt a nice sense of accomplishment when I was finished. More importantly, it really gave me an opportunity to think about what I wanted to do with my future. Too often, I have come to realize, people who have just lost their jobs don't devote sufficient time to thoughtfully considering what they really want to do with their lives. Instead, they tend to immediately focus all of their energy and efforts on finding a job similar to the one they just left. For me, the idea of becoming an entrepreneur was conceived while I was in the midst of that dirty and sweaty chore, and it was one of the best decisions I've ever made.

A TIME TO GROW

Of all the activities for combating stress, I have found exercise to be the most effective. It not only improves your physical well-being but it can greatly contribute to your psychological health as well. Medical studies have proven that exercising releases compounds such as endorphins, serotonin, and dopamine that can serve to help you battle depression and keep you motivated.[2] In the simplest terms, we just tend to feel better about ourselves when we're in good physical shape.

Back when she was in elementary school, Jacqueline instinctively understood the rejuvenating power of exercise, as evidenced by the ten-minute breaks she'd take from the demands of homework to jump on her trampoline. When she returned to the kitchen table to continue her studies, she did so recharged, refreshed, and focused. Job seekers who spend too much time networking and applying for jobs in front of their computer screens can learn from her routine and explore exercise breaks of their own.

Other ways to get the most from your transition include enhancing your skills by learning a new computer software system, getting certified in a technical skill, or learning a new language. Depending on your interests, the cost of learning a new skill can vary from a few dollars for a book or online learning program to several thousand dollars for comprehensive classroom instruction.[3] Not only would developing new skills enable you to productively channel your energy but it may also enhance your value to a prospective employer and help you land a job.

Just as there are healthy ways for combating stress, unhealthy alternatives should be avoided, including drug abuse, smoking, excessive drinking, gambling, poor eating habits, and irresponsible shopping and spending. While these activities may provide a temporary reprieve from reality, they generally contribute to greater overall stress levels as the consequences for such behaviors can be extremely harmful.

With the assistance of countless clients from a wide range of industries and professional pursuits, the following stress-relieving activities have been assembled for your review:

STRESS RELIEVERS

Aerobics	Hiking	Quality time with family
Assistant teaching	Hobby (old or new)	
Beach activities	Home cleaning	Reading—career
Biking	Home remodeling	Reading—pleasure
Camping	Home repairs	Researching career change
Charity work	Learning a language	Running
Church events		
Coaching kids' team	Learning a skill	Sports—other
	Meditation and prayer	Swimming
Consulting		Tennis
Contract work	Networking	Travel
Education and job training	Painting—art	Volunteering
	Painting—home	Walking
Gardening	Part-time job	Weight lifting
Golf	Professional certification	Yoga

Whether it's spending more quality time with friends and family, weight lifting, reading the classics, or just catching up on household chores like cleaning out your closets, delving into activities you otherwise would not have the time for can serve to reduce stress and promote clearer thinking about personal and career objectives.

Bill Horn, a business executive with Vegan To-Go in Charlotte, North Carolina, shared with me why he volunteered at a local hospital when he was in the midst of a job search:

> *For me, volunteering at a local hospital filled some of the gaps missing in my life by providing a sense of worth, accomplishment, and motivation during my transition. It improved my outlook and quality of life and brought a sense of balance to my week. I quickly learned that by helping others and my community, I was in fact investing in myself.*

While looking for a new job or exploring other career alternatives can be time-consuming, don't think you're prohibited from recharging your batteries, engaging in hobbies or interests important to you, or otherwise devoting some time to your mental and physical well-being.

Financial Survival

According to a survey from the nonprofit organization Mental Health America[3], money is the leading cause of stress, followed by health problems and employment issues. Naturally, the loss of income could greatly compound this stress factor. Irrespective of your financial security, the following topics are worth reviewing.

CONSERVING AND RAISING CASH

This is the time to thoroughly and realistically review and prioritize your household expenses. Do you need to make any adjustments to your spending habits? If so, consider cutting non-essential things such as dining out, professional lawn maintenance, travel, expensive hobbies, and plans to upgrade home furnishings. If you have been overworked or traveling a lot for your job, this is a good time to get reconnected and do things like have dinner at home with loved ones who may be far too accustomed to your absence.

When children are involved, I recommend an open approach versus trying to hide the loss of a job, provided you do not unnecessarily contribute to their stress by painting only a one-sided picture of what lies ahead. Specifically, make the effort to offset negatives, like having to cut back on spending, with positives, like how you'll now get to spend more time with them ("The good news is I get to pick you up from school"). Also, by sharing what happened and what you are going to do about it in a positive context ("So now I get to go find a job I will like even better"), you reduce the chances of them feeling somehow responsible for any increased stress around the home. As younger kids especially understand the meaning of recess and know it is always too brief, you may want to consider turning the bad news into some good news by using terms they can relate to, such as, "My recess from work won't last forever, so let's enjoy it while we can."

Now that you have some time on your hands, this may also be a good time to plan a yard sale to get rid of all the unwanted clutter stashed in the garage, attic, basement, and closets. Another option is to sell items online through sites such as eBay and Craigslist. Provided you allow sufficient time and flexibility to continue your job search, part-time, seasonal, or contract jobs represent other ways to raise cash.

TAX DEDUCTIONS

Any receipts from expenses you incur during your job search should be saved as they may be tax deductible. Typically, this includes travel related to your job search, resume writing services, fees for job boards, phone calls, and job search services such as those offered by the Navigator Institute. Pat Walker, a Certified Public Accountant in Hudson, Ohio, advises that such expenses are subject to a limitation of 2 percent of your gross income and must be related to seeking a job in the field in which you were previously employed (so if you are an unemployed accountant and you're now trying to get a job as an airplane pilot, you may be out of luck). As with anything pertaining to income taxes, however, regulations are subject to change, and there are a lot of exceptions. Accordingly, I highly recommend you check with a professional tax adviser before filing any income tax return containing job hunting expenses.

UNEMPLOYMENT BENEFITS

Depending on your location and the circumstances of your unemployment (i.e., the reason you lost your job), you may be eligible for unemployment benefits. The purpose of this program is to provide a measure of temporary economic relief to individuals who have lost their job through no fault of their own. The weekly amounts paid to eligible unemployed workers vary by state and individual earning history and range from a couple of hundred dollars to over six hundred. Recipients are usually eligible for these payments for up to six months. I recommend that you apply immediately after your job loss, as some states have a waiting period and do not make retroactive payments. During periods of severe economic retraction, state and federal governments have extended eligibility for several additional months. A great website for finding out more about applying for the unemployment benefits in your state is www.servicelocator.org.

HEALTH INSURANCE

If you had medical insurance through your previous employer, you may want to consider continuing your coverage through the provisions of the Consolidated Omnibus Budget Reconciliation Act (COBRA). COBRA allows you to keep your health insurance for up to 18 months provided you pay both the employee *and* employer costs of the plan (so it can be very expensive). The good news is that you have sixty days to enroll and it's retroactive—meaning you may want to wait until you've determined whether or not you will quickly get a new job before enrolling. Depending on your personal circumstances (e.g., number of dependents, medical history, etc.), it may be cheaper to buy your own health insurance policy.

Other options include health insurance plan options available through the Affordable Care Act (or Obamacare, as it is often called) at www.healthcare.gov or by simply typing "affordable health insurance" into any search engine and selecting from the numerous websites that appear.

CREDIT AND INVESTMENTS

While it may be tempting, I recommend extreme caution if you are considering tapping into your home equity or 401(k) account to raise cash. Not only would pulling money out of your 401(k) account involve paying taxes and penalties but this is also money you will someday need for your retirement. If you still need money after taking serious cost-cutting measures, you may instead be better off increasing your credit card debt. That's because if things go catastrophically bad, a bankruptcy court may be able to wipe out your credit card debt while keeping your retirement account safe from creditors. Also, before getting a home equity loan, see if your lender will temporarily reduce your payments or refinance your loan. In many cases, banks and mortgage companies are willing to work with customers to explore financial solutions short of foreclosure.

Durfee's Laws for Dealing with Change

You'll note that Durfee's Laws are numbered in a non-sequential order. This is because I have elected to roughly prioritize them in order of importance. Regardless of their individual ranking, however, all seventy Durfee's Laws represent some of the more important things you will need to know as you conduct your job search.

DURFEE'S LAW #1: **Project confidence.** Whether it's talking to friends, family, or whomever you choose to network with, everyone will benefit if you demonstrate confidence in your ability to land on your feet. Spouses and children should be particularly comforted by a "can-do" attitude even if some budget-tightening is required. Conversely, you may very well contribute to your own stress, depression, and ineffectiveness if you convey you have no hope of benefiting from your career transition. Furthermore, some people may be reluctant to help you network if they feel you are so "down and out" that you would embarrass them with their friends and colleagues.

DURFEE'S LAW #4: **Don't forget you're only human.** Robots don't get the blues—people do. As a result, it's only natural to experience some depression over the loss of a job. Sometimes the work or people are missed. Other times it's both of those things plus the steady paycheck and benefits. Regardless of the reasons, it's understandable that the loss of your job can get you down. Hopefully, it won't last long and you'll quickly channel your energy in pursuit of whatever the future holds for you. Just do your best to cut yourself some slack if your emotions temporarily get the best of you.

DURFEE'S LAW #12: **Forgo the victim card.** Few people would argue that life is fair, and there are undoubtedly countless past and recent incidents in all of our lives to serve as a reminder. How we react to life's injustices, however, is often a determining factor in whether we are successful and happy or bitter and downtrodden. Rarely is the question of fairness raised with more intensity or emotion than with a job loss. While there is no panacea for quickly reaching the acceptance stage of change, wallowing in one's misfortunes—regardless of real or perceived merit—is a step in the wrong direction. Bob Ravener, an author and seasoned executive with companies such as PepsiCo, Home Depot, Starbucks, and Dollar General, offers this counsel: "I can't control 100 percent of what happens to me, but I do control 100 percent of how I respond to what happens to me."

CASE IN POINT FROM THE RELUCTANT EXPERT

I have often been counseled to look toward the future and to leave the past behind. While it is true you don't want to be stuck in the past or emotionally paralyzed by your misfortunes, I think it is a huge mistake not to take the opportunity to learn from your experiences.

For example, I once got a big promotion that required me to move to a different business unit within a major beverage company. Shortly after I started my new job, I realized my boss didn't want me there. I found out later that she had wanted her friend to get my job, but the corporate office overruled her choice.

What took place was essentially a solid year of hell. No matter what I did, it seemed it wasn't good enough, and just to make things worse, she would berate me in front of my colleagues. To escape the Leona Helmsley-style of supervisory abuse that was already too familiar to me from having worked in one of her hotels while in college, I avoided my boss whenever possible and just focused on delivering results. I dug in and worked seventy to eighty hours a week and only took three weekends off for an entire year. After twelve months, I thought I was in the clear as I had led my department to the best performance of any business unit in the country. By then, however, it was too late—my boss had decided to move me out.

Candidly, it took me years to come to terms with my anger and the blatant unfairness, but eventually, I realized I had to assume some ownership for what had happened. You see, instead of avoiding my boss, I should have gotten closer to her in order to better understand her management style and her expectations of me and my department. While I don't know if that would have changed the end result, I do believe I should have made more of an effort to directly confront her animosity and to figure out how to work with her. As painful as it is to admit, that's a mistake that helped to make me smarter, stronger, and more effective throughout the remainder of my corporate career.

DURFEE'S LAW #24: **Be realistic.** A positive attitude and a confident outlook are rarely all you will need for a successful career transition. Additionally, you should dedicate significant time to the job search, including time for networking, researching employment opportunities, developing job search skills, and interviewing. Candidly assess the labor market for someone of your skill set and determine whether adjustments to your personal budget and career path are warranted. In short, be confident *and* realistic.

DURFEE'S LAW #25: **Leverage your resources.** Whether it's professional career transition support or collecting unemployment benefits, it pays to research the resources you have at your disposal. Many government and private organizations have programs specifically designed to help people find employment, address credit problems, and explore entrepreneurial opportunities—so take advantage of them.

DURFEE'S LAW #47: **Allow your mistakes to make you stronger.** If you lost your job due to something you did or did not do, learn from it. There's an old saying, "If you never make a mistake, you never learn a lesson." So rather than beating yourself up over losing your job even if it was "for cause" (e.g., a lapse in judgment or a performance issue), think in terms of how this experience can make you stronger, wiser, and more valuable to future employers. Take ownership of it, learn from it, and be better because of it.

DURFEE'S LAW #69: If it's not your fault, it's not your fault. Displaced employees commonly ask, "Why me?" or "What did I do wrong?" The reality is there are literally thousands of hardworking and loyal employees who lose their jobs every day through no fault of their own. Regardless of performance, sacrifice, or loyalty, the factors contributing to workplace changes are so great it has become commonplace for even the most talented and dedicated employees to end up jobless.

You're Not Alone

While I was not happy—and certainly never grateful—whenever notified I no longer had a job, in retrospect, I cannot deny that I learned a lot from these instances. Granted, it's a whole lot more fun and easier on the ego to share my successful job searches, but it would also be disingenuous to dismiss my imperfections or ignore the contributing forces outside of my control. In addition to learning to cope with the harsh reality of not getting jobs, including those occasions when I was the most qualified candidate, I also had to cope with having jobs taken away from me that I really enjoyed. Sometimes it was due to impersonal reasons such as restructurings, acquisitions, and economic downturns. Other times it was much more sinister. Those were the times I learned, as I know many others have, that getting great results isn't always enough to trump your boss's personal whims or selfish political agendas or the absence of organizational sponsorship.

As someone who earns a living from helping people get back on their feet after a job loss, I am now thankful that I have the insight to understand their stress, fears, uncertainties, shaken confidence, and loss of identity. These are things I understand not because I ever really wanted to but rather because I have walked in their shoes—repeatedly.

Believe me, when I was the global head of human resources for the Hard Rock Cafe, I really enjoyed traveling first class to some of the world's greatest cities and experiencing things like being transported by helicopter to massive outdoor rock concerts. But when the business strategy changed, my boss changed and my boss's boss changed, and it became clear to me that in order to achieve my career goals, I would need to change employers. Trading an ultra-cool corporate lifestyle for something far less glamorous took some getting used to, but due to my new employer's rapid growth, I ended up exponentially prospering both financially and professionally.

When discussing why I could not have launched Navigator Executive Advisors and the Navigator Institute without the lessons from my abundant career tribulations, Jim Lynde, former head of human resources for Spirit Airlines and Red Lobster, shared these words of wisdom:

> *Pain is the tuition we pay for growing. When we demand more of our spirit, our mind, and our body—that's what makes us stronger and wiser. In essence, we are tearing apart our very fiber in order to build muscle. It's supposed to hurt. But it also stretches us so that we can achieve higher levels of capacity and achievement.*

I think Jim makes a great point. Whatever the cause or the magnitude of the change confronting you, it serves as an opportunity to build personal character and professional effectiveness.

Provided, of course, that you let it.

PLEASE REMEMBER THIS

Some of the key lessons in this chapter include:

- ✔ The implied social contract that once placed a premium on loyalty and job security in the workplace has largely been dissolved.

- ✔ Globalization, new technology, mergers, acquisitions, and deregulation will continue to make job security a thing of the past.

- ✔ A healthy attitude and the willingness to understand and accept change enhances the likelihood of prospering from it.

- ✔ As demonstrated in the Career Level Pyramid, the higher you are on the organizational ladder, the longer it will likely take to secure other employment.

- ✔ Despite the emotional and financial hardships often involved, a job loss can create the opportunity for happiness and personal growth in other aspects of life.

- ✔ Techniques for reducing stress include exercising, devoting quality time to family and friends, volunteering, learning new skills, and tackling domestic chores.

- ✔ The financial impact of a job loss can be offset by cutting expenses, selling unneeded household items, engaging in part-time and project work, and promptly registering for unemployment benefits.

- ✔ Durfee's Laws assert that projecting confidence, learning from your mistakes, maintaining a realistic perspective, and acknowledging and accepting emotional lapses are critical in order to effectively deal with change.

> **"Sometimes we are lucky enough to know our lives have been changed, to discard the old and embrace the new and run headlong down an immutable course. It happened to me . . . on that summer's day when my eyes were opened to the sea."**
> *JACQUES-YVES COUSTEAU (1910–1997)*
> *EXPLORER AND OCEANOGRAPHER*

CHAPTER 2

CHASING YOUR DREAM

"I have learned that if one advances confidently in the direction of his dreams and endeavors to live the life he has imagined, he will meet with a success unexpected in common hours."

HENRY DAVID THOREAU (1817–1862)
AUTHOR AND PHILOSOPHER

Through moments of post-employment introspection, I came to terms with how desperately I tried to hang on to jobs, even when I was miserable. Bad bosses, dysfunctional work cultures, and shrinking businesses weren't always enough to give me solace when I was finally given my walking papers—not initially, anyway. But after taking some time for reflection, I accepted that I hadn't been living my dream with those employers but had clung on tightly for the stability of the predictable regimen, the steady paychecks, and to shield my ego from the sting of rejection that accompanies a job loss. It was during these times that I learned some of the most important lessons about career transitions and the opportunities they create.

Even if you haven't lost your job, these lessons can apply to you. In particular, looking at the job search process through this lens opens the door for exploring new options that may otherwise have seemed unworkable or impractical. Without the daily distractions, demands, and stress so prevalent in today's workplace, the relative serenity of unemployment allows us to take a fresh look at ourselves and our career objectives. The outcome may be a reaffirmation and continuation of our chosen career path or a decision to chart an entirely new course.

Indeed, many successful entrepreneurs would not have considered forgoing the financial security of gainful employment had they not been forced to consider other employment options. Although I always harbored an interest in running my own business, I was never willing to voluntarily walk away from the generous salaries, bonuses, benefits, company cars, and stock options to pursue an entrepreneurial enterprise. The biggest reason I stayed in corporate roles was the absence of a burning platform to compel me to accept a risk/reward ratio that included no assurance of financial success.

A combination of an organizational restructuring and the crash of the homebuilding industry changed all of that. With the elimination of my job as a vice president for a national homebuilder, I was in a sense liberated from the economic inducements that discouraged me from exploring options outside of the corporate arena. Walking away from two decades of steady paychecks wasn't initially easy, though, and for a while, I applied for jobs while simultaneously developing the concept for Navigator Executive Advisors. Before too long, a return to the corporate executive suite became less appealing as I was deriving considerable satisfaction from creating, growing, and running my own businesses. Paradoxically, the change I did not want at the time of my last job elimination is now the change I look back upon and, quite serendipitously, cherish.

Cherie Rivett, a human resources consultant who formerly worked for Frito-Lay and later held the position of Vice President of Human Resources for Universal Studios, recounted the inspirational career transition of someone she had to let go due to a downsizing:

> *Tom had said that due to business changes, he knew it was possible that he could lose his finance job. Even so, he got a bit choked up when it actually happened. He recovered after a minute and went on to tell me it had forced him to think about other alternatives. He had thought back to what his dreams were when he was in college, and he realized he really*

had not spent the last six years doing what he loved most. After his highly analytical job was eliminated, he landed a position that led him to managing golf courses. Today he gets to be involved with his favorite sport, and he is outdoors often and interacting with guests, vendors, and employees. Tom is now thriving in a way he never did when he worked indoors all day long.

While this book is primarily written for individuals searching for another job that plays to their demonstrated skills, interests, and experience, the testimonial above suggests entrepreneurial pursuits and career changes are also options worth exploring.

What's Your Dream?

In the film *Pretty Woman*, a man walks the sidewalk and yells out to no one in particular, "What's your dream?" Now may be the time to ask that of yourself. Have you really enjoyed your career so far? Has it made you happy and helped you to achieve your professional and personal goals? If so, you may want to stick with what's working, provided there's a realistic chance you can continue along the same path. If not, you may want to ask yourself the following:

- What things about my job(s) made me happy?
- What things about my job(s) made me unhappy?
- Does my line of work match my personal and professional needs and interests?
- What hobbies and interests do I enjoy? How can I match those to a job?
- What skills, qualities, talents, and personality traits represent my strong points?
- What am I not very good at or just don't like doing?

Hopefully, this simple exercise will provide you with some indication of how and where you should pursue your job search. If you have determined another job just like the one you lost is what really makes you happy, then by all means, go for it.

CLOSE ENOUGH

If for some reason you're unable to land your dream job, then at a minimum, aim for something that allows you to enjoy a large part of it. While most people will admit there are things they don't like about their job, that doesn't mean they are dissatisfied with their career choice or employer. Many teachers, for instance, are very vocal about what they consider to be low salaries. Yet they stay in the profession for their entire career because they love helping kids learn and having summers off. Similarly, hotel employees may thrive on the fast pace and lively atmosphere but dread working on holidays. My sister, Laura, worked in the bottle return area of a supermarket in Fenton, Michigan. Even though it can be a dirty and physically demanding job, her work station's proximity to the main entrance made her an unofficial greeter—something she greatly enjoyed. In an otherwise thankless job, she took considerable pride in hearing from customers that she was the only reason they didn't shop at the less expensive Walmart Supercenter across the street.

These are but a few examples of what most of the working population encounters: offsetting factors that make their jobs satisfying despite some imperfections. And while I am by no means suggesting you shouldn't strive toward achieving your ideal job, I do think it's important to understand it wouldn't be uncommon should you find yourself reconciling the differences between your ultimate career aspirations and the mixed realities of different outcomes, positions, or vocations.

Right Job, Wrong Employer

Efforts to replace a lost job often require much more than reading job descriptions. The culture of the work environment, the boss's management style, and the overall expectations of the job can greatly affect your level of satisfaction even if the work seems strikingly similar to what you did for your previous employer. Particularly when you are unemployed or in an intolerable work situation, the pressure to accept the first decent-paying job you are offered can be very compelling. Beware, however, of simply trading one source of stress and unhappiness for another.

Not only can the wrong fit greatly contribute to unhappiness on and off the job but it also can be hazardous to your health. According to a study of 6,442 civil servants in London, England, working for an unfair boss can result in a greater risk of heart attack, heart disease, and chest pain[1]. In contrast, the study found that employees with good bosses were 30 percent less likely to experience stress-related health issues.

Jeff Reeves, a speaker, author, and Human Resources executive with a number of highly regarded companies, as well as a coworker of mine at Pepsi, shared a time when he personally experienced how much more there can be to achieving job satisfaction than just the work itself:

> *After hearing me speak about the importance of HR business partnerships at a conference in San Diego, the president of a telecommunications company's business unit immediately started recruiting me to join her team in Denver. Although the entire interviewing process was poorly conducted and raised some red flags about the organization's values, culture, and commitment to their people, I was flattered by her insistence that she needed me to be her proverbial right-hand man. After some trepidation on my part, she eventually won me over and I accepted an offer. After only eight weeks on the job, however, she resigned. It turns out she was not very well liked, and for the next 18 months, I battled with being "guilty by association" because she was the one who had hired me. The stress took a personal toll on me and my family, and I vowed I would never again take a job primarily to work for one individual and without conducting greater due diligence on the organization itself.*

❷

CASE IN POINT FROM THE RELUCTANT EXPERT

I was once given a few months' notice that my job would be eliminated due to a restructuring. In the interim, I was asked to consider other opportunities in another business unit, but since I did not wish to relocate, I began interviewing locally with other employers.

I thought I was very fortunate to have soon landed a big job with another company in town. Plus the timing of my start date enabled me to pocket my entire severance check from my previous employer. So I started my new job with a fatter bank account and a big smile on my face. Unfortunately, the smile didn't last very long.

Almost immediately into my new job, I realized I was not going to be happy with either the CEO or the company's culture. They both reflected the kind of "watch your back" management style that I had experienced before and didn't want to endure again.

It turns out I was so anxious to avoid the stress of a lengthy job search that I focused on getting the job without fully considering if it was a job I wanted. As a result, I was soon miserable and kicking myself for essentially selling out my happiness.

Roe Sie, an entrepreneur and former executive with Wyndham Vacation Ownership, made sure he wasn't going to make the same mistake.

A former boss of mine became the CEO of a hot new film company in Beverly Hills and we reconnected a few years later when I moved to the Los Angeles area. As luck would have it, he was in need of someone with my background and skills, and he suggested I come to work for him. I was very excited at the prospect of working for an Oscar award-winning film company that routinely showcased the talents of some of Hollywood's top stars. For me, it was THE dream job!

While I already knew I would really enjoy working again for the CEO, I also wanted to make sure the company culture and the rest of the management team would be a great fit. As I expected, the CEO agreed it would make sense for me to meet with the other executives, and he arranged for another visit. As I soon found out, it was clear some of them had a very different idea of what my role ought to be in the organization. Without their support, I realized I simply would not be able to have the kind of impact I would need to be both successful and happy. While it was tough walking away from what initially

appeared to be such a great job, ultimately I knew it was best
for all involved. Earlier in my career I had experienced the frus-
tration and discontent that came with accepting the wrong job,
and I resolved long ago it wouldn't happen again.

Before You Change Careers

People too often rush into a completely different career, believing
they are finally pursuing their dream. Regrettably, many of these
same people end up disillusioned and, in some cases, financially ru-
ined. One reason is people have a tendency to get swept up in the
seemingly glamorous side of a profession without conducting the necessary research to fully understand everything involved. A fine-dining
restaurant, for example, may seem very appealing to a customer who
has long enjoyed the ambience, sophistication, and delicious menus of
such establishments. What a customer may not see, however, are the
operational realities of very long hours, intense competition, and the
difficulty of finding and keeping good staff. Even if restaurants somehow manage to create the elusive combination of great quality, value,
surroundings, and service, it can still be very difficult to turn a profit.

Before committing to a significant change in your career path,
I recommend that you first reach out to owners, managers, or employees in your field of interest to get their firsthand insights on
the pros and cons of the job. In addition, ask if you can spend some
time with them to actually experience the work. Another option is
to pay for the services provided by a company such as PivotPlanet
(www.pivotplanet.com), who can arrange for you to get advice from
people in jobs as diverse as florist, sports announcer, wine maker,
and alpaca rancher.

If you are set on making a career change, I strongly advise getting a real job in the business you are considering before you commit
to a substantive financial investment. While it takes a high level of
patience and a healthy dose of self-esteem for a former corporate
manager to fold shirts in a dry cleaner, serve cocktails in a restaurant lounge, or wait on customers in a dress shop, I believe there is
simply no substitute for meaningful hands-on experience.

ARE YOU WIRED FOR THE WORK?

If you are still considering self-employment or a change of career despite these caveats, you owe it to yourself to first assess your skills, interests, and technical qualifications as well as the relevancy of your previous experience. Regarding your interests and skills, a vast array of assessment tools are available online for nominal fees. Upon the completion of a 320-question self-assessment survey, the Campbell Interest and Skill Survey will compare and match your responses to the results of people employed in sixty occupations. Participants receive numerical and graphical representations of their results, narrative comments, and lists of vocations they should pursue, develop, explore, or avoid. While the report focuses mainly on careers requiring some post-secondary education, it includes other occupations as well.

In college, I marveled at what must have been a huge percentage of incoming freshmen who initially declared veterinary medicine as their major only to make a change before graduation. I don't know if it was the pay, the erratic hours, or having to stick their arms shoulder-deep up cows' rears that discouraged the pre-vet students, but clearly there was a significant disconnect between their preconceived expectations and the realities of the profession. For many reasons, I think it's a safe bet that at least half of all college students will change their majors, and some will do so more than once.

I have also witnessed colleagues land jobs for which they were simply unqualified. I'm not sure if they were intentionally misrepresenting their skills or if they thought they could get away with bluffing until they actually acquired the necessary capabilities. In most instances, their ineptitude was quickly revealed and they were soon sent packing (to make matters worse, some of them resigned from good jobs for which they were qualified only to end up humiliated and jobless).

The lessons here are to thoroughly assess how you are intrinsically wired before committing to a career endeavor that may be contradictory to who you are and what you can do. While some professions may seem appealing and very exciting, you risk making a huge mistake unless your career and personal interests are compatible with your occupational pursuits and, in many cases, your actual experiences.

The Franchising Option

While purchasing a franchise opportunity represents a viable alternative to pursuing a job with another employer, such a decision should be made with considerable caution and critical deliberation. Unfortunately, there is no shortage of stories of people who have been displaced from their jobs only to invest their life savings into franchises that have either returned insufficient incomes or outright failed. Those who do succeed, however, often express great satisfaction from their increased autonomy.

One of the attractive things about buying a franchise is it can greatly accelerate the time it takes to get a business up and running. While some individuals try to save money up front by avoiding franchise fees, they miss out on turnkey operational processes, technical support, mass media advertising, best practices, national and international customer account management, expert consulting and services, continual learning programs, preexisting vendor relationships, and volume buying power.

Tom Damewood was a veteran corporate staffing executive in the hospitality industry until his employer could no longer maintain his position following the terrorist attacks of September 11, 2001.

> *Suddenly, I was without an income, had a severance package that seemed way less than adequate, and was desperate to find a way to support my family. Times seemed very scary and I quickly learned that a fifty-four-year-old executive faces a tough battle in the job market. What I didn't realize at the time is losing that job would be the best thing to ever happen to my career. After a four-month career search that went nowhere, I concluded a Plan B needed to be explored. For me, that meant opening my own business.*
>
> *I decided that opening an executive search firm would leverage the recruiting and relationship-building skills I had developed throughout my corporate career. To address*

my weaknesses for running a business (after all, I was an HR guy—what did I truly know about marketing, finance, and accounting?), I felt purchasing a franchise through Management Recruiters International would provide the template, training, and resources I needed. While the road to self-employment wasn't always smooth, the sheer fulfillment, independence, and financial rewards have since made it all worthwhile. In fact, I finally have ended up in my dream job—after mistakenly thinking it resided somewhere in a corporate office for all those years.

There are numerous franchise websites at your disposal that can be accessed by simply entering "franchise ownership" into an Internet search engine. For my clients who have expressed an interest in purchasing a franchise, I recommend FranNet, a franchising brokerage company that administers a personal interest assessment to prospective clients to help match them with opportunities that represent the best fit. As Pat Deering, a franchise specialist with FranNet, explains, "Our proprietary profiling process allows clients to uniquely understand the question, 'Is business ownership, and franchising in particular, right for me, and if so, which business franchise?'" While many companies have information regarding franchise opportunities on their websites, you lose the advantage of being able to quickly compare among competing opportunities, and you're largely on your own in terms of assessing personal fit.

Durfee's Laws for Chasing Your Dream

Here are some important things to know when chasing your dream:

DURFEE'S LAW #9: Don't forget your happiness counts. If you are unemployed, it may be very tempting to accept the first job offer that comes along, especially if no other offers seem forthcoming. However, the short-term relief and security of a paycheck should be seriously weighed against the exceedingly important need to be happy. While financial pressures or other types of stress may make it difficult to forgo the proverbial "bird in the hand" that a firm offer represents, many people soon regret working in a dismal environment. Personal circumstances contribute greatly to such decisions, of course, but one's happiness should not be dismissed lightly.

DURFEE'S LAW #35: Don't do what you don't know. Granted there are plenty of examples of very successful and happy people who have disregarded this rule, but generally speaking, don't do what you don't know. This is particularly true if you are pursuing self-employment or entrepreneurial endeavors. Before acquiring or starting a business, make a sincere effort to obtain meaningful firsthand experience. Whenever possible, stay away from ventures that do not in some way leverage a strong combination of your existing skills, relationships, training, interests, and past experience. Otherwise, you could easily find yourself broke, miserable, and wondering why you ever got into that line of work in the first place.

DURFEE'S LAW #70: Have a backup plan. There's an old saying about the risks of putting all of your eggs in one basket. Regrettably, too many people disregard this idiom when it comes to planning their careers. As a result, they are entirely unprepared to deal with the consequences should they not achieve their primary career objectives (most people who have aspired for a career as a movie star or professional athlete can appreciate this advice). While career goals should never be abandoned lightly, neither should the realities of the marketplace. To minimize the chances you will suffer a serious emotional or financial meltdown should you encounter a major career setback, always have at least one alternative plan where you can reasonably expect to apply your skills, training, and interests.

PLEASE REMEMBER THIS

Some of the key lessons in this chapter include:

- ✔ Many successful entrepreneurs credit the loss of their job as the turning point for launching a more rewarding career.

- ✔ Before committing to a career change, conduct thorough research by engaging with and working beside people in the profession to determine whether your perception of the line of work is realistic and appealing.

- ✔ Objectively assess whether your skills, interests, and personal wiring match the requirements of the job before financially committing.

- ✔ Often overlooked in the short-term drive to secure a steady paycheck is adequate consideration of long-term happiness in the job.

- ✔ While purchasing a franchise can be risky, a wisely chosen franchise relationship can greatly shorten your learning curve and the time it takes to start earning an income.

- ✔ Durfee's Laws stress that whatever your career interests, it is important to factor in your happiness, skills, experience, and training.

"I do know how to pay attention, how to fall down
into the grass, how to kneel in the grass,
how to be idle and blessed, how to stroll through the fields,
which is what I have been doing all day.
Tell me, what else should I have done?
Doesn't everything die at last, and too soon?
Tell me, what is it you plan to do
with your one wild and precious life?"

MARY OLIVER
POET AND PULITZER PRIZE WINNER

CHAPTER 3

THE BEST RESUME WINS

"Smack the next person who tells you awards are unimportant."

JIM DURFEE
INDUCTEE, CREATIVE HALL OF FAME
THE ONE CLUB

I n an e-mail to my office, Laurie Weitz from the executive search firm Weitz & Associates in Malibu, California, remarked, "The best resume wins, at least the first round." In light of the fact that Laurie receives tens of thousands of resumes in the course of a year, I consider this to be a very powerful and credible summary of the importance of an effective resume. After all, your resume should help open doors to recruiters and potential employers and identify you as a viable job candidate.

To capture the attention of hiring managers or their screeners, a resume should be concise, clear, and compelling. It should also be relevant to the specific positions you are seeking and sufficient in content and style to stand out from the crowd of other interested candidates. Once you get an interview, your resume should then help you in the interview. What your resume should not be, however, is a detailed history of all of your accomplishments, talents, and awards.

As there seems to be no shortage of self-proclaimed job search experts who gladly charge $750 and more for their services, it stands to reason there is also no shortage of resume writing experts. And there isn't. Some resume writers are actually pretty good. Others seem to be trying so hard to be different they come up with weird or confusing formats and brazenly proclaim, "This is what employers want to see!" Well, I'm not sure which employers they are referring to, but I can tell you I'm not one of them. Furthermore, I readily dismiss anyone who tries to pass himself off as an authority unless he's spent many years sorting through stacks of resumes while under heavy pressure from impatient hiring managers to deliver qualified candidates.

As someone who has hired thousands of job candidates and—just as importantly—*not* hired tens of thousands of others, I find these experts' advice is based more on theory than on actual staffing experience. As I tell my clients, "I will share with you what I like and what I don't like. I will also share with you that your resume plays a huge role in whether or not someone like me would give your candidacy more than passing consideration." I also let my clients know that as the head of human resources responsible for staffing a couple of start-up operations, I would get particularly impatient with poorly written resumes. Literally, there were times when I had in front of me thousands of resumes, and the great majority received five to ten seconds of my time before I forwarded them to either the reject file or the further review file. Whether clients accept or reject my counsel, of course, is entirely up to them. The same is true for you.

Either way, it's important to know there simply is no one right way to write a resume. The formats I recommend in this chapter represent my preferences based on my real-world experiences. Inevitably, I will have clients who challenge my recommendations based on something else they have read or heard, and that's perfectly okay. At the end of the day, you should be the one deciding the style that works for you, your profession, and the industry you are targeting. Whatever format you decide upon, I urge you to remember that a resume essentially serves as an introduction and not an entire autobiography.

The Billboard

To illustrate why concision, style, and content are important for a resume, imagine you are driving seventy-five miles per hour on a highway and you see a billboard up ahead. Given your speed, you will have only a few seconds to grasp its purpose. If there's too much information on the billboard, its message will be lost because you won't have time to read it. Conversely, if it contains too little information, you will be left clueless and wondering why it's even there. In some ways, your resume is not unlike a billboard advertisement in that you have a very small window of opportunity to create favorable interest among the targeted market (i.e., prospective employers).

Taking the analogy a step further, let's say the billboard is for an automobile. The auto manufacturer who paid for it certainly doesn't expect you to buy its car based solely on what you saw or read while barreling down the highway. However, the manufacturer does hope to pique enough interest to entice you to visit one of its showrooms, where a salesperson will make a comprehensive and convincing sales pitch. In a nutshell, that's what a good resume does—it generates enough interest on the part of the seller (you) to get you in front of the buyer (the employer) so you can pitch yourself as a strong candidate for the job. Accordingly, your resume needs to create a brief and compelling "call to action" on the part of the recruiter.

RESUME MECHANICS

The mechanics of resumes are typically divided into seven distinct sections. Depending on your career interests and the expectations of your profession, they are:

1. Name and Contact Information (Required)
2. Professional Objective and Profile (Required)
3. Experience and Qualifications (Required)
4. Education (Optional)
5. Accreditations/Associations/Awards/Interests (Optional)
6. Technical Skills (Optional)

The number, type, and location of these sections will largely depend on the position and your background. For instance, recent college graduates may focus heavily on Education and Associations and dedicate little attention to Experience and Qualifications. Similarly, an administrative assistant may draw attention to his or her computer capabilities by adding a Technical Skills section to the top of the resume and omitting the Education section altogether. For individuals with considerable relevant work experience, I recommend giving the Experience section priority over Education, Associations, and Technical Skills.

Joe Filimon, a Principal with the global executive search firm of Navigator Search Advisors, explained why he advocates organizing resume sections so that employment history and experience are sequentially ordered beginning with the most recent:

> *From a style perspective, I always prefer a chronological resume to a competency-based resume. Alternative formats give me the impression that a candidate has moved around too much or has something else to hide. I'm sorry, but the reality is if I can't quickly and succinctly follow career progression and corresponding achievements by position, I'm inclined to disregard the resume altogether.*

Regardless of the order, each of these sections summarizes the information that will largely determine an employer's initial interest in you and will help them decide if further consideration, such as an interview, is warranted.

NAME AND CONTACT INFORMATION *(REQUIRED)*

Key Lessons

1. Use a bold and large font (e.g., 16- to 24-point) for the name, 10-point font for the mailing address, and 12-point font for the e-mail address and phone numbers. Subsequent section headings should be consistently applied using at least a 14-point font but no larger than a 16-point font.

2. Including one's street address is optional, but I do recommend including your city and state, except in situations where you are planning to relocate for the job and do not wish to reveal that you reside outside of the employer's area.

3. Whereas this individual's full name may be David Bennett Royal, he goes by Dave. This makes it easier for the recruiters or potential hiring managers to know who to ask for when placing a call and reduces the risk someone will mistake them for a telemarketer and handle the call dismissively or curtly. Using the name you are widely called is both acceptable and practical, provided you avoid whimsical nicknames that could project an unprofessional image. In addition, I emphasize to my clients that your resume is not your tombstone, so it's okay to lighten up and forgo using a middle name or initial.

4. Note the e-mail address suggests to the recruiter this is Dave's personal e-mail and not an address shared with a spouse. Also, the e-mail address is void of any potentially detrimental innuendos regarding the individual's personality or behavior (e.g., hotmama@Domtbd.com, partyhound@Domtbd.com, etc.).

5. Clearly delineate home, business, and cell phone numbers so recruiters can better anticipate who may be answering the call. For instance, if they call a cell number versus a home number, they will likely ask, "Is this Dave?" versus "Is Dave at home?"

6. Add a LinkedIn profile badge to invite recruiters who receive your resume online to review your profile with one click. Directions for adding this feature are available in the "Your Public Profile URL" section of your LinkedIn account. Recommendations for writing an effective LinkedIn profile are covered in the next chapter.

PROFESSIONAL OBJECTIVE AND PROFILE *(REQUIRED)*

Senior hospitality executive with a proven track record for proactively and aggressively achieving marketplace leadership, product and process improvement, sustainable financial growth, and unparalleled guest and employee satisfaction. Qualifications include capabilities in the areas of:

- Timeshare Sales and Marketing
- Product and Brand Development
- Asset and Franchise Management
- Global Operations
- Call Center Operations
- Culture and Change Management
- Service Standards and Execution
- Talent Planning and Development

Key Lessons

1. Bold your targeted career focus (e.g., senior hospitality executive) to make it easy for the recruiter to discern your career interest.

2. Use 12-point font for the main text. Bullet points should also be in 12-point font but can be reduced to 10-point font if it is necessary to save space.

3. Reference the industry to match the job posting (e.g., hospitality).

4. Limit this section to two or three sentences.

5. Refrain from describing your capabilities in subjective terms such as "hard worker," "team player," "high integrity," and "self-motivated." They may sound nice, but such personal descriptions are clichés that add nothing to your credentials. Plus, they take up space that can be better utilized for promoting relevant work experiences and accomplishments that will better match the key words of a job-posting screening filter.

6. Insert six to eight bullet-pointed skills and competencies that are most relevant to the position you are applying for, based on information discoverable from job descriptions, position postings, employer websites, media articles, and other sources. Bullet points also allow for easy customization of your resume as they can be quickly changed to match the requirements of different positions.

3

CASE IN POINT FROM THE RELUCTANT EXPERT

One of the things I always want to see in a resume is the Professional Objective and Profile section just below the name and contact information. I call this the "billboard within the billboard" as it summarizes key information about the applicant in the already abbreviated format of the resume itself.

While I sometimes have clients argue this approach potentially limits their opportunities within an organization, I can only tell them what I typically do as a recruiter when in possession of resumes without this section—I delete them or toss them in the reject pile.

When a single job posting generates literally thousands of resumes, I want to sort through them as quickly and efficiently as possible. And if someone doesn't provide a brief overview of their qualifications, I am simply not going to spend the time to determine if the job I have open fits their particular interests and skills. My feeling is, if they don't know what they want to do, I'm not going to figure it out for them.

This may seem harsh, but it is reality. Your goal is to get recruiters and hiring managers to review as much of your resume as possible. To entice them to do this, make it as easy as possible by including a Professional Objective and Profile section. Otherwise, your resume may not be afforded anything more than a cursory glance.

EXPERIENCE AND QUALIFICATIONS *(REQUIRED)*

<u>**RITZ-CARLTON CLUB**</u> Boca Raton, FL — 2005 – Present

Vice President of Marketing — *2010 – Present*
Director of Marketing — *2005 – 2010*

Reporting to company President and promoted to Vice President with system-wide responsibilities for developing and implementing lead generation programs for a *$200M* international timeshare resort company with *35,000+* owner/members. Also led *200-employee* corporate telemarketing and customer service operation charged with vacation travel package sales.

- Established telemarketing operations as a critical source of new leads (from *10%* to *31%* of tour flow) through improved employee scripting, training, incentives, and retention.

- Established and expanded relationships with strategic hotel and cruise line travel partners that contributed to annual revenue increase of *$35M* from *$12M*.

- Partnered with direct mail marketing firms to create, test, and monitor programs with weekly volume of *100,000+* solicitations while improving base response rates by *17%*.

- Supervised nationwide special lead generation activities including planning, staffing, and advertising coordination for *25 events* annually.

Key Lessons

1. As Ritz-Carlton Club represents a prominent brand in the hospitality industry, it will warrant top billing over job titles. However, if your job titles are more impressive than the brand (or if the brand is relatively unknown), reverse the order (see resume example below for non-management professional). Just be consistent, and don't flip-flop the position and employer headings throughout the Experience and Qualifications section of your resume.

2. Capitalize, bold, and underline the name of the employer to help it stand out, and use 12- to 14-point font.

3. Bold and italicize job titles to help them stand out from both the name of the employer and other text. It is appropriate to list job titles together if they reflect a promotion within the same department, provided the duties were essentially expanded versus significantly changed. Otherwise, each job title will warrant a separate description of responsibilities and bullet-pointed accomplishments.

4. Use 12-point font for the main text.

5. Include the title of your supervisor, provided that position is impressive in scope and responsibility.

6. Start with one or two sentences to briefly describe your overall job duties and provide a description of the employer.

7. Use bullet points to draw attention to key accomplishments.

8. Include and italicize substantive quantifiable data.

9. Important: Overusing bullet points risks reducing their effectiveness, so use them sparingly for jobs of limited current relevance. For example, a more recent job may warrant four to six bullet points, whereas a job from fifteen-plus years ago with lesser responsibilities may warrant one or two.

EDUCATION *(OPTIONAL)*

Executive Development Program:		
Financial Analysis for Non-Financial Managers	*University of Chicago*	**2012**
Master of Business Administration, Marketing	*Michigan State University*	**1993**
Bachelor of Arts, Hotel Management	*Michigan State University*	**1992**

Key Lessons

1. Begin with the degree and area of study if they are more impressive than the institution. Conversely, reverse the order if the institution is more impressive than the degree (for example, Ivy League institutions generally warrant top billing).

2. Depending on which is listed first, bold either the degrees and areas of study or the institution(s).

3. It is acceptable to sparingly insert non-degree certifications and programs, provided they are sufficiently substantive to enhance, and not distract from, the credibility of the college degree(s).

4. If the area of study is unrelated to the position being applied for (e.g., you have a degree in zoology, but you are applying for a job as a logistics manager in an unrelated industry), consider mentioning only the institution and the level of degree earned (e.g., Bachelor of Science versus Bachelor of Science in Zoology). Similarly, if your degree is from a well-known for-profit school, you may want to just list the degree without naming the entity. While these schools seemingly do an effective job of marketing themselves to prospective students, recruiters and employers often give them little credence, particularly among the executive ranks.

5. While including the year a degree was earned is a personal decision, I generally recommend adding it, provided it is within twenty-five years of the present date.

6. If you attended college but did not fulfill the requirements to graduate, it is appropriate to name the institution, followed by "Earned course credits toward a degree in Business Administration."

7. If you have not completed high school or if your formal education falls substantially short of what a prospective employer is seeking, you may want to omit this section from your resume.

ACCREDITATIONS/ASSOCIATIONS/AWARDS/INTERESTS *(OPTIONAL)*

ACCREDITATIONS & AWARDS	
Award:	Best Resort Marketing; American Resort Development Assoc., 2013
Award:	President's Award of Excellence; Marriott Corporation, 2012
Certificate:	Six Sigma Green Belt, 2010
Certificate:	Global Institute for Leadership Development, 2010
Certificate:	Project Management Leadership Institute, 2009

Key Lessons

1. Accreditations, affiliations, awards, and interests are advisable when the position, industry, or prospective employer holds the membership, award, or certification in high regard. Memberships in organizations should not be listed if they are potentially controversial or risk alienating recruiters or hiring managers (e.g., involvement with a political party). Awards should be relevant and meaningful and may instead be cited in the text of the Experience and Qualifications section.

2. Personal interests should be avoided or used sparingly unless they have a high level of applicability to the role and industry. For example, listing golf as a hobby will likely be more relevant in a business development role, where entertaining clients represents a significant job requirement, versus in an operations management role in a factory (unless the employer happens to be manufacturing golf clubs).

3. In light of increasingly robust diversity hiring objectives, listing organizations with predominately female and minority memberships can have its advantages. For example, executive adviser Vic Benoit advises African American executives to join the National Black MBA Association and to list the membership in this section to draw the attention of recruiters seeking to increase diversity representation within their organizations.

4. Omit this section from your resume if it does not add meaningful value to your career pursuits. Otherwise, it risks becoming clutter that distracts from the more salient sections of your resume.

TECHNICAL SKILLS *(OPTIONAL)*

COMPUTER SKILLS

Microsoft Word, Excel, PowerPoint, Publisher, Outlook, Java, SAP, Access, WordPerfect, Windows 3.1, 95, 98, NT, PageMaker, .NET, Quicken, C++, Harvard Graphics, PeopleSoft, Oracle, and various mainframe systems.

Key Lessons

1. Computer and technical skills should only be included when they are highly relevant to your career pursuits. For example, this section is generally important for someone pursuing a technology position as an administrative assistant but will add little value— and may even be detrimental—for someone seeking a senior executive position where the position's success is measured by strategy development and leadership skills versus proficiency with various software systems.

2. Omit this section from your resume if it does not add meaningful value to your career pursuits.

REFERENCES

I do not recommend including the oft-used statement, "References are available upon request" as this is nothing more than a statement of the obvious. In general, I also do not recommend including the names and contact information of your references unless the individuals are well known, highly respected, and relevant to your profession or targeted employer.

PERIODS OF EMPLOYMENT

Whether you decide to include the months along with your years of employment is really your call. While I personally have only cited years on my own resume, some recruiters get suspicious when the corresponding months are not included. On a personal level, it doesn't appear leaving out the months has worked against me during my own job searches, and I also don't care if they are included when I review resumes. Nonetheless, if you have had no employment gaps that lasted over a month, you may choose to play it safe and include them in your resume.

FONT SIZE AND TEXT ALIGNMENT

I frequently see resumes that are difficult to read because in an effort to cram in a lot of information, the applicant has made the font size too small. This is a bad idea! You want to make your resume easy for a recruiter to read, and anything less than a 12-point font size for the main text (larger sizes for headings) is a risk. If you can't fit everything with a 12-point font size, then I recommend you remove content, reformat the resume, or add another page. Also, there's a tendency to use the justify feature to neatly align the right-hand side of the text. Instead, I recommend aligning the text only along the left-hand side of the page. While not as uniform, it makes the resume more readable as it's less likely recruiters will lose their place as their eyes move from line to line.

Action Words

Action words (or verbs) in the resume are intended to demonstrate that you get things done and take ownership of your job. While action words will vary based on career pursuits and industry, here are a few you may want to consider using when articulating your accomplishments:

Achieved	Implemented	Planned
Advised	Improved	Presented
Collaborated	Increased	Promoted
Contributed	Initiated	Provided
Coordinated	Instituted	Reorganized
Created	Integrated	Restructured
Designed	Led	Secured
Developed	Maintained	Started
Established	Managed	Supported
Exceeded	Negotiated	Surpassed
Executed	Obtained	Targeted
Generated	Optimized	Upgraded
Grew	Orchestrated	
Identified	Partnered	

If you are currently employed and applying for another job, I recommend you change the words to present tense. Also, avoid repetition as using the same word too often risks negatively affecting the credibility of the accomplishment or causing the recruiter to lose interest in your resume.

Competencies

Competencies are skills, behaviors, or capabilities that have been identified as important to the performance of particular jobs or within specific companies, industries, or workplace cultures. Employers typically determine the competencies they are seeking in job candidates by identifying those possessed by the top performers in the same or similar positions. Essentially, they aspire to hire individuals who share the same competencies, or strengths, with the expectation that these individuals will also achieve a high level of performance.

Competencies may vary greatly from position to position, profession to profession, and industry to industry. For example, the competencies "Creativity" and "Thinks Outside the Box" may be very important for a position with an advertising agency, whereas "Results-Oriented" and "Customer Focus" may be more important for someone selling industrial supplies.

When assessing your own competencies, it is important to: (1) accurately identify your strengths through assessment tool results, your own insights, and the perspectives of people who know you well and (2) determine which competencies are important for a targeted position through a careful review of the job posting and, if possible, from individuals who have insider perspectives on the role and the workplace culture. Once you have done this, determine the competencies you have in common with the position, and modify your resume accordingly (see "Customizing and Modifying Your Resume" later in this chapter).

A sample list of competencies includes:

Administrative Efficiency	Flawless Execution	Problem Solving
Business Acumen	Honesty and Integrity	Project Planning
Change Management	Innovation	Quick Learner
Creativity	Inspires People	Results-Oriented
Customer Focus	Leadership Skills	Sense of Humor
Delegates Authority	Manages Ambiguity	Sense of Urgency
Delivers on Commitments	Multitasking	Strategic Thinker
Develops Talent	Organization Skills	Strong Work Ethic
Drives Execution	Organizational Savvy	Team Player
Embraces Quality	Partnership Skills	Thinks Outside the Box
Employee Champion	Proactive Planner	Treats People with Respect

Key Words

In light of the fact that an employer may get hundreds or even thousands of resumes for a single job opening posted on the Internet, key words are used in electronic filtering systems to identify matches between the content of the resumes and the desired candidate profile. These key words are important as they generally lead to further consideration by the person responsible for screening the resumes. Depending on the position, key words may or may not differ from action words. The reason is key words simply represent the specific words and terminology a recruiter is seeking in a candidate's resume. So while key words may represent competencies, skills, and action words, they may also include industry jargon, professional certifications, and past employers (e.g., a beverage company may be looking to hire someone with work experience at Coors Brewing, Pepsi, E. & J. Gallo Winery, or Coca-Cola).

Key words for a Human Resources position, for example, may include: Diversity, Talent Management, PHR, European Works Councils, Recruiting, Business Partner, EEOC, Dispute Resolution, etc. For an administrative assistant, the key words may include: Excel, PowerPoint Presentations, Meeting Planner, Travel Coordinator, CEO, CFO, etc.

How do you find out which key words may be important for a particular job opening? In addition to generally accepted industry or professional terminology, key words can usually be found in the job description for the posted position. Recruiters do not want to reveal the key words to candidates as doing so will neutralize the effectiveness of filtering, so the best candidates can do is make an educated guess as to which ones they should include in their resumes.

Customizing and Modifying Your Resume

Before the introduction of home computers, inexpensive printers, and the Internet, resumes were often produced at professional print shops. Producing resumes in this manner was expensive and time-consuming. The process also made it very prohibitive to customize or modify a resume for a specific job opening. As a result, Professional Objective and Profile sections were often very broad, and many resumes lacked relevance to the specific job opening. Similarly, the key words contained in a resume may have been key for some positions but not others.

Now that technology has provided the masses with the capability to inexpensively and quickly change and send resumes, it would be a mistake not to take full advantage of it. Invest the few minutes required to attempt to match your resume to the specific requirements of a position by adding, omitting, or altering your professional objectives, accomplishments, certifications, key words, etc., in order to increase the likelihood a recruiter or electronic filtering system will identify you as a candidate warranting further consideration. Just be sure you do not compromise accuracy and truthfulness when modifying your resume.

CURRICULUM VITAE

In the U.S., a curriculum vitae (CV) is generally used in place of a resume by individuals seeking teaching or research positions at colleges, universities, and institutions of science. A CV differs from a resume in that it tends to focus much more on academic assignments, achievements, publications, and awards. Sample CVs can easily be found online, but I recommend you stick with a resume unless you are seeking a job as a professor or researcher.

INTERNATIONAL RESUMES

Americans are often surprised to see that resumes from outside of the United States generally include personal information such as nationality, age, marital status, children, and place of birth. (These are commonly referred to as CVs rather than resumes, and CVs in Europe are not limited to academia as they are in the U.S.). Cultural differences and the absence of American-style employment discrimination laws make the European CV both acceptable and widespread. For example, while recruiting for the position of Executive Vice President for a hotel company, I received a CV from a European candidate whose resume contained his photograph. While photographs are acceptable in professional biographies and LinkedIn profiles in the U.S., they are not acceptable for a resume. Steve Mitchell, an entrepreneur, consultant, and former global human resources executive with companies such as Kimberly-Clark, CHEP, and Honeywell suggests:

> *When applying for a job with a European hiring manager and European candidates, it is to your advantage to make your resume look similar in format and content as the other resumes the hiring manager is reviewing. If not, you may be rejected from the process simply for a lack of comparative information.*

WORD OR PDF?

When sending your resume electronically, I advise sending it as a PDF file because it provides a sharper look and is essentially tamper-proof. Unlike formats with an automatic editing feature, a PDF file also won't inadvertently bring to the attention of the recruiter any typographical errors or fragmented sentences. Should PDF not be compatible with a hosting website, then a Word format is generally required. Fans of Macintosh computers should not e-mail resumes before making sure the necessary compatibility features are activated to ensure that the resumes will appear as intended when received by recruiters using a Microsoft system.

Entering or Re-entering the Workplace and Changing Careers

For individuals who have either little or no applicable work experience because they are young, have been absent from the workplace (e.g., homemakers returning to the workforce after divorce), or are pursuing a different field of endeavor, the resume should focus less on experience and more on skills, competencies, education, and non-workplace accomplishments such as volunteer work, personal experiences, and hobbies. Depending on the situation, it is appropriate to locate the sections for Education, Accomplishments and Competencies, Technical Skills, and Accreditations/Associations/Awards/Interests near the beginning of the resume versus toward the end. The focus should be on demonstrating how your personal attributes, skills, interests, and training make you an ideal candidate for a job despite the limited actual or recent professional experience.

Employers will frequently train someone for a job provided the candidate can demonstrate some admirable accomplishments, transferrable skills, and a passion for the work. For example, a hotel may be interested in hiring someone without industry experience for their convention services department if the candidate successfully organized big volunteer fundraising events. Similarly, a company may hire and subsequently train a restaurant manager for a sales position if the candidate were to demonstrate the level of energy, enthusiasm, and personality possessed by successful salespeople. In addition, there are countless stories of individuals who have made major career changes by demonstrating how their hobbies have prepared them for success in corresponding or related industries.

Professional Biography

In addition to the resume, a professional biography, or bio, can further serve to market your candidacy to potential employers. While the resume is the more valuable of the two as it provides essential information about your career goals, work history, skills, and accomplishments, the bio allows you to share information that would not normally be included in a resume. For instance, bios generally include things such as your photo, hobbies, personal information, and memberships or interests unrelated to work. A bio should provide much of the content used to create a LinkedIn profile (see page 94) with the added benefit of giving recruiters a more complete impression of who you are as an overall person.

For a professional bio to be effective, it should reiterate some of the more critical skills and experiences referenced in the resume, but present them in a journalistic or storytelling format. The bio also serves as an opportunity for you to stay fresh in the minds of recruiters and hiring managers if you e-mail it several days after submitting your resume. Providing a bio as supplemental information tends to be more impactful than reaching out with a "just checking in on the status of my candidacy" approach.

Matt Durfee
PROFESSIONAL BIOGRAPHY

Matt Durfee is the founder and president of Navigator Executive Advisors, Inc. (www.navexec.com) and the Navigator Institute (www.navinstitute.com)—career services firms providing executive search, outplacement, and executive coaching and leadership development to employers such as *Avis Budget*, *Heineken*, *Universal Studios*, *Hard Rock*, *Hostess Brands*, *Wyndham*, and small-cap and nonprofit organizations. Prior to launching the firms in 2006, Matt held chief human resources officer, senior vice president, vice president, and human resources management positions in a number of the world's most admired companies including *PepsiCo*, *Hard Rock Cafe*, *Frito-Lay International*, *Bank One*, *Nestlé*, *Coca-Cola Enterprises*, and *Marriott International*. His expertise in career and leadership transition, change management, and executive development is supplemented with extensive experience in roles ranging from the business unit level to the Board of Directors.

Matt's international experience includes European Works Councils, extended in-country projects, and temporary duty with the U.S. State Department and U.S. Council for International Business to represent national employer interests at the United Nations' International Labor Organization conference in Geneva, Switzerland. With notables including Elizabeth Dole, Nelson Mandela, Lech Wałęsa, Lane Kirkland, and Lynn Morley Martin in attendance, Matt's leadership was instrumental in developing formal international labor standards for the hotel and restaurant industries. As an active "Ambassador" for *Business Leaders for Michigan* with William Clay Ford Jr. serving as chairman, Matt is one of a small number of C-suite executives with Michigan roots dedicated to helping the state achieve Top 10 status for job, economic, and income growth. In 2014, he was also appointed to a two-year term on Michigan State University's International Alumni Board Advisory Council.

Matt earned his master's degree in labor and industrial relations from Michigan State University, where he also graduated with a bachelor of arts in political science, and he subsequently completed an executive program in financial analysis at the University of Chicago Booth School of Business. His national newspaper column for American City Business Journals, *Navigating Your Job Search*, appeared in 40 U.S. markets with over four million readers.

When not working, Matt is an avid hiker and founder of the *Bucket List Hiking Club* (www.bucketlisthiking.com) for executives seeking reflection, exercise, and professional networking. In 2011, he accepted an invitation to join the *Society of Antiquaries of Newcastle upon Tyne*. Founded in 1813, it is England's oldest provincial society dedicated to the region's history and archaeology. Matt was also a Producer for the feature-length films *Scare Zone*, winner of five film festival awards, and *Characterz*, starring Mitchel Musso.

Matt Durfee can be contacted at (407) 581-6885 or mdurfee@navexec.com.

Key Lessons

1. Use a bold and large font (e.g., 16- to 24-point) for the name and 12-point font for the text.

2. If using a photo (optional), use something that reflects the expectations of your professional field. For instance, someone in the finance field would have a more conservative look in terms of business attire and background, whereas a creative director may project a much more casual image. A nice smile is almost always more appealing to recruiters than a stern or dispassionate expression, particularly when the job involves a high level of customer contact as with sales positions.

3. Use full sentences, paragraphs, and good grammar.

4. Summarize professional accomplishments that you wish to highlight from your resume along with hobbies, interests, memberships, accomplishments, and other pieces of personal information that portray an image compatible with the expectations of your career objective.

5. Italicize substantive quantifiable data, businesses, and organizations that convey credibility and to which you wish to draw the reader's attention.

6. Include your e-mail and telephone contact information.

Cover Letters

While many individuals devote great care and thought to every word of their resume, it is not uncommon for the cover letter to be an afterthought lacking in both professionalism and effectiveness. Huge mistake! Just as with a personal introduction, you only get one chance to make a good first impression. For a resume, the cover letter is the introduction, and the quality of it, or lack thereof, may determine whether or not the resume gets reviewed.

To help ensure your cover letter compels the recruiter to review your resume and extend further consideration to your candidacy, begin by naming the person who helped you network into the organization (e.g., a current employee, friend of the hiring manager, etc.). If no one provided direct assistance, then reference where you learned of the individual, organization, or opening (e.g., a colleague, friend, newspaper article, job posting, etc.).

Next, it is important to highlight a few of the key qualifications relevant to the position for which you are applying. The cover letter should also not be too lengthy or detailed as this could discourage the recruiter or hiring manager from reading it. Rather, it should be succinct and sufficiently compelling so as to entice a hiring manager to review your resume more thoroughly than he or she normally would.

EXAMPLE 1
Cover letter—Referral from a friend of hiring manager or recruiter

---

Subject: Friend of Jim Stoddard

Dear Mr. Harbin,

Jim Stoddard, my former supervisor at Universal Studios, recommended I contact you regarding the position you have open for a **Human Resources Manager** at your corporate office. Given he is familiar with the requirements of this position from when the two of you worked together at SeaWorld, Jim thought my five years of theme park experience as his corporate Human Resources Manager would represent an ideal match for this opportunity.

As you will note from the attached resume, my accomplishments include the development and implementation of an innovative employee retention program that reduced voluntary turnover by *34 percent* and saved *$700,000* in recruiting expenses. I also possess the specialist skills in employee relations, non-exempt staffing, and customer service training listed as job requirements in the CareerBuilder posting.

Mr. Harbin, so that you can "put a name to a face," would it be okay if I dropped by your office for just 10 minutes to introduce myself?

Thank you!

Jessica Leigh

Cell: (555) 765-4321

Key Lessons

1. Use "Friend of Jim Stoddard" as the subject matter to draw the recipient's attention and provide instant credibility.

2. Jim Stoddard's name and the open position are bolded to capture the recipient's attention and interest.

3. Mention how you know the recipient's friend.

4. Reference a credible and relevant employer (in this case, Universal Studios).

5. Insert at least two key accomplishments and italicized numbers to demonstrate measurable and impressive results.

6. Underline applicable skills to help them stand out from both the plain and highlighted text.

7. Ask for only 10 minutes to introduce yourself (Note: If the request is granted, be prepared for a longer meeting and bring copies of your resume).

8. Extend an enthusiastic and presumptuous "Thank you!"

9. If the recipient does not respond, follow up with a phone call referencing the e-mail.

EXAMPLE 2
Cover letter—Unknown recruiter and no contacts from networking efforts

---

Subject: Follow-Up: Human Resources Manager

A colleague recommended I contact you regarding the position you have open for a **Human Resources Manager** at your corporate office.

As you will note from the attached resume, I offer five years of applicable Human Resources experience at **Universal Studios**, and my accomplishments include the development and implementation of an innovative employee retention program that reduced voluntary turnover by *34 percent* and saved *$700,000* in recruiting expenses. I also possess the specialist skills in employee relations, non-exempt staffing, and customer service training listed as job requirements in the CareerBuilder posting.

I would greatly appreciate the opportunity to introduce myself in person. Would it be possible to schedule a time for us to meet?

Thank you!

Jessica Leigh

Cell: (555) 765-4321

Key Lessons

1.   Use "Follow-Up: Human Resources Manager" as the subject matter to draw the recipient's attention and suggest a call to action.

2.   Use "a colleague" as the referral source to state you may have been referred by a colleague of the recipient. Otherwise, cite the source and change the wording to, "After reviewing the job posting on CareerBuilder, I felt compelled to reach out to you regarding the position of . . ."

3.   Place the title of the open position in bold to capture the recipient's attention and interest.

Also see Key Lessons 4–9 above.

EXAMPLE 3
Cover letter—Following up on a request for your resume

Subject: Follow-Up: Jessica Leigh

Dear Mr. Harbin,

It was a pleasure speaking with you today regarding the **Human Resources Manager** opportunity at SeaWorld. Per your request, I am attaching my resume for your review and consideration.

Please note I offer five years of theme park experience as the corporate Human Resources Manager for **Universal Studios**. Among my accomplishments is the development and implementation of an innovative employee retention program that reduced voluntary turnover by *34 percent* and saved *$700,000* in recruiting expenses. I also possess the specialist skills in employee relations, non-exempt staffing, and customer service training you mentioned in our discussion.

Mr. Harbin, I would greatly appreciate the opportunity to discuss the opportunity in person. Would it be possible to schedule a time for us to meet?

Thank you!

Jessica Leigh

Cell: (555) 765-4321

Key Lessons

1.   Use "Follow-Up: Jessica Leigh" as the subject matter to draw the recipient's attention and serve as a reminder as to the reason for the e-mail.

2. Reference your discussion and remind the recipient that he requested your resume (Note: Respond to such requests as quickly as possible!).

Also see Key Lessons 4–9 from Example 1 above.

Resume Examples
EXECUTIVE AND MANAGEMENT

The following example represents the actual resume format of a corporate executive and former client. To conceal his identity, I replaced his employers with fabricated names, but I ask you to think of them as brands warranting top billing over job titles (see Key Lesson 1 above in the "Experience and Qualifications" section).

BRANDON LOUIS

1995 Longhorn Drive
Orlando, FL 32819
brandonlouis@Domtbd.com

HOME: (407) 555-8661 | View my profile on **Linked in** | CELL: (407) 555-7321

CAREER OBJECTIVE AND PROFILE

Executive-level human resources position in an organization that will leverage my demonstrated ability to create strategic human resources solutions for improving company *performance, customer service*, and *employee satisfaction*. I am particularly interested in **generalist or talent management** assignments with responsibilities for:

- Organizational Development
- Staffing & Selection Assessments
- Employee & Labor Relations
- Succession & Talent Planning
- Operational Efficiencies
- EEOC & Employment Compliance

PROFESSIONAL EXPERIENCE

STEMMLER HOTELS San Jose, CA   2005 – Present

California's largest independent hotel developer and operator with 32 properties, 11,000 employees, and $1.7B in revenues.

Regional Vice President, Human Resources   *2009 – 2014*

Reporting to chief HR officer with responsibilities for staffing and talent management, leadership development, employee relations, compensation, and process and productivity improvement.

RESUME CONTINUES

- Developed Employer of Choice talent strategy for *5,400* employees at *16* properties in Southern California and Mexico. Awarded AHMA's top award for *Best Place to Work*.

- Led extensive upgrading of talent level for human resources staff of *28* professionals.

- Championed diversity initiative that contributed to *38% increase* in female and minority management staff over three-year period.

- Successfully orchestrated two NLRB-sanctioned union-avoidance campaigns.

- Created retention incentive for top 10% managers that reduced attrition by *22%*.

Vice President, Talent Management   *2005 – 2009*

Executive in charge of the staffing and talent management processes for *11,000* employees and managers.

- Reduced corporate office staffing costs by *27%* (*$650,000* annually) through development of comprehensive sourcing strategy and improved hiring processes.

- Centralized and aligned recruiting activities of *8* recruiters located throughout the U.S. and Mexico, resulting in elevated brand awareness, image and staff synergies.

- Created a comprehensive college relations plan that resulted in *45%* increase in offer acceptance rates.

TWIN EAGLES COMPANY Las Vegas, NV   1995 – 2005

Director of Employee Relations   *2002 – 2005*

Managed a staff of *7* professionals and advised field management on all employment-related issues for *25,000* employees and managers in *350* restaurants.

- Improved company efficiencies for resolving over *1,000* employee disputes per year while reducing department expenses by *$175,000*.

- Upgraded management training programs for performance coaching and corrective action, resulting in an annual average savings of *$300,000* in settlement costs.

- Implemented company-wide alternative dispute resolution process and developed metrics to track effectiveness.

Director of Staffing   *1999 – 2002*

Responsible for company-wide staffing hiring strategy, processes, and staff leadership.

- Redesigned selection and hiring processes, resulting in reduction of front-line employee turnover from *135%* to *89%* and management turnover from *35%* to *18%*.

- Reduced cost-per-hire by *$500* for management hires while improving management trainee turnover by *27%*.

- Partnered with minority organizations to identify new sourcing strategies for diverse candidates, which led to recognition by *Fortune* magazine as one of the 50 Best Companies for Minorities.

RESUME CONTINUES

Manager of University Relations and Employment   *1997 – 1999*

Developed and implemented management and faculty internship programs to strengthen relationships with key universities.

- Designed and implemented company-wide university recruiting program at *25* campuses, resulting in a *250%* increase in college trainee hires (*34* hires in 1999).
- Led project team in design of the company's employment website.

Area Employment Manager   *1995 – 1997*

Partnered with unit management to staff 112 restaurants located throughout the southeastern U.S. Forecasted hiring needs, developed staffing evaluation tool, and assisted in new restaurant openings. Key member of troubleshooting team for underperforming restaurants.

STANTON HOTELS CORPORATION   1990 – 1995

Human resources and front-line operational responsibilities including serving as the executive committee member responsible for all departmental programs and services at *400+* employee hotels including recruiting and staffing, employee relations, compensation administration, worker's compensation, and employee training and development. Also managed labor relations for three unionized employee bargaining units.

Human Resources Manager, Los Angeles, CA   *1993 – 1995*

Employment Manager, Newport Beach, CA   *1992 – 1993*

Food and Beverage Manager, Orlando, FL   *1990 – 1992*

EDUCATION

Master of Human Resources and Labor Relations *1995*
Michigan State University
Concentration in Organizational Change Leadership

Bachelor of Arts   *1990*
University of Miami
Studies in Political Science

NON-MANAGEMENT PROFESSIONAL

In this example, a Computer Skills section has been added and prominently placed immediately after the Summary. This format is designed to highlight the technical and software skills listed as critical in many administrative assistant job postings.

JACQUELINE LOREN, CPS

View my profile on **Linked** in

CELL: (863) 555 – 4229   E-MAIL: Jloren@Domtbd.com

SUMMARY

Professional **executive administrative assistant** with extensive experience supporting senior executives in all administrative areas including *maintaining business calendar and scheduling activities*; *designing presentations, templates, and documents*; *coordinating extensive travel,* and *planning meeting events*.

COMPUTER SKILLS

Microsoft Word, Excel, PowerPoint, Publisher, Outlook, working knowledge of Access, WordPerfect, Lotus 1-2-3, Windows 3.1, 95, 98, NT, PageMaker, Quicken, Harvard Graphics, PeopleSoft, Oracle, and various mainframe systems.

PROFESSIONAL EXPERIENCE

BREAKER RESTAURANTS INC. Phoenix, Arizona **2008 – Present**

EXECUTIVE ASSISTANT TO SENIOR VICE PRESIDENT, STRATEGIC DEVELOPMENT

Maintained executive's calendar; created documents, reports, and presentations; coordinated travel and meeting arrangements.

- Organized office to increase efficiency, including both paper and computer files for over *250* project plans.

- Implemented new procedures to increase departmental staff's administrative effectiveness, resulting in *$90,000* annual payroll savings.

- Coordinated physical relocation of department staff of *28* employees with minimal disruption to workflow.

- Responsible for coordinating program content at monthly best practices staff meetings.

- Awarded corporate office Professional of the Month in workplace of *800* employees.

CALAIS RESORT GROUP Orlando, Florida   **2003 – 2008**

EXECUTIVE ASSISTANT TO EVP OF HUMAN RESOURCES

Coordinated and disseminated information flow; maintained executive's calendar; created documents, reports, presentations, training materials,

RESUME CONTINUES

and manuals; handled travel and meeting arrangements; ensured smooth operation of all departmental functions.

- Designed and produced training manuals on leadership skills for company-wide domestic and international sales force of *4,500* professionals; edited text to ensure accurate, clear message and sourced graphics to enhance visual appeal.

- Developed employee communications process including memos, letters, and presentations to disseminate information on new policies, procedures, and benefits to *2,500* new hires annually. Project costs came in *24%* under a budget of *$62,000*.

- Created forms such as a disciplinary action report, payroll action form, and new hire orientation checklist to ensure consistency in the administration of core practices.

- Supported human resources needs of *3* start-up operations, including training and mentoring of staff.

BELL COMMUNICATIONS INC. Detroit, Michigan **2000– 2003**

***ADMINISTRATIVE ASSISTANT** TO REGIONAL HR DIRECTOR*   *2001– 2003*

HUMAN RESOURCES COORDINATOR   *2000– 2001*

Human resources generalist duties charged with administering various benefits plans; creating and placing want ads; screening resumes; conducting new hire orientations; coordinating performance appraisal process and annual employee survey.

- Maintained personnel database and files for approximately *150* employees.

- Identified and eliminated error in continuing to pay terminated employee, which saved company a projected loss of *$125,000* and resulted in change of policy that prevented any reoccurrence of such errors.

- Researched temporary employment services and centralized temporary help needs through the human resources department, reducing costs by *$30,000* (*25%*).

EDUCATION AND CERTIFICATIONS

CERTIFIED PROFESSIONAL SECRETARY (CPS)

Earned CPS designation from International Association of Administrative Professionals upon successful completion of course and examination.

MONTGOMERY COUNTY COMMUNITY COLLEGE Rockville, Maryland

Associate Degree in Business Administration

Magna Cum Laude, GPA 3.87

WHITING BUSINESS COLLEGE Cleveland, Ohio

Certificate in General and Legal Secretarial Studies

(Completed one-year course in six months)

FRANKLIN COVEY COURSES

Seven Habits of Highly Effective People

Time Management

NOTARY PUBLIC, State of Florida

RE-ENTERING WORKFORCE/JOB GAP

When there has been a significant break in employment (e.g., having left the workforce to raise children), the resume format below is advisable. In this instance, Competencies and Accomplishments and Education both appear before Experience, and the employers are presumed to be well-recognized brands (otherwise, the job titles would be listed first). Also note volunteer work has been added to the Experience section to bridge the gap between the last period of employment and now. Importantly, this format should only be used when there has been a sustained and generally acceptable gap in employment.

Tiffany Dane

ORLANDO, FLORIDA

View my profile on **Linked** in

CELL: (407) 555-3355   **E-MAIL:** Tiffanydane@domtbd.com

Career Objective and Summary

Finance management position in an organization that will leverage my successful track record and demonstrated leadership in business & financial analysis. In addition to my technical and management skills, I also offer specific expertise in the *hospitality*, *manufacturing* and *defense industries*.

Competencies and Accomplishments

- **Financial reporting:** Directed financial reporting and analysis for 6 customer service call centers and identified efficiencies resulting in 18% overhead reductions.

- **Budgeting and forecasting:** Designed and implemented system-wide forecasting and budgeting systems for 23 site operations in U.S. and Canada.

- **Technology:** Collaborated with IT to drive $225,000 in annual cost savings while enhancing reporting capabilities and accuracy.

- **Leadership:** Recipient of President's Award for cultivation of team environment as measured by company-wide top 10% scores in both employee satisfaction and talent retention.

- **Project management:** Led 12-person, multi-department implementation team for installation of SAP software, resulting in successful activation three months ahead of schedule and 16% below budget.

- **Business analysis:** Designed a rolling 13-month financial reporting package to measure and analyze performance on moving averages and to reduce impact of cyclical trends of business.

RESUME CONTINUES

Education

Bachelor of Science
Appalachian State University
Concentration: Accounting

Experience

VOLUNTEER SERVICE Portland, Oregon   2007 – Present

Project Leader / Event Coordinator / Volunteer

Dedicated volunteer for numerous non-profit organizations including the Portland Rescue Mission, and the Humane Society and serving as a PTA member and events coordinator for 800-student elementary school. Combined fundraising event participation resulted in annual receivables in excess of $125,000.

Bluewater Hotels & Resorts Portland, Oregon   2000 – 2007

Business Manager / Sr. Financial Analyst / Business Analyst

Provided financial reporting, statistical analysis, and program management for 23 resorts, hotels, and regional sales offices.

- Led and executed program to analyze call center customer referral leads, mass marketing campaigns, and tour referrals that translated into *$3.5M* in incremental annual sales.
- Developed and programmed automated payroll model that reduced processing costs by *45%* and increased accuracy from *94%* to *99%*.
- Provided financial and statistical reporting on a daily, weekly, and monthly basis for key metrics including occupancy rates, sales revenue, and EDITDA.
- Presented financial analysis and rolled out annual budget information and process to senior and middle management.

General Package Corporation Seattle, Washington   1997 – 2000

Sr. Financial Analyst

Budgeting, forecasting, and monthly P&L report generation for *$330M* business unit of international industrial shipping company.

- Budgeted, forecasted, and generated monthly P&L statements and analysis.
- Designed five-year, long-term business plan.

Border Technologies Gaithersburg, Maryland   1993 – 1997

Financial Analyst

- Designed and developed company's monthly income statement and cash flow forecast for nine worldwide divisions with annual sales of $750M.
- Developed profitability model and ongoing analytical support.

Computer and Software Skills

Oracle Financials, PeopleSoft, Hyperion, SAP, Lawson, Microsoft Word, Excel, Access, SAMS (Sales and Marketing System).

RECENT COLLEGE GRADUATE

For recent college graduates with limited professional experience, a one-page resume with the Education section following the Career Objective is appropriate.

LAURA LYNN

Lauralynn@Domtbd.net ♦ Linden, MI ♦ CELL: (555) 810-0610

CAREER OBJECTIVE

A **hospitality management** position that will leverage my extensive frontline & operational support experience, formal education, training and strong desire to deliver unparalleled guest satisfaction. I am particularly interested in the *hotel/resort*, *food & beverage* and *travel/tour* industries.

EDUCATION

UNIVERSITY OF NEVADA – LAS VEGAS   **2015**

Bachelor of Science: Hotel, Restaurant, and Casino Management
Dean's List: Academic Honor Roll (4 years)
Senior Adviser and Committee Chair: UNLV Hospitality Society

PROFESSIONAL EXPERIENCE

Provided exceptional and personal service to guests and staff members in various front-line and support capacities including:

- **Food and beverage:** Food server, bartender, front-line cook (lunch and dinner), banquet server, dishwasher, and busser in hotels and free-standing restaurant operations.
- **Room operations:** Front desk clerk and bell attendant for seasonal Mobil 4-Star resort with championship golf course.
- **Leadership:** Supervisor and lead trainer for beverage staff and front office reception desk.
- **Guest service:** Designated to resolve guest complaints that progressed beyond front-line staff. Awarded Employee of the Month for "professionalism and exceptional guest service" (August 2008).
- **Accounting:** Responsible for daily guest room ledger, reconciliations, cash handling, deposits, and financial reports.

FIREPLACE BAR & GRILL Henderson, NV   **2011 – Present**
Casual-style restaurant and bar with 350-seat banquet facility.
Bartender, food server, front-line cook, banquet server, and stewarding roles.

FENTON LAKE RESORT Lake Fenton, MO   **2009 – 2011**
400-room property and only Mobil 4-star resort on Lake of the Ozarks.
Front Desk Clerk, Night Auditor, Bell Attendant (summer seasonal staff)

Durfee's Laws for Writing a Great Resume

Here are some important things to know when writing your resume:

DURFEE'S LAW #6: **Don't do what George did.** George O'Leary was a highly successful football coach for Georgia Tech when he resigned in December 2001 to accept the job he had dreamed about—head coach for Notre Dame. After much fanfare and personal elation, he was forced to resign five days later. Why? It was discovered he had lied about his academic and athletic background on his resume. O'Leary claimed to have a master's degree in education and to have played college football for three years, but background checks showed those claims weren't true. Prior to submitting his resignation, he reportedly asked, "What am I going to tell my mother?"[1]

DURFEE'S LAW #8: **Double check and triple check.** Very simply, mistakes and typographical errors can be deal killers. They can knock you out of consideration regardless of the position for which you are applying. Before you distribute your resume or send a cover letter, double check and then triple check for typos and other errors. I strongly recommend you ask someone else to proofread your resume to get the perspective of a fresh set of eyes.

DURFEE'S LAW #13: **Quantify accomplishments.** Prospective employers consider a number of factors when determining which candidates match the requirements for an open position. While skills, experience, and education are all important, the demonstrated ability to get measurable results will add significant credibility to your qualifications. For instance, while many salespeople may be able to talk a good game by highlighting their activities (e.g., "Called on key customers in major markets"), I am always more impressed with statements quantifying specified accomplishments (e.g., "Increased sales revenue by 45% annually over a three-year period"). So while activities are nice, results are a whole lot better.

DURFEE'S LAW #20: **Summarize the unimportant.** For individuals who have changed careers and their previous experience is not relevant to their current career aspirations (or if they are concerned about age discrimination), one tactic is to summarize the earlier jobs and experiences under the heading Previous Experience at the bottom of the Experience and Qualifications section. For example, "Prior to 1992, I gained valuable computer experience and was promoted to various roles of responsibility including system analyst, programmer, and billing coordinator." If age is not a concern, you can add the span of years, such as, "From 1994 to 1998, I gained valuable experience. . . ." In this manner, you are submitting a factual resume without revealing too much about your age or past jobs.

DURFEE'S LAW #31: Keep it short. The resume is not intended to represent a comprehensive history of all of your accomplishments, talents, and awards. Depending on your years of experience, background, professional or occupational standards, and career pursuits, the resume may be as short as one page (e.g., young college graduates) and as long as three (e.g., seasoned executives). Anything more than three pages may be too cumbersome and detailed and cause the recruiter to end up setting it aside in favor of more reader-friendly resumes.

DURFEE'S LAW #37: Use key words. Given an employer may get a large number of resumes for a job opening posted on the Internet, key words help to get your resume electronically identified as a potential fit (which will lead to further consideration by the person screening the resumes).

Depending on the position for which you are applying, key words may or may not differ from action words. The reason is key words simply represent specific words and terminology a recruiter is seeking in a candidate's resume. So while key words may represent competencies, skills, and action words, they may also include industry jargon, professional certifications, and previous employers or accounts. You can generally identify potential key words for a specific opening in the job description for the posted position.

DURFEE'S LAW #38: Own your resume. Despite the claims and critiques of what seems to be an endless supply of so-called resume writing experts, there simply is no universal "right way" to write a resume. Unsurprisingly, it is not uncommon to get confused given the contradictory advice you can expect from multiple sources. So while I have gone to great lengths to help you develop what I consider effective and professional resume formats, ultimately, you will need to decide what works for you, your situation, and your comfort level. Even then, expect to continually modify, update, and edit your resume as you incorporate new or different styles, content, and concepts.

DURFEE'S LAW #41: Get rid of the squiggly lines. Before sending a resume electronically, always be sure to use the spell-checking feature so you can remove the squiggly red and green lines that highlight possible spelling and other errors (such as fragmented sentences). Even if highlighted words and sentences are correctly spelled and formatted, the red and green lines serve as a distraction for the reader and suggest an absence of detail-orientation on the part of the sender. To minimize the chance those lines won't show up on the recipient's end, you may want to first cut and paste your resume from one document to another before sending (sometimes that helps), or send your resume as a PDF file.

DURFEE'S LAW #63: Add a LinkedIn profile badge. A LinkedIn profile badge in the contact information section of the resume invites recruiters to view your LinkedIn profile with one click. As the great majority of recruiters utilize LinkedIn to search for potential candidates, this feature enables them to easily review your profile—something they most assuredly will do anyway. Provided you have created an effective LinkedIn profile (see chapter 4), the convenience of this feature stands to increase the likelihood that it will be viewed and will add to your appeal.

DURFEE'S LAW #68: Omit and protect. On rare occasions, it may make sense to leave a job off the resume provided you don't hide it. Huh? For instance, I joined an international logistics company only to have my position eliminated in a restructuring 20 days later. Rather than include such a short stint on my resume and risk it diverting valuable interviewing time away from more relevant experiences, I would mention the job in interviews by simply saying, "I didn't even bother putting it on my resume as I was there such a short time." By always bringing up the job in the interview and including it on the application, I was able to focus the interviewer on what was important while protecting myself from potential claims the omission was somehow dishonest. Should you be concerned that an omission may open the door for your integrity to be called into question, the safest approach is to list every job on your resume or use the approach provided above in Durfee's Law #20: Summarize the unimportant.

The Application

Some candidates don't understand why they're asked to complete an application when they have provided the recruiter with a world-class resume. The reason is the application provides the employer with important information not typically contained in the resume. This includes inquiries regarding salary, reasons for leaving prior jobs, reference contact information, names of family members currently working for the employer, and felony criminal convictions. In addition, applications often include legal disclaimers and authorization for background checks.

Regardless of whether you submit an application on a paper document or electronically, you are expected to complete it accurately and truthfully. Failure to do either risks raising suspicions about your integrity. Furthermore, omissions and falsifications can be considered grounds for termination even if not discovered until many years later. Accordingly, even if something was deliberately excluded from the resume (e.g., a job lasting only a few weeks), I advise including it on the application.

CRIMINAL RECORD

Most job applications have a section asking something along the lines of, "Have you ever been convicted of a felony?" with "Yes" and "No" boxes and a space to write an explanation if the former option is checked. If the company conducts criminal background checks and a false response was provided, there's a very good chance the conviction will be revealed and the employee will be immediately terminated.

If you have a criminal record, I recommend an honest and straightforward approach rather than trying to cover up the past and risk the humiliation of getting fired shortly after being hired. You are also much better off targeting employers who do not require their employees to be bonded.[2] For instance, financial institutions such as banks and credit card companies often require extensive criminal background checks for prospective employees, and there's usually very little leeway for making exceptions (bluntly speaking, don't even bother applying if you have a felony conviction). The better bet would be to target smaller employers or positions where employees have limited access to sensitive financial or confidential material, products, or data.

When filling out a paper application, an alternative to checking the "Yes" box is to write in, "Prefer to discuss in person," in the space provided. This improves the chances you will at least be afforded the opportunity to explain the circumstances with an interviewer. This is advantageous as sometimes an employer will make an exception for a convicted felon, provided the crime isn't relevant to the job and the applicant seems sincerely remorseful for his or her past actions. Conversely, checking the box could result in the automatic rejection of your application without any further consideration. Another option some applicants have success with is to neither mark a response to the question nor write a comment and hope the omission is overlooked by the interviewer.[3] The reason this approach has worked for so many applicants is many human resources departments do a lousy job of paying attention to the responses on applications, and omissions can easily go unnoticed.[4]

PLEASE REMEMBER THIS

Some of the key lessons in this chapter include:

- ✔ The resume is essentially a marketing tool to help you get and do well in interviews.

- ✔ The mandatory sections for your resume are Name and Contact Information, Professional Objective and Profile, and Experience and Qualifications. The optional sections are Education, Accreditations/Associations/Awards/Interests, and Technical Skills.

- ✔ Quantifiable accomplishments should be included whenever possible and italicized to draw the recruiter's attention.

- ✔ An effort should be made to match action words, key words, and competencies with job postings in order to improve the chances your resume will not be filtered out by electronic screening systems.

- ✔ Resumes can and should be customized to better match career interests, skills, and experiences to the posted requirements of specific positions.

- ✔ Resume and CV styles and formats can vary depending on profession, experience, and career aspirations.

- ✔ An effective LinkedIn profile is just as important for marketing your capabilities as an effective resume.

- ✔ The cover letter is a critical component of the application process and should be personalized whenever possible.

- ✔ The application is a formal document generally requiring more specific information than the resume.

- ✔ Durfee's Laws highlight the importance of factual information, measurable results, and the absence of typographical errors in resumes, cover letters, and applications.

> "Advertising says to people, 'Here's what we've got. Here's what it will do for you. Here's how to get it.'"
>
> *LEO BURNETT (1891–1971)*
> *FOUNDER, LEO BURNETT WORLDWIDE*

CHAPTER 4

THE ART AND SCIENCE OF NETWORKING

"It's not what you know; it's who you know."

Anonymous

My uncle, Duane Jones, shared the above words of wisdom one summer day when I was bagging groceries in Holly, Michigan, prior to starting my senior year at Lake Fenton High School a few miles down the road. While I can't recall the specific topic of our conversation, I do remember thinking this comment on how one gets ahead in the world of work was meant somewhat cynically. After all, shouldn't working hard and doing a great job be enough to get ahead in life? Today, as I think of all the talented people I know who have lost their jobs mainly because they didn't have the equivalent of a corporate godfather to protect them, I realize my uncle was very insightful. In this chapter, we'll explore how that old saying applies to networking.

With respect to seeking employment, networking is the process of making contacts and finding out about job opportunities that you may not have otherwise found on your own. It calls upon you to draw on your direct contacts (e.g., friends, family, vendors, former coworkers, etc.) and to reach out to and establish new or secondary contacts (e.g., people you do not yet know). The goal of networking is to enlist the support of others, not only to make you aware of potential job opportunities but, ideally, to also endorse you as a candidate. Tami Mann, Director of Corporate Staffing for Wyndham Vacation Ownership, adds, "Networking is a sincere act of exchanging information, adding value, and fostering a relationship of trust."

Without question, a great percentage of jobs are found through networking. In contrast to showing up at the human resources office without an introduction or responding to an online job posting along with hundreds of other interested individuals, networking offers returns that include:

- Exponentially expanding the number of people who will refer jobs to you.
- Making you aware of unadvertised job openings.
- Opening doors for you by way of credible and impactful introductions.
- Placing you in direct contact with hiring managers.

Joe Gonzalez, Managing Partner of BCA Executive Recruiters, a human resources executive search firm based in San Diego, said networking is a vital component of his efforts to find top talent for his clients:

> The executive search industry is primarily built on networking. Sure, there are many other responsibilities we have in a search, but if not for our relationships, we are worthless to our clients. So if a multibillion dollar industry is built on this one thing, do you think maybe it is important enough to carve out ten minutes a day for it?
>
> We currently have incredible technology tools to help us network, such as LinkedIn. It gives us the ability to grow our network like never before. The theory is well known that through six degrees of separation, everyone on this planet is connected. When limited to the context of profession or industry, it is probably much more like three degrees of separation. I encourage everyone to focus on this starting today, and the sooner in your career you get started, the better.

Noel Ferguson, an entrepreneur and executive coach who previously held senior vice president roles with Marriott International and La Quinta Inns & Suites, shared his cautionary perspective on how job seekers may be spending their time on the least effective activities:

> *From what I have seen, people are more likely to spend the majority of their time in front of their computer visiting Internet job boards. While this may provide the illusion of productivity, the reality is comparatively few jobs are found this way. What this suggests is a disproportionate amount of time is being spent applying for jobs online at the expense of more effective job search activities such as networking.*

The Story Line

One of the first priorities in preparing to network is to get your story line down. By this, I mean, how will you concisely, positively, and factually respond to the often-asked question, "Why did you leave your last job?" The story line is critical for a number of reasons, including that you need it to respond to one of the first questions you may be asked by everyone from your next-door neighbor to a corporate recruiter. During the interviewing process, an effective response will also help you progress from the "What happened?" stage to a more productive discussion about how your skills, experience, and interests match the needs of the prospective employer.

The story line may reflect a circumstance out of your control such as job elimination due to downsizing, a merger, or a shift in business strategy. It can also be used to more positively position a termination resulting from poor performance or misconduct. Regardless of the reason you may be looking for another job, Barbara Wilcox, Chief Talent Officer for Orange Lake Resorts, advises, "Never, ever speak badly about your past employers, companies, bosses, or leadership."

LEVEL 1, 2, AND 3 RESPONSES

Your story line should be delivered via progressive levels of detail, starting with a response that is short, broad, and easily understandable (which I refer to as a Level 1 response). Only if pressed for more detail should you offer Level 2 and Level 3 responses. For example:

Level 1 Response

Brian: Sorry to hear you lost your job at the Gudith Company, Mike. What happened, anyway?

Mike: Well, the same thing that a lot of people seem to be going through these days—my job was eliminated due to a recent re-structuring.

Level 2 Response

Brian: Really? Gee, I thought I read that Gudith is a growing company.

Mike: That's true in some areas. Unfortunately for me, some of that growth is through acquisitions, and they consolidated my business unit with a company they bought last year. As part of the consolidation, they no longer needed two controllers.

Level 3 Response

Brian: That's too bad. But if they still needed one controller for the consolidated business, how come you didn't get that job? After all, you've worked there for eleven years.

Mike: The company Gudith acquired is twice the size of my business unit, plus they have a lot of outstanding accounting issues we inherited from the acquisition that necessitated keeping the other controller in place. Although I was disappointed I didn't get the newly created job, I can understand why it made sense for them to give it to the other controller. They really do need to tap into her institutional knowledge of the other company's past issues if they are going to successfully merge the two businesses. Anyway, this gives me the opportunity to grow my career by taking what I learned at the Gudith Company and applying my experience to another company—maybe even in a different industry.

Notice how the responses get increasingly longer and more detailed? Clearly, Mike would have preferred limiting the exchange to a Level 1 response (which is what he tried to do). Given that was not an option, his preparation enabled him to progressively elaborate in a confident and credible manner that demonstrated he was moving forward in his career transition with a positive and professionally mature demeanor.

I encourage you to take a few minutes at this time to create your own Level 1, 2, and 3 responses to the question: "Why did you leave your last job?" Try to keep your responses concise, credible, and, of course, factual. Avoid the common mistake of launching into Level 2 or 3 responses when a Level 1 response may be all you need. This is easy to do if you remember to simply pause after each response and don't volunteer any more information unless pressed to do so.

Developing a Targeted Approach

Before you start networking, first identify and target the employers you'd really like to work for, and then list all of the sources who could potentially help you get in the door. Do this without any reservations or self-imposed disqualifications, such as having recently heard the employer had a downsizing or was not hiring. The reason you should still explore potential opportunities is that you and your source connected to the organization simply may not know what the organization has in mind now or in the near future. Organizational changes including downsizings often result in the creation of new positions, and your specific skills and experience may match the needs of unannounced job openings.

Next, develop lists of people you would personally like to contact including direct contacts (people you know and who know you) and secondary contacts (people known by your direct contacts but not you). Keep your list of targeted employers in mind when soliciting secondary contacts. For example, in this situation, Mike has reached out to his friend Susan, who has agreed to help him network:

Soliciting secondary contacts from direct contacts

> "Thanks for your assistance, Susan. Also, I've always been intrigued about the possibility of working at Disney. Do you happen to know of anyone over there who may be able to help me find out about job openings in finance or accounting?"

Be sure to ask direct contacts if they will make an introduction for you or, at a minimum, allow you to reference them when you reach out to these secondary contacts.

Durfee's Laws for Networking

Here are some important things to know when networking:

DURFEE'S LAW #1: Project confidence. (Note: With just a few modifications, this Durfee's Law was introduced in Chapter 1. Given that it's equally relevant to this chapter's topic, I felt it was worth repeating). Whether it's talking to friends, family, or whomever you choose to network with, everyone will benefit if you demonstrate confidence in your ability to land on your feet. Conversely, some people may be reluctant to help you network if they feel you are so angry or "down and out" that you would embarrass them with their friends or professional colleagues. In fact, your attitude is so important that if you're having difficulty coping emotionally with your current predicament (e.g., an unexpected or unfair job loss), you may want to take some time before you begin reaching out so you can, at a minimum, put on a believable "game face."

DURFEE'S LAW #2: Spread the word. While unemployment used to be widely considered a cause for embarrassment, those days are long gone (just think of how many people you know who have lost their jobs through a restructuring, downsizing, or other uncontrollable event). If you are one of the increasingly rare individuals with a short list of former employers, pick up the newspaper and you'll undoubtedly read about some major downsizings even in an overall healthy economy. So rather than trying to keep your unemployment a secret, spread the word to your friends, family, acquaintances, and former coworkers. Since so many people have been in the same situation, you will likely find a lot of them will earnestly keep an eye out for opportunities that may be of interest to you. Remember to be clear about what kind of job you are looking for, and always be positive (Durfee's Law #1).

This tactic has served me well over the years as I have received countless calls from search firms who got my name from friends and professional associates who knew I was looking for a new job. A past job of mine as the Vice President of Human Resources for Centex Homes resulted from a call directed to me by my friend, Jim Lynde. The headhunter initially called Jim to find out if he would be interested in the job, and when he said he wasn't, he gave the person my name and contact information along with a very positive recommendation. Had I not let Jim know I was in the market for a new job, who knows if the headhunter would have ever contacted me?

DURFEE'S LAW #11: Find the insider. The odds of being considered for a position are greatly enhanced if you have someone inside the organization willing to help open doors and help you bypass the standard hiring process hurdles. Even if the source does not know you well, or even at all, he or she may be willing to forward your resume to the hiring manager at the request of a mutual friend or acquaintance. Conversely, sending a resume without any internal sponsorship usually means it will get reviewed with minimal attention, if at all.

Over dinner not too long ago, Jim Whitaker, a business development executive with Bolthouse Farms and a former Pepsi colleague, remarked, "It's not the quantity of your network that matters; it's the quality of your network." As we compared notes on the whereabouts of some of our former colleagues, it became clear that if he were ever looking for a new opportunity, he would have little problem finding insiders at consumer products giants like Sara Lee, Kimberly-Clark, Coors Brewing, Dean Foods, and Diageo. When those individuals changed employers, Jim made a point of maintaining his relationships with them, and many of them are now senior executives for those companies.

Durfee's Law #15: Don't fade away. Once you have created your lists of contacts and reached out to them, don't think that's sufficient. Keep them in the loop on your progress (e.g., job prospects, interviews, etc.) by following up with them regularly so you are fresh in their minds. Otherwise, they could very easily get distracted by their own responsibilities and forget about sending you job leads. (Note: To avoid becoming a nuisance by over-communicating to your contacts, limit your correspondence to every three weeks).

CASE IN POINT FROM THE RELUCTANT EXPERT

4

One day when I was a Senior Vice President for a resort company, I got a phone call from a gentleman named Roger who got my name through networking. I had never met this individual, but we established an instant and cordial dialogue once he mentioned we had both worked at Pepsi a couple of years earlier.

The reason for Roger's call was his job as the Chief Financial Officer for an international logistics company had recently been eliminated, and he was wondering if I would mind forwarding any job leads to his attention. I said I would and while he hadn't asked if we had any jobs at my company, I nonetheless offered to check. He also asked if it would be all right for him to stop by my office for just a few minutes to introduce himself in person and to drop off his resume. While we only met for about fifteen or twenty minutes, it helped to further establish a connection.

While I regularly receive requests for networking assistance, what made Roger so memorable was his excellent follow-up skills. For the next several months, he would send me short and informative e-mails every four weeks or so, updating me on his job search. He shared some basic information about jobs he was pursuing as well as other opportunities that hadn't worked out. Because he didn't fade away after our initial meeting, I found myself increasingly trying to help him find another job—rooting for him, even. Once Roger did land a job, he closed the loop by sending me a note telling me where he would be working and thanking me for my support.

In contrast, most people seeking networking assistance make it a one-time event. That is, they reach out once and then disappear. As a result of their failure to keep me engaged in their job search process, I quickly forget about them or assume they have found another job. The lesson? If you fade away, so will your networking support.

DURFEE'S LAW #16: **Never stop networking. Ever.** People often make the mistake of building and maintaining a network only when it suits their immediate needs. A lack of interest in helping others or failing to sustain and grow a healthy networking pipeline when there is no apparent self-serving reason to do so is short-sighted and often breeds lasting resentment that stymies future requests for assistance. Simply stated, no one likes to feel used, and effective networking—when earnestly nurtured over the long term—can prevent that from happening. Besides, just because you may have landed a new job today doesn't mean it won't go away tomorrow.

Jan Cannon, an HR executive who has worked for companies such as Cranium, Trendwest Resorts, and Sur La Table, once had a conversation with an unemployed executive with a distinctly unflattering view of networking:

> *This individual told me outright he thought networking was dishonest. His reasoning was you were reaching out to people only because you wanted something from them. I responded that while it was true he did want something—help finding a job—there was nothing dishonest about it as long as he stated up front the reason for establishing contact. I also pointed out that he should offer to return the favor somewhere down the road, either to that person or to someone they know. Ironically, he then came around to asking for my assistance, and it led to an interview with the company of the wife of a consulting client.*
>
> *By his own admission, he now has a much better appreciation for the power of networking.*

Ray Stitle, the Chief People Officer at Monogram Foods in Memphis, Tennessee, offered the following firsthand advice on the topic:

> *We all know how important it is to keep our network fresh and relevant, but doing so is difficult and requires effort and time. We tend to do better when we are searching for talent or looking for our own opportunities—in short, when our*

own interests are top of mind. The bigger challenge is helping someone else by responding to their call when it seems you are just too busy to fit it into your schedule.

During my last job campaign, I made many calls and reached out to several previous associates, managers, business leaders, and search professionals. I can count on one hand how many returned my call in a prompt manner. Learning from this and previous situations throughout my career, I have vowed to make every effort to return calls as soon as possible. I also keep trying until I make contact with the individual. It's also worth mentioning that some of my most rewarding days have ended after a conversation with a friend or associate whom I helped take a step closer to his or her next career goal.

5

CASE IN POINT FROM THE RELUCTANT EXPERT

Networking should not be a one-time event. Rather, it should be an ongoing, never-ending process you engage in for the remainder of your career.

In today's world, you never know when your job is going to go away. As harsh as that may sound, even the most stable employers have been rocked by globalization, mergers, acquisitions, technological advances, or funding cutbacks. Even employees of once-safe government and academic institutions are no longer immune.

I remember getting a phone call from a former colleague when I held the position of Global Vice President of Human Resources for Hard Rock Cafe. Even though I hadn't talked to this individual for a couple of years, I was happy to help him network as he had just lost his job. Given we had a good relationship when we worked together at Nestlé, I went out of my way to make some phone calls on his behalf and to send him some job leads. He was very appreciative of my efforts, and eventually he landed another job.

Before he started with his new employer, I asked him to keep in touch and to send me his new contact information. He never did. I really don't know what happened to him but I do know this—I won't ever help him again.

By abruptly disappearing, he made it clear he had no interest in me other than what I could do for him. In short, he was only a taker and not a giver. Sadly, had he kept in contact, there's a good chance we could have helped each other throughout our careers—and not just for job leads either. A strong network can be leveraged for all kinds of things, including best practice sharing, vendor recommendations, business development, and getting the inside scoop on just about anything.

By treating networking as a short-term proposition or a one-way street, you're likely to alienate the very people who can be tremendously helpful to you. Very simply, treat networking as an integral source of your overall career success—regardless of how secure you may think your job is.

DURFEE'S LAW #22: **Create the lists, then create the lists.** While responding to Internet job postings and even newspaper ads should not be discounted, word-of-mouth is a very effective means of finding jobs—that is, of course, if you make the effort to connect with as many people as you can. To begin with, create a list of all your former coworkers, bosses, subordinates, and vendors you have worked with. Secondly, create a list of all your friends, acquaintances, and social contacts. Once done, you can start direct networking by reaching out to people whom you know and who know you. When in contact with these individuals for job leads, also ask them if they would introduce you to people they think can help with your job search (this represents your list of secondary networking sources). If they are hesitant or lax about making a timely introduction, ask instead for permission to at least reference their names as you reach out to their contacts.

DURFEE'S LAW #30: **Leverage LinkedIn.** If you don't know someone inside the organization you are targeting for employment opportunities, find someone who does and solicit their assistance to get you a personal introduction to the key decision maker(s). The website LinkedIn (see page 92) is tremendously helpful in this regard as its primary purpose is to foster greater professional and business connections among its worldwide membership. Social websites such as Twitter and Facebook are also great networking venues.

DURFEE'S LAW #39: Don't ask for a job. As eager as you may be to find other employment, avoid the temptation of outright asking people for an interview or a job. Instead, ask for assistance with networking as they will likely be much more agreeable to such a request. Besides, just by asking for networking assistance, you have opened the door for them to consider you for any jobs they may have open.

DURFEE'S LAW #42: Show your appreciation. Once someone has helped you with your job search—even to a minimal extent—immediately thank them for their assistance. For individuals who have been particularly helpful with networking, mailing a nice thank-you note shows your sincerity and will help them to remember you for jobs that may later come to their attention. Once you have accepted a new job, follow up again to let them know your search is over, and provide some details about your employer, your responsibilities, and how they can contact you. Extending such courtesies may open the door for future networking and even friendships.

DURFEE'S LAW #49: Call in your IOUs. Think of individuals you helped find jobs or provided some other form of assistance (e.g., church, fundraisers, school events, etc.). How about people you helped at your former employer who are still there, such as other employees or vendors? Now is not the time to be shy about asking for some help in return. If you have made a sincere effort to lend a helping hand so that others could achieve their goals, in most cases, they will gladly reciprocate. Before they can return the favor, however, you must first let them know you are in a career transition (see Durfee's Law #2).

DURFEE'S LAW #55: Identify references early. As soon as possible, begin lining up your references—don't wait until you have a pending job offer. By asking others to be a reference, you are accomplishing a few important objectives. First, this is a great way to establish your network as such requests open the door for you to explain why you may need references. Once you've shared that you are looking for a new job, it then becomes a very smooth and natural transition to ask for their help with networking. Second, people who are asked to be your reference may be flattered you have such trust in them and, in turn, may be especially interested in helping you network. Third, a reference request should give you a more accurate understanding of who you should use as a reference—and who you should not. It's much better to find this out early in the job search process so you aren't scrambling later to find suitable references and holding up your job offer in the process.

DURFEE'S LAW #57: Establish lots of references. Although you will generally not need more than three or four references, I recommend you proactively secure the commitments of six to ten people as that will improve the reach and effectiveness of your networking. Besides, there is no downside to this approach as it is very doubtful these contacts will have their feelings hurt if they aren't later called by a prospective employer seeking to use them as a reference.

DURFEE'S LAW #67: Help headhunters (search firms) before you need help. It is quite common for someone who just joined the ranks of the unemployed to call a search firm and solicit their assistance in finding another job. It is also quite common to feel disappointed when the search firm seemingly shows little interest in helping. Usually, this is a reflection of the reality that headhunters only get paid from clients looking to fill jobs and not by individuals looking to find jobs. To improve the odds a search firm will make a more meaningful effort to present you to their clients when you need a job, first try helping them fill jobs when you are not searching for employment. By assisting them with their networking efforts, you begin building positive and helpful relationships that may pay big dividends in return should you ever find yourself seeking their assistance.

Professional E-mail Addresses

As mentioned in the previous chapter, I strongly recommend you establish a professional e-mail address, particularly if the one you use for personal correspondence risks conveying the wrong message to networking sources and employers. For instance, your friends may not think twice about e-mail addresses such as

hotmama@domtbd.net or partyhound@domtbd.com, but potential employers may.

When I was a human resources executive in the job market, I
created mattdurfeeHR@domaintbd.net for all of my job search correspondence. Not only did this address clearly include my name to
make it easy for recruiters to identify me but adding the "HR" suffix
also gave it a professional connotation. By establishing a separate
job search account, I also reduced the risk that important e-mails
would get lost among personal correspondences.

Personal Business Cards

As the information on business cards issued by your former employer
may no longer be valid, it is advisable to make personal business
cards for your job search. Personal business cards enable you to not
only share information when a resume is not available or appropriate
but they also effortlessly invite you to ask for the recipient's business
card in exchange. The value of getting someone else's business card is
that you can use it to follow up for networking assistance (e.g., "It was
great meeting you at the Little League park on Saturday").

In addition to a myriad of printing companies, all national office supply store chains sell business card templates that allow you
to design and print business cards inexpensively with basic home
office computer equipment. When designing your business card,
include your name and all of the standard contact information plus
a reference to your professional objectives or qualifications. For

Hewitt Judson
ATTORNEY-AT-LAW

*Corporate Law including International Trade,
Mergers & Acquisitions, Antitrust Regulation*

CELL: (407) 555-0123   E-MAIL: HJCorporatelaw@domaintbd.com

instance, a former Vice President of Marketing may use titles such as Marketing Executive or Marketing Consultant, whereas a corporate attorney may go with something like what is shown on the sample business card on the previous page.

LinkedIn

Launched in 2003 by Silicon Valley entrepreneurs, LinkedIn (www.linkedin.com) is the premier global networking website for business connections. With literally hundreds of millions of registered users in over two hundred countries, LinkedIn opens doors for introductions and connections by leveraging the principles of the six degrees of separation. Members can readily reach out to others with whom they may have a common association, such as fellow college alumni, friends, or previous employers, and request to be connected. Once a request is accepted, both parties can view each other's lists of connections, which contain personal and professional details about their contacts. This is particularly valuable to job seekers, as they can request introductions to people they see are working for companies where they'd like some help getting in the door. In addition, recruiters regularly use LinkedIn's messaging capabilities, group forums, and job posting feature to identify and contact potential candidates.

Scott Steiger, Chief People Officer for Michelman Inc. in Cincinnati, Ohio, came to appreciate the immense potential of LinkedIn after his spouse was affected by a downsizing.

> *My wife, Jen, is a fellow HR professional, and when she was engaged in a job search, she sent me an invitation to join her on LinkedIn. Historically, I have not been a huge proponent of using social networks such as LinkedIn as I considered them to be too invasive. However, in a short period of time, Jen made numerous contacts and even got referrals from some fairly senior people. Additionally, she was contacted by a recruiter that identified her as a job candidate from the background contained on her LinkedIn profile.*
>
> *As a result, I soon engaged a "social strategist" consultant at my company to assess how we could use technology*

as a tool to support our business strategy for sales and marketing, as well as to reduce our reliance on recruiters. In a remarkably short time, I became a firm believer that online social networking is here to stay, and you'd be making a huge mistake if you didn't embrace it and make the most of it.

YOUR PROFILE

LinkedIn is so vital to networking that one of the first things my outplacement firm does with new clients in career transitions is help them create effective profiles. Usually this means revising their current profile, although there are times when individuals who have worked for the same employer for a long time need to create an account for the first time. For the latter, LinkedIn's basic service is free, and their website provides easy-to-follow instructions for signing up. Regardless of your status, it is important to devote the same thoughtfulness and attention to detail that goes into the resume and professional biography.

Jerry McGrath, a Managing Partner with DHR International in New York City, summed up the value of a LinkedIn profile as follows:

> *This is your story, so make sure it is complete by sequentially including your location, employment history, and dates. If I'm going to represent you as a candidate, I'll need to know everything, so fill in any gaps. Also, this should be an objective, versus subjective, representation of who you are as a professional, so don't overthink it by including too much information that wouldn't appear on your resume.*

Furthermore, Dave Rowe of Aspen Rain Associates, cautions, "Be certain that your resume matches your LinkedIn profile as any discrepancies will raise a red flag."

The main sections of the profile include summary, background, experience, skills, education, recommendations, connections, and groups, with secondary areas for contact information, additional information, and other users that the profile owner follows.

SUMMARY

The summary section contains the user's name, position, past and present employers, location, education, and functional specialty area. As with a professional biography, a photo is acceptable, and there is also a feature allowing for an optional background photo. Unlike social networking sites like Facebook, however, LinkedIn is intended for professional networking, and therefore, your photo should be appropriate for your profession.

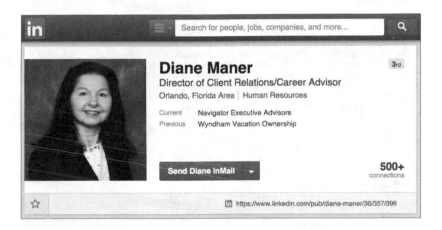

The summary section also shows how many LinkedIn connections the user has and the degree to which they are connected. Users who are directly connected to another user (a 1st connection) can access LinkedIn's messaging feature without paying for an upgraded account. This is a huge benefit for job seekers soliciting networking assistance and a compelling reason for having a large number of direct connections. Additionally, a direct connnection offers the added benefit of enabling you to access the contact information tab, where many users provide their e-mail addresses.

BACKGROUND

Similar to the Professional Objective and Profile section of a resume, the background section is essentially another billboard that should succinctly convey your current position or professional level, skills, experience, interests, and education. However, whereas a resume is often in the hands of passive recruiters who may not be particularly interested in your reviewing credentials, anyone reading your LinkedIn background is likely to be more actively interested in you since he or she wouldn't otherwise devote the time. As a result, you can afford to provide more detail than you would in your resume. In this case, limit your background summary to no more than three short paragraphs.

Background

 Summary

Diane serves as both Director of Client Relations and Director of Operations and is responsible for client coaching, recruiting, training and alliance partner relations. During her distinguished career, she has held key management positions with several of the most prominent names in the hospitality and resort industries including the Peabody Hotel Group, Grenelefe Golf and Tennis Resort and most recently Wyndham Vacation Resorts as Regional Director of Human Resources. Diane holds a degree in Psychology & Philosophy and has served on several executive boards including the Polk County Workforce Development Board.

EXPERIENCE

The experience section isn't that dissimilar to the Experience and Qualifications section of a resume. The main differences are that the format doesn't invite as much content or style capabilities such as italicizing. In addition, company logos and website links are pervasive, and recommendations from past or former colleagues are prominently displayed.

LinkedIn provides a friendly format for this section, and the content can easily be cut and pasted from your resume. Not only is this approach efficient but it also ensures consistency and accuracy.

SKILLS

This section enables both you and your connections to identify and select your skills from a lengthy menu, which are then displayed to any viewers of your profile.

The abundant volume of content and the lack of credible authority with respect to how the skills are awarded mean recruiters generally give little credence to this section of the profile. Regardless, it is worth having some skills listed if for no other purpose than that the absence of content risks inviting unwarranted and unfounded speculation as to the reasons.

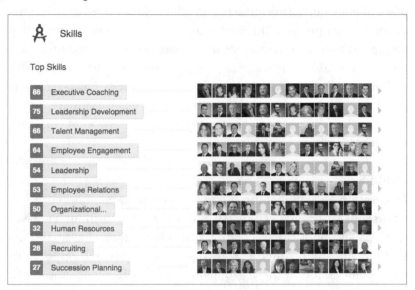

EDUCATION

References to education should follow the same guidelines contained in the corresponding section for resumes in the previous chapter. Accordingly, include the name and link to the institution(s) along with your field of study if they carry academic and vocational merit for your particular profession. Consider leaving out the name of the school if the degree was acquired through a for-profit online school.

RECOMMENDATIONS

Professional recommendations from colleagues in your profile (see the "Experience" section above) are nice to have, and although they carry more weight than the skills section, it is doubtful they will have much influence with recruiters as it is well known that such endorsements are often solicited by users and amount to little more than professional pleasantries. Once again, however, it is advisable to have at least a few recommendations so as not to draw unwelcome attention.

CONNECTIONS

As the name implies, this section of your profile provides a snapshot of all of your LinkedIn contacts and allows your direct connections access to their profiles. This information is valuable to users seeking to expand their own network for purposes such as assistance with job searches or business development. Given the global popularity of LinkedIn, it is important to achieve a network of at least a few hundred connections as anything less may suggest you are out of touch with respect to social networking and the power of this multifaceted service in particular.

GROUPS

In addition to establishing individual connections, LinkedIn has thousands of groups ranging from everything to industry associations and political associations to college alumni associations and job-sharing forums. For anyone seeking new job opportunities, membership in these groups tends to be fairly open and can exponentially increase job leads and open doors to insiders within targeted organizations. As with any approach to networking, the results are contingent on the time, effort, and discipline that you expend.

ADDITIONAL INFORMATION AND FOLLOWING

The section for additional information provides a place for referencing hobbies, memberships, training programs, technical certifications, personal details, and other interests. Meanwhile, in the section for following, you can also follow other users such as companies, not-for-profit organizations, and colleges. As recruiters will be able to review both sections and therefore draw conclusions about your potential fit with an employer, refrain from following any organizations or institutions that may be considered controversial, political, or a conflict of interest as it could jeopardize your candidacy without you even knowing it.

GETTING CONNECTED

After your profile is in sufficient shape to project the image of a capable professional, you will be ready to expand your LinkedIn network. To do so, note in the example of the summary section (page 95) that at the top of the page is a field to search for the names of individuals with whom you would like to connect. This is a particularly helpful feature should you not have the contact information for those individuals on the list of contacts you created earlier in this chapter (Durfee's Law #22).

If you do not know of anyone at a company that you'd like to target, you can simply type in the name of the organization and the department where you'd like to explore opportunities. For example, over 175,000 individual or group LinkedIn profiles appear when you type in "GE marketing." The results page will reveal the profiles of direct and indirect connections that you have with people either currently or previously employed or associated with GE marketing. As the sheer volume of profiles can be too great to reasonably filter for helpful connections, narrow the search with a more targeted approach based on factors such as function, segment, level, or location. For instance, by changing the same search to "GE marketing aviation Florida," the list of contacts is reduced to fewer than six hundred users.

If you do not have a direct connection to a user in an organization that you have identified as a potentially valuable networking resource, LinkedIn allows you to send an invitation to most users.

✉ Invite **Steve** to connect on LinkedIn

How do you know Steve?

○ Colleague
○ Classmate
◉ We've done business together

[President & CEO at Navigator Executive Advisors, Inc. ∨]

○ Friend
○ Other
○ I don't know Steve

Include a personal note: (optional)

Steve - I see from your profile that you and I share a direct to
connection to Sarah King as well as to Michigan State Alumni
Association. With your approval, I'd like to add you to my
LinkedIn contacts.
Thanks and I hope you are doing well at GE.

Important: Only invite people you know well and who know you. Find out why.

[Send Invitation] or Cancel

In these situations, the Send InMail button in the illustration on page 95 is replaced with a Connect button. A user will first need to accept your invitation to connect before you can send free messages to him or her. One exception is that you can send a limited message in the invitation itself. To do so, click on the Connect button, which will take you to a page where you will be asked how you know the individual. Do not be concerned if you don't share a common employer or college as you can use your current or a past employer. After responding to the first section, you will be invited to include a personal note—which I highly recommend you provide to show that you are not simply spamming for LinkedIn connections. Whenever possible, the note should reference a common connection along with any shared groups, institutions, etc.

Note that this initial correspondence does not contain any reference to your job search. This is because the goal is to first establish a direct connection, and asking for networking assistance at this stage of the process risks having your invitation declined as it may be perceived as too much of a bother. Instead, first establish the connection so that you can later seek to obtain the user's work e-mail in the contact information tab.

If your invitation is accepted and the user has provided an e-mail address, scripts for soliciting networking assistance are provided later in this chapter and will guide you as you write your follow-up e-mail. If your invitation has been accepted but the e-mail address is not provided, send a LinkedIn message using the same language. While perhaps not as effective, you now have the benefit of being a direct connnection, which means there is no limit to the size of your message, as there is in the initial invitation (LinkedIn limits the size of messages contained in an invitation to three hundred characters). In the event your invitation is not accepted, resend the request every two weeks (doing so any more frequently risks alienating the user).

For direct connections that you already have, first check if they have included their e-mail address in the contact information tab, as it is preferable to reach out to your contacts that way rather than through LinkedIn's messaging service. This is true for a couple of reasons: the length of a message isn't restricted, and most people check their work e-mails frequently throughout the day, whereas they may only sporadically read their LinkedIn messages.

Steve Steury, a principal with Navigator Search Advisors, always prefers sending e-mails to prospective candidates for this very reason. "As beneficial as LinkedIn's messaging feature is," he said, "I have much better success getting responses from executives through their work e-mail, as that is something they constantly check even when they are out of the office and on vacation."

LinkedIn offers such great potential for networking that hundreds of books have been written on how to optimize the service. If you're not already well versed with it, I highly recommend you invest the time to become at least sufficiently proficient.

Other Networking Venues

In addition to LinkedIn, there are a number of activities, events, and organizations to be considered when developing a networking strategy. Some are specifically intended for job seekers, whereas others are primarily intended for different purposes. You might consider exploring the following options.

PROFESSIONAL NETWORKING CLUBS

Networking clubs and associations have grown dramatically in popularity over the last several years. Generally, they offer a distinctly formal yet open solution for meeting the demands of those seeking to gather and exchange contacts and information. The effectiveness, relevance, and costs of these associations vary greatly, so it is advisable to obtain recommendations from current and former members prior to making a financial commitment. Information regarding clubs can easily be acquired from your network and online, including from LinkedIn groups.

TRADE ASSOCIATION MEETINGS

Trade associations represent a very valuable venue for networking in your career field. Attendees of trade association meetings are often keenly aware of posted job openings as well as those not widely known (e.g., jobs that have just become open or are about to become open). If membership is required for attendance and a fee is required, you should first find out if a membership purchased in your last job is still valid or if a discount is available while you are in transition. Otherwise, you may ask a friend or former colleague if you can attend as their guest. You can also contact the meeting's leader to ask if you can attend a session before you determine whether to purchase (or renew) a membership. Should you attend a trade association meeting, always dress professionally, and bring plenty of resumes and personal business cards.

BUSINESS AND TRAINING SEMINARS

Not only do business and training seminars enable you to develop or retain valuable skills but they can also be another great source for networking. As most of the attendees will likely be employed, there is ample opportunity to make connections and network. However, before soliciting the other attendees for job leads or other networking support, make the effort to develop more personal yet professional connections. As a rule of thumb, "Make friends in the morning, and get leads in the afternoon." As with networking clubs and all of the other networking venues covered above, always dress appropriately, and bring your personal business cards.

RELIGIOUS INSTITUTIONS

Churches and other places of worship have always been great places for networking, and many business relationships are established and fostered in these settings. Some religious institutions have even established support groups and forums specifically for members seeking job search assistance.

CHARITY AND VOLUNTEER ACTIVITIES

In addition to helping people deal with the stress of a job loss, participating in charitable and volunteer activities with organizations like Rotary International offers great networking opportunities. As very positive relationships can develop among fellow volunteers, efforts at networking can be particularly effective. The collective and often contagious spirit of being surrounded by people who are lending a helping hand to others doesn't hurt either.

SOCIAL GATHERINGS

Whether it's your kid's soccer game, the annual family reunion, or a round of golf with friends, social gatherings can serve to keep you actively engaged while exposing you to new contacts and updated leads. Knowing what I do for a living, countless people have come up to me at Little League games or Girl Scout meetings to solicit my advice on job search strategies—and I'm perfectly fine with it. Conversely, disappearing from the social scene because you are discouraged or embarrassed about being out of work can have devastating consequences on networking efforts, as the old adage holds true: "Out of sight, out of mind."

ALUMNI ASSOCIATIONS

Many universities and colleges earnestly try to support their alumni with job search assistance. While the support extended to alumni is usually limited compared to that given to current students, colleges and universities often offer free career transition programs.

Nick McLaren, Senior Director of Development for Michigan State University's College of Social Science, explained:

> *No longer are four years of education enough to succeed after graduation, and that includes situations when our alumni find themselves looking for employment. We encourage them to utilize the MSU Alumni Association Career Services resource, which offers webinars, workshops, seminars, and professional events, as well as to participate in online interactive groups created for our nearly 500,000 alumni.*

Networking Scripts

For some individuals, the most difficult part of the job search process is reaching out and letting people know you'd like their help in finding a job. The following scripts are intended to ease the burden by providing you with some key lessons and examples that are adaptable to most situations. While presented here in e-mail form, the scripts can easily be used for phone calls as well.

EXAMPLE 1
Direct Contact—Seeking assistance due to upcoming restructuring

---

Subject: Networking Help?

Hi, Bob—

It was great running into you at the school fundraiser on Saturday and to hear that you and the family are doing well.

Also, I wanted to reach out to you to let you know I will be leaving the Marsden Company in a few weeks, and I'm wondering if it would be all right if I reached out to you for some networking assistance. Marsden was recently acquired by the Maupin Corporation, and my position is being eliminated. They have asked me to stay on to help finish some projects but it looks like June 1 will be my last day. Although I'd like to find another management position in Media Relations, I would also be interested in opportunities in customer service or government relations.

Anyway, would it be okay if I forwarded my resume to you just in case you hear of anything you could send my way?

Thanks, Bob!

<Insert contact information, and be prepared to respond to requests for additional information including reasons for leaving, industry preferences, relocation preferences, etc.>

Key Lessons

1. If possible, always send your first e-mail from your work e-mail address as it enhances the credibility of your story line (e.g., you are leaving in good standing), but make sure to include your personal contact information and send a blind copy to your personal e-mail.

2. Using "Networking Help?" as the subject line draws the recipient's attention without appearing overbearing or overly demanding.

3. Instead of going straight into business, first include a short courtesy message to reinforce your personal relationship. In the case of someone who is more of an acquaintance, remind them of how you know each other.

4. Don't ask for a job, and keep the e-mail short, informative, and upbeat.

5. Ask permission to network before sending your resume. Not only is this courteous but it also invites additional dialogue with the individual and lets you know if he or she is willing to offer assistance.

6. Extend an enthusiastic (and presumptuous) "Thank you!"

7. If the individual does not respond, a follow-up phone call referencing the e-mail is recommended versus sending a reminder e-mail.

EXAMPLE 2

Direct Contact—Seeking assistance due to voluntary or involuntary termination of employment

---

Subject: Networking Help?

Hi, Dwinn—

It was great running into you at the school fundraiser on Saturday and to hear that you and the family are doing well.

Also, I wanted to let you know I recently left the Marsden Company, and I'm wondering if it would be all right if I reached out to you for some networking assistance. I had a great run at Marsden, but it was time for me to do something different. I'm still very interested in finding another management-level position in Media Relations as well as in customer service or government relations.

Would it be okay if I forwarded my resume to you just in case you hear of anything you could send my way?

Thanks, Dwinn!

<Insert contact information, and be prepared to respond to requests for additional information including reasons for leaving, industry preferences, relocation preferences, etc.>

Key Lessons

1. Note the individual references their time at the Marsden Company in positive terms and does not give any details as to why he or she is no longer employed (such information is best shared in a follow-up discussion, preferably in person or over the phone). Also see Key Lessons 2–7 above.

EXAMPLE 3
Direct Contact—Seeking assistance at a targeted company

Subject: Networking Help?

Hi, John—

It was great running into you at the school fundraiser on Saturday and to hear that you and the family are doing well.

Also, I wanted to let you know I recently left the Marsden Company after a restructuring, and I'm wondering if it would be all right if I reached out to you for some networking assistance at Evalyn Wayne Enterprises. While I know you're in a different part of the business, I am hoping you could introduce me to a contact in the Media or Government Relations department.

If you would like, I would be happy to first forward my resume to you so that you can get a better understanding of my experience, skills, and career objectives.

Thanks, John!

<Insert contact information, and be prepared to respond to requests for additional information including reasons for leaving, industry preferences, relocation preferences, etc.>

Key Lessons

1. Note the individual briefly references a plausible reason why he or she left the Marsden Company. If the reason for termination is involuntary, no details should be given as to why the employment ended (such information is best shared in a follow-up discussion, preferably in person or over the phone). Also see Key Lessons 2–7 from Example 1 above.

EXAMPLE 4
Secondary Contact—Seeking assistance at a targeted company

Subject: Friend of Barbara Byers

Hi, Rick—

I'm a friend and former colleague of Barbara Byers, and she suggested I contact you in case you would be so kind as to help put me in contact with the individual in charge of media relations at Evalyn Wayne Enterprises.

I worked with Barbara at Rohen Equity as a Media Relations Assistant prior to being hired as the Manager of Media Relations for the Marsden Company.

I am currently exploring other career opportunities, and I would greatly appreciate the opportunity to network with the Media Director at Evalyn Wayne.

Would it be possible to get his or her name and contact information or maybe even an introduction?

Thanks, Rick!

<Insert contact information>

Key Lessons

1. Using "Friend of Barbara Byers" as the subject matter draws the recipient's attention and provides an instant connection opportunity. Also see Key Lessons 2–7 from Example 1 above.

EXAMPLE 5

Secondary Contact—Seeking assistance in a specific field or profession

Subject: Follow-Up: Rick Branham Referral

Hi, Mark—

Rick Branham was kind enough to suggest that I contact you as I network to find other career opportunities in Media Relations. Prior to being hired as the **Manager of Media Relations for the Marsden Company in 2009**, I was the Media Relations Assistant at Rohen Equity for three years. While I'd like to find another management-level position in Media Relations, I would also be interested in opportunities in customer service or government relations.

Mark, I would greatly appreciate the opportunity to get your thoughts on any employers that you think may have an interest in someone with my experience and skills. So that you can "put a name to a face," would it be okay if I dropped by your office for just 10 minutes to introduce myself?

Thanks, Mark!

<Insert contact information>

Key Lessons

1. Using "Follow-Up: Rick Branham" as the subject matter draws the recipient's attention, provides an instant connection opportunity, and suggests a call to action. Also see Key Lessons 2–7 from Example 1 above.

2. Rick's name and the sender's most recent position are in bold to capture the recipient's attention and interest.

3. An in-person visit puts "a face to a name," and it elevates the networking to a more personal level, which increases the likelihood the contact will remember you for job openings both inside and outside the organization. This tactic will often give you the inside track into the hidden job market.

4. Ask for only ten minutes of their time to introduce yourself. However, be prepared for a longer meeting, and bring copies of your resume.

PLEASE REMEMBER THIS

Some of the key lessons in this chapter include:

✔ The goal of networking is to enlist the support of others to find out where the jobs are and to get help with introductions and endorsements.

✔ An effective story line explains the reason for your job search in concise, positive, and factual terms.

✔ A targeted job search strategy, a professional e-mail address, and personal business cards are networking fundamentals.

✔ LinkedIn is a tremendously powerful tool for global networking, and an effective profile is essential for generating interest among employers and recruiters.

✔ Networking venues are numerous and include trade association meetings, professional networking clubs, places of worship, and alumni associations.

✔ Requests for networking assistance should be customized to the recipients and absent of any direct requests for employment.

✔ Durfee's Laws in this chapter are extensive and encourage an open and vast communication strategy supported by online networking, a long list of references, continual updates to contacts, and direct connections with influential internal sources.

"Knowledge is of two kinds. We know a subject ourselves, or we know where we can find information upon it."

SAMUEL JOHNSON (1709–1784)
ENGLISH AUTHOR AND POET

CHAPTER 5

FINDING YOUR NEXT JOB

"A man standing on a hilltop with his mouth open will wait a long time for a roast duck to fly in."

CONFUCIUS (551 BC – 479 BC)
PHILOSOPHER

As referenced in the preceding chapter, networking is a powerful and effective means for searching for employment opportunities. It is, however, just one of many sources at your disposal. While technology has ushered in powerful Internet job boards and employer career opportunity portals, comparatively old-school venues such as job fairs, search firms, college career services, and even newspaper help-wanted advertisements are still viable and even essential sources for finding your next job.

In this chapter, we will explore the various ways to learn about job openings and how to increase your odds of catching the interest of recruiters.

The Elevator Pitch

If you were riding in the elevator with a staffing manager and he or she asked, "What do you do?" how would you respond before the doors opened and you parted ways? Such a scenario illustrates the concept of the elevator pitch. For purposes of job fairs, interviews, networking, and other job search activities, you should always be prepared to give a thirty-second statement that briefly highlights your skills, experience, and career interests in favorable, but not overly boastful, terms. For example:

> *I specialize in increasing sales and market share for companies. Most recently, as a brand manager with American Express, I developed and rolled out a new private banking service for their premier customers, which exceeded plan goals by over 200 percent in the first year alone. At this time, I'm very interested in pursuing opportunities that would leverage my skills and experience in financial services, consumer products, or wherever there's the desire to grow a product or business.*

Your elevator pitch should showcase your talents and be sufficiently open-ended so as to potentially expand your career opportunities into a broad range of professions or industries. If it's too narrowly focused (e.g., "I'm a hotel sales manager"), you may miss out on opportunities where your skill sets are transferable. If it's too broad (e.g., "I'm a people person"), it risks being ambiguous and nearly worthless.

At this time, I recommend you set down this book, grab a blank sheet of paper, and draft your thirty-second elevator pitch. I also encourage you to practice your speech in front of a mirror until you feel comfortable with both the content of your remarks and your delivery. While this exercise is awkward for some people, I am convinced it will help prepare you for such brief encounters during your job search. As a prelude to the incessant discipline I preach in the next chapter on preparing for interviews, there's simply no substitute for the practice and preparation required to get this right.

A Measure of Focus

While it may be tempting to indiscriminately apply for every job you hear about, I urge my clients to be relatively selective. In particular, I encourage them to pursue opportunities that are at least somewhere in the ballpark of what they are seeking, rather than blasting out their resumes to everyone everywhere. Otherwise, they risk getting aimless job leads that do little more than waste their time and inhibit the pursuit of what they really want.

While I do encourage you to keep an open mind and explore new industries and career paths, an overly random approach (such as pursuing jobs to which your skills are not readily transferrable) puts you at risk of being contacted for jobs that can cause unwanted distractions, confusion, and hassle. For example, if you are a trained civil engineer and really enjoy that type of work, does it really make any sense to submit your resume for a job selling insurance?

Internet Job Sources

Internet job boards serve employers in much the same way newspaper advertisements have for countless generations. That is, an employer posts a job opening and waits for interested applicants to respond. The main differences are that everything is done electronically and the job posting can be seen at the same time by virtually anyone around the world. Internet job sources also vary from general sites that post jobs for most vocations to specialist sites that cater to narrower segments delineated by profession, industry, income level, race, and age.

All of the major Internet job boards are very easy to use. Once you have applied for a position and submitted your resume, you can usually track your application's status to see if it has been received by the employer. On most sites, you can also choose to make your resume accessible to other employers and elect to receive notifications for newly posted positions. In addition to job postings, some websites include basic career transition articles and tips covering topics such as resume writing, interviewing, and local job fairs.

Here are some of the more popular job boards:

- www.careerbuilder.com
- www.monster.com
- www.theladders.com
- www.indeed.com
- www.linkedin.com
- www.ziprecruiter.com
- www.simplyhired.com
- www.craigslist.org
- www.glassdoor.com
- www.usajobs.gov

In addition to the above, many people claim success finding jobs through social networking forums such as Facebook and Twitter.

THE NUMBERS GAME

My clients frequently share their frustration when they apply online for jobs they think they're perfect for and then don't get a response. "But I have everything they are looking for!" they tell me. Many times, they ask if they should go ahead and apply on the employer's website as well. The answer I give is "Yes." By applying on both websites, my clients have everything to gain and nothing to lose.

To illustrate, when I was in a corporate job and looking to fill a position, I generally had the job opening first posted on my employer's website and then on a leading job board. Not only did I never penalize anyone for posting their resume on both sites but sometimes their resume would end up on my desk from one source but not the other. That suggests one of their two submissions had been overlooked and had it not been for their decision to post their resume on both sites, I never would have seen it.

Also, when applying for jobs online, it may be helpful to know you are essentially dealing with a numbers game. What I mean is hundreds and sometimes thousands of other candidates may have applied for the same job. With that kind of response rate, there's a very good chance that despite your qualifications, experience, and interest, there may be ten or fifteen other applicants who are even more qualified than you are. While that may sound discouraging, people still do find jobs on Internet job boards, so don't give up on them entirely.

The volume of applicants further serves to reiterate the importance of the networking skills introduced to you in the previous chapter. If the employer is identified in the job posting, leverage networking sites such as LinkedIn, Facebook, college alumni associations, and your own contacts to find someone who will put you in touch with the hiring manager. As your resume won't be electronically screened out if you go this route, you stand a much greater chance of being considered. If your efforts at networking aren't successful, then it makes even more sense to apply in as many ways as possible including, if feasible, visiting the employer's facility.

When visiting the employer's location, have your thirty-second elevator pitch ready, and ask if you can meet with the individual even if it's just to drop off your resume and introduce yourself. If you get the runaround, at least try to get the hiring manager's name and contact information so you can follow up via e-mail or regular or express mail. If you seem to have hit a dead end despite your best efforts, you're better off changing course and devoting your time searching for other opportunities.

BLIND JOB POSTINGS

In order to avoid getting overwhelmed by an influx of eager job seekers directly calling or visiting an employer's office in response to a job advertisement, it is not uncommon for jobs to be posted without revealing the employer's identity. These are often referred to as "blind postings," and you should know there is always a risk you could send your resume to employers in whom you have no interest, including your own if you already have a job and are looking to make a change.

Another problem with blind ads is that they make it difficult to launch targeted networking activities. Difficult, perhaps, but not necessarily impossible, as sometimes employers will give clues as to their identities in the job description. For instance, they may provide general information about their industry, location, products, size, customer base, values, history, or facility that can help you pinpoint the likely employer. Even if you cannot identify a specific employer, there is nothing preventing you from using your networking skills to reach out to all employers closely matching the criteria. If you think the job was posted by one of five or six employers, for instance, then try to ascertain and contact the likely hiring manager for each.

Employer Websites

Most large employers have a link on their main website designated for careers or employment opportunities. In much the same way positions are posted on job boards, these sites are designed to make it easy for you to explore their job openings and for you to submit your resume. Great websites for locating multiple employer job postings that may not be listed on the traditional job search sites are www.indeed.com, www.ziprecruiter.com, and www.simplyhired .com. These websites use an aggregating platform to gather job postings from both employer websites and other job boards and post them on their own.

If you find a job on an employer's website and decide to apply for it, you should know many employers place a premium on a candidate's ability to follow instructions with respect to the stated application process. If you are required to answer prescreening questions, sometimes referred to as "knockout" questions, when you submit your resume, it's essential you answer honestly.

Kent Keoppel, an entrepreneur and former Executive Vice President for Wyndham Vacation Ownership, shared his findings when filling a position on his staff:

> I am a big fan of online screening as the process can significantly reduce the time we would otherwise spend on sorting out applicants who are unqualified but have elected to submit their resumes anyway. When we posted a job for a Human Resources Director, I made sure we included ten weighted qualifying questions concerning education level, years of experience, industry background, etc., along with a comment box for providing their thoughts on the overall role of HR. The comment box question is really important to me as it offers some insights into how they would respond to an open-ended question.
>
> Of about 250 applicants, we didn't even look at 200 because their responses did not meet the minimal criteria for the position. Those included a number of candidates who scored well on the questions but failed to submit an answer in the comment box.
>
> Of the fifty resumes we reviewed, thirty-five were rejected because of insufficient work or industry experience or some other job-related consideration. We went ahead and phone screened the remaining fifteen candidates and called five of them in for in-person interviews. We eventually hired our new HR Director from that final group.

I cannot stress enough how important it is for applicants to follow instructions. When they don't, it gives me the impression they are lazy or don't care or are just sloppy when it comes to details. And if they don't answer the qualifying questions honestly, they are just wasting everyone's time because we will eventually find out the truth as the screening process progresses.

Once again, hurdles such as these make it even clearer that you should rely on your networking skills to minimize the risk your resume will get lost or rejected in a vast electronic holding bin along with hundreds or thousands of other resumes e-mailed to the employer's website:

Office Visits

Depending on the level of the job you are seeking, it may also be appropriate to visit the employer's human resources office. If you go this route, you may be directed to apply on their website or to fill out an application on-site either on paper or at a computer kiosk. It's possible you may be interviewed, so dress appropriately and bring along a few copies of your resume just in case.

There are, however, much more strategic and creative approaches to getting your foot in the door of a company's human resources office. Ron Wilensky, retired Senior Vice President of Human Resources for Marriott's timeshare company, revealed an approach he once used that proved to be highly effective:

Several years ago when I was Vice President of Human Resources for a major rental car company, I was ready to make a change to a company with a well-respected brand and reputation for world-class HR services. I compiled a list of targeted companies, developed a thirty-second "elevator speech," and began my job search.

Among the companies at the top of my list was Marriott Corporation. Since I did not know an insider who could endorse me and get my resume to the right person, I decided to do some research and get the name and direct phone number of their senior HR executive.

I called the headquarters office and told the operator I wanted to compliment an employee in human resources and asked to be switched to the department's Senior Vice President. She readily gave me his name, and I asked, "By the way, what is his phone extension for when I call back?" Now that I had his name and extension, I could call him directly both before and after normal business hours. The following week, I planned to call early in the morning, before his administrative assistant arrived to screen his calls.

It was 8:10 a.m. when I called for the third time. Sure enough, he picked up his own phone, and I was ready to go with my elevator speech. At the end of the call, he suggested we should get together for lunch the next time I was in the Washington, D.C., area (the location of Marriott's worldwide headquarters). I conveniently found a reason to be in the area one week later and took him up on his offer. Although he did not have an immediate opening, this created the connection that eventually led to a very rewarding twenty-year career with the company.

Industry and Association Websites

Whereas many job boards post opportunities for practically everyone, there are numerous niche websites dedicated to specific industries and professions. Looking for a job in the construction or building supply industry? Then check out www.constructionjobs. com. How about a job in human resources? If so, the Society for Human Resource Management lists hundreds of jobs on its website, jobs.shrm.org.

Other profession-based job boards include:

- **Advertising and Marketing:** www.talentzoo.com
- **Call Center:** www.callcenterjobs.com
- **Consulting and Freelance:** www.elance.com

- **Finance:** www.efinancialcareers.com
- **Health Care:** www.healthcarejobsite.com
- **Hotels:** www.hcareers.com
- **IT and Technology:** www.dice.com
- **Law:** www.lawjobs.com
- **Non-profit:** www.idealist.org
- **Retail:** www.allretailjobs.com

Regardless of your individual career interests, chances are there is a website specializing in your field of endeavor. Simply insert your profession or industry followed by the word "jobs" into any Internet search engine, and a list of websites should appear.

Job Fairs

On the surface, the relevance of job fairs seems to depend only on your job level or profession. For instance, a Systems Engineer may not see the value of attending a job fair marketed for hospitality professionals, particularly when the advertised job openings list only cooks, food servers, housekeepers, etc. Dismissing such events as irrelevant, however, could be premature for a number of reasons:

1. The information booths are typically staffed by the employer's human resources department. Given that these employees typically have broad recruiting responsibilities, they often have other openings that they are trying to fill. So while they may not be expecting to find a Systems Engineer at a hospitality job fair, it's doubtful they will turn you away if your skills and experience match those of a current opening. You will also stand out from the crowd given your markedly different resume and career interests.

2. Job fairs also give you the opportunity to network with the recruiters in attendance. If they don't have an opening of interest to you, it is perfectly appropriate to ask if they know of any organizations that may.

3. Job fairs enable you to find out about organizations and employers unfamiliar to you. For instance, you may learn of a new company coming to town or of an employer planning to expand.

Be forewarned that a job fair can be very trying and very taxing if there is a large turnout. Even though you may have to wait in long lines with a motley crowd, do your best not to get frazzled. Dress professionally, bring plenty of resumes, and be prepared to pitch yourself in relevant, concise, and positive terms (see the section on elevator pitches in Chapter 6). Also, be sure to get the employer representatives' business cards so you can follow up after the job fair. Lastly, while leaving the kids at home may seem like a no-brainer, trust me, it's not for some people!

Search Firms and Employment Agencies

For executive-level positions in particular, search firms are especially well equipped to provide a much more targeted level of placement support. While they may not be searching for someone with your skills and background at the same time you are seeking employment, it is advantageous to register in their candidate databases to increase the likelihood you will be contacted should their needs change. And since there are literally thousands of search firms, you may want to begin with the larger firms, boutique firms specializing in your field, and firms with whom you may have already established a relationship (for instance, as a hiring manager, you hired them to conduct a search).

SEARCH FIRMS

Many individuals who are unfamiliar with search firms often express disappointment when they reach out to them for job search assistance and receive little encouragement, support, or interest in return. Why is that?

Very simply, search firms work for and get paid by employers who have specific jobs they need filled. So while they may have some interest in reviewing your resume, they won't earn a fee unless your skills, background, and career interests match a preexisting job requisition and their client hires you. With the exception of certain sectors, such as technology, where demand exceeds labor supply and employers are perpetually recruiting for talent, search firms will rarely devote any effort to searching for a job on your behalf.

Nonetheless, it is still a good idea to send them your resume or register in their databases in the event a client should enlist their services to find someone just like you. Here's a list of some of the largest executive search firms:

- **Korn/Ferry International** (www.kornferry.com)
- **Egon Zehnder International** (www.egonzehnder.com)
- **AIMS International** (www.aimsinternational.com)
- **IIC Partners** (iicpartners.com)
- **Spencer Stuart** (www.spencerstuart.com)
- **Heidrick & Struggles** (www.heidrick.com)
- **IRC** (www.ircsearchpartners.com)
- **Russell Reynolds Associates** (www.russellreynolds.com)
- **Boyden** (www.boyden.com)
- **Stanton Chase** (www.stantonchase.com)

Another option for reaching out to search firms is to register on a database sponsored by the Association of Executive Search and Leadership Consultants (https://www.aesc.org). BlueSteps (www.bluesteps.com) is unique in that it not only provides additional candidate profiles for most of the largest executive search firms to consider but it also serves as a major database (and sometimes, the primary database) for approximately eight thousand search professionals in over seventy countries. There is a fee to register with BlueSteps, and you should only consider joining if you earn a salary of at least $100,000 annually.

EMPLOYMENT AGENCIES

In addition to firms catering to executives, there are also thousands of national and local firms specializing in administrative and non-exempt positions. Many of these employment firms have expanded their services from strictly temporary agencies to include placement services for permanent staff. Temporary assignments also can lead to permanent roles with the same employer, and I have personally hired a number of executive administrative assistants this way. An added benefit for both the temporary employee and the employer in these arrangements is the opportunity to determine if the working arrangement is to each other's liking before any permanent hiring decisions are made.

To find employment agencies in your location, enter "temporary employment agencies" and your city into any Internet search engine, and select the applicable agencies in your vicinity.

Newspaper Advertisements

While not nearly as dominant as they were prior to the introduction of the Internet, of course, newspaper help-wanted ads are still in existence and are still useful. Employers advertising in this medium tend to be looking for local talent and may ask applicants to apply on their websites or in person at a job fair or office.

A few years ago, Rick Larson, now an employment law attorney and SVP with Winning Work Teams Inc., landed the position of Chief Administrative Officer for the Nickelodeon Suites Resort by responding to a small advertisement in the local newspaper. While he did so with minimal expectations, he was pleasantly surprised to learn it was a big job with big pay. If an executive position for a growing and internationally recognized brand could be found in a local classified ad, then clearly they are still relevant.

Government Agencies

Unlike most other organizations, government agencies serve two useful job search purposes in that they hire employees as well as help people find jobs. Regarding the former, a great place to search for jobs with the U.S. Federal Government is www.usajobs.gov, and www.governmentjobs.com lists jobs at the state and local levels.

WORKING FOR THE GOVERNMENT

Most federal jobs are filled by the individual government agencies, and there are two classes of jobs—those in the competitive civil service and those in the excepted service. The former places a heavy emphasis on equal employment in the hiring process, whereas the latter includes jobs with agencies such as the FBI and CIA, to which those requirements do not apply. Most jobs have online applications and do not require taking a civil service exam.

Even if you do not think your profession or skill sets would be of value in the public sector, you may discover opportunities that represent a career fit. This became apparent to me several years ago when I ran into my friend Bill Dehart during a visit to my hometown. As Bill had been in sales for most of his career, I figured he must have embarked on a different path when he told me he had accepted a job in Michigan's state government. On the contrary, he now holds the title of Promotional Agent with the Department of Corrections and is a representative for the office furniture products manufactured by inmates in the state's correctional institutions. Granted, his customers are other state agencies, but his selling skills are nonetheless an essential requirement of the job.

WORKFORCE SERVICES

If you cannot find or are not interested in a job with the government, most agencies offer services to help you find jobs and develop some essential skills such as resume writing and interviewing. Quality and service levels vary greatly across agencies and locations, so if you aren't satisfied with the state government's services, for instance, you may want to look into programs offered by the county government.

Several years ago, I was fortunate to have worked with an incredibly service-oriented and talented government agency when I was the Director of Human Resources responsible for opening what is now the Vinoy Renaissance St. Petersburg Resort & Golf Club in St. Petersburg, Florida. It was slated to open in the midst of a recession that was wreaking havoc on the entire travel industry, and my budget fell way short of what was needed to hire over five hundred employees in job categories ranging from the marina's dockmaster to fine-dining chefs. Just when I was on the brink of despair, Dick Koch from the Job Service of Florida paid a visit to my office to see if his agency could be of any assistance.

What transpired from that point on was an exceptional example of private industry and government working together to get the right people hired for the right jobs and at the right time. Dick quickly marshaled the Job Service's resources and ensured his team screened and referred only those job applicants who met the high standards we had set for the luxury resort. Not only were we able to hire the necessary staff on schedule but as a testament to the quality of the hires, the company's scoreboard for guest service soon ranked the resort as the No. 1 property in the entire chain. As a regular visitor to the resort over twenty years later, I still encounter employees who likely would not have been hired had they not registered with this government agency.

Whether or not this represents an exceptional example of the favorable role government agencies can have on your job search is subject to debate. Nonetheless, I would recommend you at least look into such services, as they may be in a position to help you get your foot in the door of even the most selective employers.

Campus Services
CAREER CENTERS

If you are attending or have attended college, your campus career services center could be a great resource for learning critical interviewing and job search skills. Most colleges offer workshops and one-on-one counseling to help students find and secure post-graduation employment. These programs are especially helpful for graduating students when visiting employers interview them in the center's facilities.

I have found student placement efforts vary greatly in terms of scope and organizational structure. Some colleges, for instance, have a centralized approach to career services and coordinate the recruiting activities for all of the institution's degrees and majors. Others assign placement support responsibilities to the specific academic departments. For example, the business and engineering departments may arrange for recruiters to visit with their respective students entirely independently of one another.

Whether you have access to the career centers for counseling, recruiters, or both, I encourage you to take full advantage of these resources. Chances are you will never again in your entire career have so many resources available to you or such convenient interviewing opportunities as when you are about to graduate from a college with an established and effective career center.

EMPLOYER INFORMATION SESSIONS

If you are getting ready to graduate from college, find out about information sessions and receptions hosted by visiting employers. The events are usually held the evening before the employer is scheduled to interview upcoming graduates. For the employer, it provides an opportunity to share information regarding the organization's operations, history, future plans, products, and services— as well as, importantly, the skills and experience the employer is seeking in its candidates and the expectations the employer has for students. This information can be very helpful in preparing you for an interview as well as assessing your overall interest and fit.

Having hosted a number of these functions for various employers, I was often able to get a sneak peek at the talent we would be interviewing the next day. Accordingly, it's important to take these events very seriously and to find the opportunity to spend a few minutes with the host and preferably the person who will be interviewing you. Meeting your interviewer beforehand can reduce anxiety during the interview, and it potentially gives you the opportunity to stand apart from the twelve to fifteen other students with whom the recruiter will be interviewing the following day.

Vern Horstman, a Director of Human Resources with companies such as Ford, Visteon, Aerojet, and now L-3 Communications, recalled a reception he and fellow student Sue Gladstone attended while pursuing their graduate degrees in Labor and Industrial Relations at Michigan State University:

> *I remember being a graduate student and getting an invitation to a pizza party and beer and wine reception sponsored by Frito-Lay. Although I was early in my graduate school career, I felt that attending these types of sessions gave me the chance to network with both alumni and corporate recruiters so I would be better prepared when my time came to interview.*
>
> *During the presentation, I was intrigued to hear about not only Frito-Lay's cutting-edge approach to human resources but also the company's approach to R&D. I particularly remember an instance when the recruiter attempted to impress his audience by proudly pointing out the technical*

advances his firm was making in the area of potato genetics. As he showed a slide of a young potato seedling growing in a test tube, a unified gasp of awe came from the audience. However, one of the other students sitting next to me was amused by the presentation and snorted, "Potato genetics?" under his breath and started giggling. Apparently, he had had a few too many glasses of wine at the reception and couldn't quite figure out how so many people could be so impressed with such a wet little weed. His giggling became a little contagious, and Sue and I, along with a few others sitting nearby, found ourselves trying to maintain our composure as well. Needless to say, the snickering did not endear the student to the corporate recruiters.

In contrast, a few of the students who took the event more seriously asked pointed questions and garnered face time with the recruiters immediately after the presentation. A couple of these students ended up receiving job offers from Frito-Lay prior to graduation.

Durfee's Law for Finding Your Next Job

Here is something important to know when looking for your next job:

DURFEE'S LAW #40: **Do it all.** Sometimes individuals may see the same job posted both on a job search site and on the employer's website and wonder which they should respond to. The answer is simple—apply to both. In addition, extract whatever helpful information you can from the job posting in an effort to establish networking contacts who may be able to get your resume in the hands of the recruiter, the hiring manager, or both.

Tom DeLuca, a Vice President of Human Resources with AIG, shared his perspective:

> *Even with the abundance of talent available in a weak economy, we are pursuing every avenue to identify top talent in our space. As part of this effort, we maximize online search vehicles and*

*have relationships with some of the larger job boards. We have
also identified LinkedIn as another source, and we're exploring other postings and candidate search tools.*

PLEASE REMEMBER THIS

Some of the key lessons in this chapter include:

✔ While online job boards and social networking sites have greatly
altered how people find jobs, traditional resources remain viable
sources of information and support.

✔ The volume of applicants received by job board postings means
networking is increasingly important for getting your resume in
front of the recruiter or hiring manager.

✔ When applying for a job directly on an employer's website, pay
particular attention to the instructions for submitting your resume, and be sure to provide accurate information.

✔ The elevator pitch is important for job fairs, networking, and
other encounters.

✔ Although search firms will be of limited immediate assistance
unless they have been hired by an employer to find someone with
your career profile, registering in their databases and establishing
good relationships may pay off later.

✔ Irrespective of your profession and career level, government
agencies are both prospective employers and valuable sources for
job leads.

✔ Graduating college students should take advantage of campus
career centers for interview training, information sessions, and
recruiter visitations.

✔ Durfee's Laws advocate using multiple approaches when applying
for a job even if it's with the same employer.

"Two roads diverged in a wood, and I—
I took the one less traveled by,
And that has made all the difference."
*ROBERT FROST (1874–1963)
POET AND PULITZER PRIZE WINNER*

PREPARING FOR INTERVIEWS

"The more you sweat in training, the less you bleed in battle."
U.S. Navy SEAL maxim

I magine a very ambitious individual. Someone who wants to win. Someone who wants to win badly. This is the kind of person who has clear goals and knows what he wants to achieve. Now suppose this person enters a local 10K race. He has always been athletic (and quite fast) and greatly enjoyed the thrill of competition. Indeed, he won many races in high school and has a box of trophies to prove it. Now, dressed in the latest sportswear and new running shoes, he confidently steps up to the starting line. The big race begins and, burning with desire and full of adrenalin, off he goes—only to finish toward the rear of the pack, out of breath and quite embarrassed in front of his family and friends who showed up to root him on.

What happened? Very simply, he overlooked a critical and universal ingredient for success in virtually all endeavors—adequate preparation. Despite how badly he wanted to win, he could not make up for the fact that, in this contest, he had not properly trained and was simply out of shape. This is the way it goes with interviewing.

Attention, Graduating College Students

While the contents of this book are intended for job applicants with all levels of experience, the following chapters are particularly important to recent or soon-to-be college graduates. This is because it's highly unlikely that ever again in your career will you have so many potential employers converging in one place (e.g., the campus career center) and in such a concentrated timeframe with the sole purpose of recruiting you or someone like you.

Whether you have five campus interviews or twenty-five, you will soon find that subsequent job search activities will be much more sporadic and less frequent. In a curious twist of fate, all of this attention and interest comes at the precise time when most college students lack the fundamental interviewing experience and sheer appreciation of the overall selection process to perform very well as job candidates. And despite the best intentions of campus career centers, few staff members possess sufficient staffing experience to impart practical guidance, particularly with respect to the critical nuances important to trained private sector recruiters. This is something I know all too well, as the seeds of my job search skills were planted during my very first campus interview when my lack of foresight, training, and preparation resulted in repeated despair and disappointment.

While I certainly appreciate the sheer mental fatigue brought about by years of lectures, studying, and testing, I beg you to muster up the energy to truly focus on the key lessons of this chapter and the remaining contents of this book. You have likely worked very hard and spent tens of thousands of dollars to pursue your career aspirations. You owe it to yourself to learn the skills that will enable you to embark on your chosen career path with as many options as possible.

The Three Essentials

While the interview can be a very demanding event in its own right, the key to achieving a desirable outcome is largely determined well before the actual interview ever takes place. Whether you blow or ace an interview will largely depend on how willing you are to do the required prep work up front.

For the purposes of effective interviewing, proper preparation requires discipline, practicing the right things, and commitment.

DISCIPLINE

Unwisely, interviewing preparation is often put off until a formal interview is scheduled. That can be a big mistake as many interviews are often the direct result of networking or pre-screening activities requiring effective interviewing skills in order to reach the next level of consideration. In other words, if you wait until a formal interview is scheduled to develop your skills, you may never get a formal interview.[1] So, regardless of whatever else you may have going on, start developing your skills now, and don't let up until you have landed your next job.

PRACTICE

Once you have identified the interviewing style and content best suited for your career interests, it's essential you take the necessary steps to keep refining your skills. Doing so requires regular practice and may include mock interviews (e.g., with a friend or career transition coach), practicing alone in front of a mirror, and interviewing for jobs of limited interest primarily to gain valuable interviewing practice.

COMMITMENT

While developing your core skills is critical to effective interviewing, the preparation and commitment do not end there. In order to effectively interview for specific opportunities, research how your skills and experiences match the needs of prospective employers. The research should include insights into an organization's history, background, financial reports, industry trends, competitors, new products or services, and short- and long-term plans. It is also advisable to research the specific individuals you will be interviewing with by means of employer websites, LinkedIn, Facebook, Jigsaw, ZoomInfo, and Internet search engines. To learn more about senior executives of publicly traded companies, check out the expansive directory that is available for a fee at www.hoovers.com.

For a real-life example, I like to share the story of a corporate attorney who went online and researched the Senior Vice President of Human Resources for a company he would be interviewing with the following week. At an opportune time in the interview, he referenced a speech the executive had given at a conference concerning the challenges of recruiting non-casino executive talent to the Las Vegas area. The candidate then asked for an update on the issue, and the executive gladly obliged. While many factors contribute to a successful interview, I cannot help but think this exchange had something to do with him receiving an offer from the company.

The Recruiter's Mindset

In case you're still not convinced that preparation is important, you should know that many recruiters (whether in-house staff or search firm professionals) will look for reasons not to hire you. While this may seem counterintuitive, the reality is they desperately want to avoid the embarrassment of having endorsed what is commonly referred to as a "bad hire." Moreover, because they are the employer's gatekeepers for new talent, the rest of the organization expects them to be flawless when making staffing decisions.[2]

To reduce the chances of having their professional competency called into question, recruiters frequently will try to find reasons to reject your candidacy. Only after coming up empty will they transition to a more accommodating mindset of how, why, and where you could fit into the organization. Evoking a "last man standing" scenario, Joe Davis, a senior construction and development executive who was once my colleague at an international resort company, captured this sentiment when he said, "Selection is often the process of elimination."

What the Interviewer Wants to See and Hear

In an interview, it's really all about the fit. The interviewer wants to determine whether you would be a fit for the job, the work environment, and the culture. So what does that mean for you? It means it's to your advantage to know what the interviewer is looking for before you begin the interview.

Because jobs, skills, and cultures can differ greatly from one employer to the next, even in the same industry, there are no common criteria that apply to all situations. However, there are a number of things many good interviewers generally want to hear from an applicant. As you prepare and rehearse your answers to the questions provided later in this chapter, think of how you can match your experience, skills, training, accomplishments, and interests to the following attributes.

Ability to handle change. Things are changing fast, and employers need people who can keep up. Think of changes you have experienced and what you have done to adapt to and even thrive from them.

Attitude. Be honest—are you upbeat and someone who can fix problems or a whiner and a complainer? If you are the former, think of specific examples you can use in your interview to showcase these behaviors. If you are the latter, I suggest that you consider self-employment as nearly all employers desperately want to avoid hiring someone with such a disposition.

Be the solution. Interviewing is more than just telling prospective employers about your skills, experience, background, and reasons you want to work for them. Importantly, you should make the connection between what you offer and the employer's most pressing needs.

When coaching displaced managers and executives for Navigator Executive Advisors, Noel Ferguson drives home this point:

> Especially during tough economic times, job applicants must be able to convincingly position themselves as a "compelling solution" to a specific business challenge faced by the employer.

Competency, creativity, and effectiveness. Many employers need people who are creative, can independently solve problems, and can just get stuff done. Be prepared with specific examples demonstrating how you use your drive, passion, intellect, and talent to achieve meaningful and quantifiable results.

Critical thinking. Making effective decisions in business is one of the things that sets people apart. For instance, do you take the time and make the effort to thoroughly consider all the factors involved when making a decision? Do you include the stakeholders in the process? Are there advantages to involving the stakeholders, or do you tend to rely on your own judgment and experiences? Think of specific incidents for all of the above in case you're called upon to provide examples in an interview.

Enthusiasm. Too many times, a candidate focuses on his or her technical fit for a job without demonstrating sufficient enthusiasm for it. If you give it enough thought, you should be able to sincerely appreciate and articulate the upside of just about any job.

Integrity. Employers want to hire people with high integrity whom they can trust. If asked to give specific examples of when you demonstrated high ethical standards, what would they be?

Level 2 responses. Remember the three levels of responses for the story line in Chapter 4? For the purposes of interviewing, the Level 2 response is the preferred option, which means you should provide a sufficient level of detail but not too much. As a general rule, rehearse your responses to keep them within sixty to ninety seconds in length. If the interviewer asks for more information, respond accordingly (e.g., a Level 3 response). While you may be eager to share all the details about some matter of great relevance or importance to you, long-winded answers risk frustrating and annoying the interviewer.

Susan Chadick, co-Chief Executive Officer of Chadick Ellig, an executive search firm in New York City, advises:

> *When asked what time it is, don't explain how to make a*
> *watch. In anticipation of an interview, be clear on what points*

of information you want to focus on, and remain within that plan. For an analogy, consider a dinner plate; focus on the steak and only add the peas, potatoes, salad, and roll if that is what is required. Provide additional information if it is asked for, but don't ramble and lose the primary point.

Steve Steury, a Principal with Navigator Search Advisors, agrees.

We reach out to many "passive" potential candidates on the assignments our firm handles. As such, we often have an exploratory conversation prior to seeing a resume. Those who do the best in these situations are the ones who can confidently and succinctly state how their background, experience, and results support a strong match with all of the position requirements. This initial conversation is often quite brief, but it is also a mini interview that gives me an indication of their ability to do well in a formal interview with the client. In a recent such conversation, I needed to continually help the person close a point and move on. This is a common and strong indicator that the candidate would get eaten alive in the interview process.

Loyalty. Ironically, while employers increasingly show little loyalty to employees, they still expect loyalty from employees. If you have had many jobs, be prepared to explain the reasons, and don't hesitate to let them know if your job changes were due to a restructuring, downsizing, new ownership, business issue, change in strategy, etc. If you would have stayed with a previous employer had it been an option, it's okay to share that, provided: (1) you don't come across as too distraught, broken-hearted, or bitter; (2) you don't talk too much about how "great" your former employers were; and (3) you let them know how excited you are about the job for which you are interviewing. To put it into another context, think in terms of being on a first date and inquiring about old girlfriends or boyfriends. If your date's response is filled with seething hostility, turmoil, or a sense of great loss versus a more tempered and mature response, you may deem the person not emotionally ready to move on and come up with an excuse to cut the date short.

Gabe Lazzaro, Global Vice President of Human Resources and Talent at Astadia Inc. and Managing Partner at GSL Enterprises, understands from firsthand experience how the concept of loyalty has changed over the years.

> *Although loyalty, to me, is key to managing a successful business, I am also realistic about the fact there are way too many variables these days that make it hard for any one person to be loyal to organizations in the way we once expected. I consider myself a loyal employee; however, I have also been downsized on three different occasions during my career due to economic considerations through company acquisitions. From the company's viewpoint, it was nothing personal and all business, but loyalty only ran so deep when it came to the financial aspect of the equation.*

Maturity and honesty. If a previous job didn't work out, be prepared to explain in a manner that is not overly critical of the circumstances or that places the blame solely on someone else (such as a bad boss). Take some degree of ownership over the experience, and discuss how it has made you more capable and insightful.

Dan Barr, the Founder and President of the executive search firm Barr Resources, cautions against trying to conceal potentially important information from recruiters.

> *"I am not a prosecutor, and the candidate isn't on trial,"* he said. *"If the candidate appears evasive and unwilling to answer, I often conclude they're hiding something. Being direct and forthright is the better approach."*

Results and awards. From your resume and other resources, identify the quantifiable results and meaningful awards relevant to the position, and be prepared to share that information. Leon

Lachance, Director of Human Resources for Digital Risk, created the SAIL approach for ascertaining a candidate's career achievements and lessons:

> **S**ituation: Why should the employer care? Describe the situation in a way that resonates with interviewers.
>
> **A**ction: What action did you take and why?
>
> **I**mpact: What were the direct and indirect impacts of your action? Can they be quantified?
>
> **L**essons: What did you learn from this experience? How will this benefit the employer?

Awards must also be relevant to the interviewer. If you were recognized as a top performer or were instrumental in securing a prestigious award for your employer, be prepared to share that. Sometimes it's acceptable to highlight an award not directly related to your profession, provided it supports your candidacy through a demonstration of personal attributes such as character, abilities, and values.

Successes. The best predictor of future success is past success, so think of what you wrote on your resume and how you can demonstrate a consistent pattern of successes. If you are re-entering the workforce after a prolonged hiatus, consider personal examples such as volunteer work where you were in charge of a successful fundraising event.

Teamwork. Very few jobs are designed with such high levels of independence and isolation that some degree of teamwork isn't required. Franz Hanning, CEO of Wyndham Vacation Ownership, places a high level of emphasis on this attribute.

> *"Aside from the obvious skill set required to do a job well, I'm interested in how a person is going to fit within a team structure," he said. "I believe chemistry is just as important in the boardroom as it is on the ball field."*

As you construct your responses, be sure to add some "we"s along with your "I"s to demonstrate that you are realistic about how things get done and that you can work with others. The exception to the rule is for behavioral questions when the interviewer specifically wants to know what you accomplished.

Putting It All Together

Perhaps the most common interview line is, "Tell me about yourself." By making this request, the interviewer hopes to get a sense for the individual's background, accomplishments, communication skills, personality, and track record. Oftentimes, the answer also gives the interviewer insights into the applicant's personal upbringing, situation, and values that he or she could not otherwise discover without asking potentially discriminatory questions.

Jon Knotts, a human resources executive with Time Warner Cable, encourages job candidates to keep their responses relevant to the position for which they are interviewing:

> Many times, candidates will answer the question with a litany of information that doesn't tell me anything about how it relates to the job. For instance, some people will only share personal facts like, "I've been married for twenty years and have four kids." If they choose to volunteer personal information, then they should put it in a context that helps me understand why it matters. A better answer would include something about how quickly technology is changing in the cable industry and how heavily [their] family of six relies on these TV, Internet, and security services in their daily activities.
>
> And even if they don't currently have all of these services, it would be a good idea for them to let me know that they understand and appreciate the value that our products and services provide to our customers.

In terms of what a candidate could and should share when asked to tell an interviewer about themselves, the following example from a candidate interviewing for a hotel management position illustrates an effective response:

Well, I was born and raised in the Myrtle Beach area. My parents owned and operated a casual-style restaurant, and I started helping out there after school when I turned fourteen years old—provided I didn't have softball practice or a student council meeting. From an early age, I knew I wanted to be in the hospitality business. I just loved the pace, the camaraderie, the customer contact —all of it.

So when I got accepted to Florida International University's Hotel and Restaurant Management program, I was thrilled. In addition to the academics and making the dean's list, I got the chance to work at the Nuzzo Beach Resort, where I was able to get some rooms division experience as a front desk clerk. That's really when I knew I wanted to be a hotel general manager.

After graduation, I joined the Maner Hotel Company and worked at four different hotels and resorts as a management trainee, assistant banquet manager, room service manager, front office manager, and sales manager. I've always excelled at guest relations, and as a result, I have earned the Manager of the Quarter award three times. Currently, I'm the assistant GM at the Asencio Resort & Golf Club in Orlando, which is one of only three five-diamond properties in the entire chain. I was recently recognized for managing the $35 million renovation and leading a team that helped move us to the top 5 percent ranking in guest satisfaction for the first time in four years. While I really like working for the company and was very honored to receive the President's Award for Outstanding Performance last year, I would like to stay in the Orlando area until my daughter graduates from high school in four years.

Unfortunately, in order for me to become a GM, I'd have to move to the Midwest, and I would really prefer not to relocate my family at this time. So when I was contacted about the GM opening at the Grand Homan Hotel—it is such a prestigious property—I jumped at the opportunity. Frankly, I can't think of a better fit for someone with my combination of experience, skills, and career interests.

Is that okay, or would you like me to go into more detail?

Key Lessons

1. Include as many behaviors from the "What the Interviewer Wants to See and Hear" section above as possible.

2. Provide some illuminating and pertinent personal information so the interviewer gets to know the whole you. If elements of your upbringing are relevant to the position, share them (in this case, Myrtle Beach is a well-known resort town, and the candidate gained valuable foodservice experience at an early age).

3. Share both your passion for the business and any related academic credentials.

4. State your qualifications by referencing specific jobs, experiences, employers, skills, achievements, and awards.

5. Reference both individual and team accomplishments.

6. Reveal why you are in good standing with your current or former employer(s).

7. Provide a plausible explanation as to why the position interests you.

8. Don't speak badly of your present or past employers. (Note: A rare exception may be if an employer has garnered widespread public notoriety or disdain and it's clearly in your best interests to distance yourself.)

9. Express enthusiasm for the opportunity while reiterating why you are the ideal candidate.

10. Keep your initial response to less than two minutes.

11. Ask if your response was satisfactory, and offer to provide additional information.

Durfee's Laws for Preparing for Interviews

Here are some important things to know when preparing to interview:

DURFEE'S LAW #3: **Study like it's a final exam.** Develop an extensive list of potential interview questions, both basic and behavioral, and draft your responses. Once you feel comfortable that you have fully leveraged the lessons from this book, create a study guide to prepare for future interviews. This includes reviewing and rehearsing your answers before every interview, every time. I also recommend creating a small cheat sheet of relevant key metrics to keep in your pocket or portfolio for you to review immediately before interviews or during breaks.

6

CASE IN POINT FROM THE RELUCTANT EXPERT

The need to thoroughly prepare for an interview is a lesson I learned the hard way as a graduate student at Michigan State University.

While en route to meet with the recruiter from Chevron's corporate office at the campus placement center, I remember feeling prepared for the interview. After all, I had done my research on Chevron, and I was proudly sporting my brand new business suit. Enthusiasm certainly wasn't an issue because at that time, working for a big oil company was near the top of my list.

I remember greeting the recruiter with an adequate balance of etiquette and energy and waiting to be invited before I took a seat. From that point on, it was a disaster.

The first thing that happened was he asked me to fill out an index card with some basic information. At that moment, I realized I hadn't brought a pen. By asking to borrow his, I was in no uncertain terms making the statement, "I didn't come prepared to this interview."

I could have potentially recovered from this setback had I spent some time anticipating and preparing how to respond to some basic questions. Instead, I pretty much fumbled and stammered and babbled during the entire interview. No matter how basic the question, I simply was not able to offer a thoughtful, concise, and impactful response. I guess I thought a combination of spontaneity and charm would suffice. I was badly mistaken.

From that point on, I vowed I would never go into another interview without being adequately prepared to respond to a long list of possible interview questions. Throughout my career, I have studied for every interview with the same focus and diligence as I would for a final exam, and I highly recommend you do the same.

Prior to retiring as the Senior Vice President of Human Resources for Holiday Inn Club Vacations, Dan Carricato established his own proven process for preparing for interviews:

> *As a child, I recall my dad telling me the old story about the musician that arrived in New York City with his violin under his arm. He went up to an elderly man on Broadway and*

asked, "How do I get to Carnegie Hall?" The man's response was "Practice, practice, practice." So it is with preparing for the interview.

I recall every job interview I've ever had . . . mainly because I practiced for each of them several times before the actual interview and then evaluated my performance in each of them afterwards.

Before the interviews, I would write down the toughest questions I could imagine being asked of me. After gathering my thoughts about how I would respond, I would then think of how the interviewer might interpret my answer and, subsequently, my potential follow-up comments. I would then ask a trusted friend to role-play the interview with me and provide constructive criticism.

After the actual interview, I always conducted my own postmortem to consider what went right and where I could improve my skills. While there always seemed to be at least one question I hadn't bargained for, I was usually still able to offer a concise, honest, and direct response.

DURFEE'S LAW #7: Be prepared to go deep. Organizations are increasingly applying behavioral and structural interview processes that require candidates to provide actual supporting evidence. What that means for you is that a single or cursory answer to a question may not be sufficient. For every question, be prepared to provide greater detail and specific examples to illustrate your skills, experience, and accomplishments.

DURFEE'S LAW #10: Interview often. To develop your interviewing skills, consider interviewing for positions even if the location or industry may not initially appeal to you. The experience will help prepare you to interview for positions where your interest level is higher, plus you may end up pleasantly surprised to find the position is much more attractive than initially expected.

This actually happened to me a couple of times in my career. The first is when I flew to New Jersey for an interview with

Prudential Healthcare. While I really wanted to stay in Florida and wasn't particularly keen on the thought of moving to New Jersey, I also didn't want to rule out the opportunity. In the midst of the interview, the Senior Vice President of Human Resources asked, "We haven't posted it yet, but would you be interested in a job we have coming open in Jacksonville, Florida?" Had I not accepted the interview for the job in New Jersey, where I did not want to go, I would not have had the inside track for the job in Jacksonville, where I did want to go.

I also got a call from a headhunter for a job with First USA (now Chase) for a position I very nearly declined because I didn't think the job was big enough and the salary was quite a bit less than what I had been earning. At the very last moment, I figured I needed the interviewing experience, so I agreed to the interview. It turned out to be one of the most rewarding and enjoyable jobs in my career. Not only did they upgrade the position to the level of vice president but the salary was a full 33 percent more than what the headhunter initially said was the targeted pay. In addition, the company had a great culture, great people, and great benefits.

DURFEE'S LAW #18: **Learn from your interviews.** After you have concluded an interview, take a few minutes to capture what went well and what you could have done better. Did you fumble any answers or lose your concentration? Whatever you did right or wrong, make note of it, and incorporate those lessons into your preparation for future interviews. Not only will you be better prepared but you'll likely be more confident too.

DURFEE'S LAW #21: **Research their company (and yours).** Failure to properly research a prospective employer can have dire consequences in an interview. Simply stated, if a company realizes you have not bothered to find out about them, why should they bother finding out about you? After all, the employment process should represent a two-way street, where each party does its part to determine whether there's a mutual match. Given the high-speed information age we live in, it is a rare occurrence that you aren't able to research any given company or organization.

Use Internet search engines to find out about the employer's products, services, financial reports, leadership team, market updates, analyst ratings, and press releases (make sure you know the same things about your current or former employer as well). Additional information can be found through employee and industry blogs, by using the website Glassdoor (www.glassdoor.com), and by directly searching for individual executives on the Internet. Finally, don't overlook the time-tested and proven method of networking with people who may have honest and valuable insights, including employees, former employees, and vendors. Often this is where you will get the real scoop on the organization's culture, people, history, benefits, and growth plans.

John Sprouls, Chief Administrative Officer for Universal Parks & Resorts, advises,

> Research the company and the people you're meeting with; understand what they do and what's important to them in their business. If you don't care to know what we do before you meet me, I doubt you'll ever get the opportunity to find out by joining us.

DURFEE'S LAW #28: Visit the employer's operations. In addition to the research available online, if the employer's enterprise is open to the public, you should make every effort to visit the location in person. Not only will this be invaluable should you be asked about their operations but it also will help you come up with some questions that let the interviewer know you are a customer.

This advice served me well several years ago when I received a call from Cecelia Gonzalez of the search firm BCA when she was charged with recruiting a Corporate Director of Employee Relations for the Red Lobster restaurant chain. I earnestly expressed my interest in the job, and she arranged for an interview the following week. In the interim, I contacted Roger Green, who, in addition to being both my friend and mentor for over twenty years, had also worked at Red Lobster's corporate office earlier in his career.[3] After I shared my excitement and got his insights on the organization,

Roger asked me when I had last visited a Red Lobster. Once I confessed that it was too long ago to remember, he expressed to me, in very clear terms, what a grave error I would be making if I went into the interview unprepared to talk about the restaurant chain's menu, service, clientele, and atmosphere. Candidly, I was embarrassed that I had not thought of something so obvious, particularly since several Red Lobsters were in close proximity to my home.

So before the interview, I made a point of having lunch and dinner at two different Red Lobster locations. I have no doubt the perspectives from those visits, which I shared in my interviews, were instrumental in my receiving a very nice job offer.

DURFEE'S LAW #44: Ask about pre-employment testing. More and more organizations are adding pre-employment testing to their selection processes. The testing can be wide-ranging and include tests of technical skills, intelligence quotient (IQ), general knowledge, occupational interests, and personality traits. When the interview is being scheduled, ask if any pre-employment testing will be administered. (Just be sure to clarify you are not asking about drug testing, as that may raise some concerns about your character.) Then allow yourself adequate time to study any subject areas where you may be rusty. For example, do you know or remember how to multiply and add fractions? What about geometry or algebraic equations such as $x - y / x^2 = ?$ If not, you may want to prepare by picking up a math book or visiting an online site such as www.ixl.com.

CASE IN POINT FROM THE RELUCTANT EXPERT

Another lesson I learned the hard way was when Capital One flew me to Virginia for an interview at its corporate headquarters. A headhunter made all the arrangements and gave me the scoop regarding the company and the position. As always, I spent considerable time anticipating some likely interview questions and preparing my responses.

I thought the interview was going quite well until the interviewer asked me to take a test that I thought would be a simple personality assessment. Instead, I was very surprised when a young Human Resources assistant gave me what appeared to be the first math test I had seen in nearly twenty years. Literally, it ranged from geometry to multiplying and dividing fractions to calculating algebraic equations.

While the test wouldn't have been particularly difficult had I remembered any of the basic formulas from my college days, the reality is I hadn't. I simply had not been required to perform algebraic calculations throughout my professional career, and algebra just wasn't a subject I had naturally retained or, quite candidly, was ever very good at.

The outcome was predictable and somewhat embarrassing. The headhunter later told me that while Capital One's senior HR executive really liked me, my test scores were below their acceptable hiring level.

Ironically, four months later, another headhunter encouraged me to go to Delaware to interview with First USA, one of Capital One's major competitors in the credit card industry. Much like Capital One, First USA also required me to take an algebra-type test, but this time, I aced it. The difference? I simply asked the headhunter, "What kind of pre-employment testing should I expect?"

By knowing what was expected of me prior to the interview, I was able to dig out my old college algebra books and refresh my memory on some of the basic stuff I had long ago forgotten. So whenever possible, don't go into an interview blindly. Find out in advance what will be expected of you so that you can prepare accordingly.

DURFEE'S LAW #53: Google yourself. Executive search firms and corporate recruiters are increasingly using the Internet to conduct research on job candidates. While reliable statistics are unavailable, anecdotal evidence suggests the findings are regularly being used to disqualify candidates. As a result, make sure your Facebook and LinkedIn accounts do not contain any photos or posts that could be looked upon unfavorably by potential employers. For Internet findings outside of your control, beat recruiters and hiring managers to the punch by entering your name in any Internet search engine, combined with key words such as your city, profession, employers, and associations. Knowing in advance what they may discover gives you the opportunity to prepare thoughtful responses should the need arise.

DURFEE'S LAW #54: **Know your resume.** As surprising as it may seem, sometimes an interviewer will know more about what is on a resume than the candidate. Perhaps it's because the candidate has not looked closely at the resume for a while or simply forgot something that drew the attention of the interviewer. Regardless, being caught off guard by a question originating from the content of your resume can raise questions about your preparedness, focus, and honesty. Before every interview, re-read your resume, and pay particular attention to dates of employment, responsibilities, and accomplishments.

Basic Interview Questions

Below are basic questions you should expect to be asked in an interview. Keep in mind your responses give you the opportunity to highlight how your skills, achievements, interests, experience, and personal qualities position you as a compelling solution to the employer's specific needs or challenges.

When considering your responses, don't forget to employ the SAIL approach. Also, due to the generic content of the questions, I encourage you to supplement the list with questions specific to the position and industry for which you are interviewing (e.g., What percent of sales calls did you close? Which payroll systems are you proficient with? What problems did you experience with your call center provider?).

- Tell me about yourself.
- Why did you leave your last job?
- Why are you interested in this position?
- What are your short-term and long-term career objectives?
- What do you consider to be your strong points?
- What would your former bosses say are your developmental needs (or weaknesses)?
- How would your former employees describe your management style?
- Tell me about your greatest work accomplishments.

- Tell me about a time you when you learned from a mistake or failure.

- If you could choose your ideal job, what would it be?

- Describe the best boss you ever worked for.

- Describe the worst boss you ever worked for.

- How is your experience relevant to this position?

- What are your compensation expectations?

- What do you like doing when you are not at work?

- What else would you like me to know about you?

What Are Your Weaknesses?

One of the more difficult questions you may have to respond to is about your weaknesses (bullet #6 above). This question is particularly tricky because if you don't offer an answer, it suggests you are either hiding something or you have low self-awareness—both of which can knock you out of contention for the job. Conversely, a response that reveals something too severe can disqualify you as well. The goal, therefore, is to offer something that's sincere yet not damning.

With respect to the latter, Ron Wilensky, now an Executive Vice President at Navigator Executive Advisors, recently conducted a practice video interview with a senior marketing executive who responded to the question by saying his biggest weakness was "dealing with corporate politics." As corporate politics are a reality for almost everyone who performs at the executive level—whether they recognize it or not—Ron worked with the client to identify another developmental need that wouldn't be as poorly received.

Sarah King, Executive Vice President of Human Resources for Wyndham Vacation Ownership, isn't as interested in the shared weakness as she is about the candidate's willingness to act upon it.

> *"I don't necessarily care that a candidate has a weakness— we all do," she said. "Rather, what I look at is the individual's level of self-awareness, receptiveness to feedback and coaching, and desire to grow and improve."*

When interviewing for a job opening on his staff while an Operations Manager at Disney World a few years ago, Bert Garcia received a response from a candidate that he found acceptable:

> *I asked the applicant what he thought his weaknesses were, and he said, "Sometimes I guess I'm just too impatient. When I want something done, I want it done right away. I'm learning to make more of an effort to understand what prevents people from delivering on their commitments because that's one of the things that really disappoints me." I ended up hiring the individual because I appreciated his openness and drive for results. Besides, it's always much easier to reel someone in than to try to light a fire under them.*

Behavioral Interview Questions

While particularly applicable for those applying for leadership and senior management positions, the following are questions all job candidates may be asked. And while they're typically more difficult to answer than basic questions, the same techniques apply with respect to preparedness and delivery. (Note: As you will see, the following are more akin to requests or directives than questions. For the sake of simplicity, however, let's just consider them questions.)

- Describe a circumstance when you realized the need to change your behavior from your original approach.

- Describe a time when you had to persuade an individual or group to accept an idea they were initially opposed to.

- Describe a time when you led a project that involved a lot of people or departments and how you ensured success.

- Describe a work circumstance when you continued to champion a project or cause when others had given up.

- Describe a work circumstance where you went above and beyond what was expected.

- Describe a time when you had to overcome challenges or barriers in order to achieve a business goal.

- Describe a time when you have succeeded in an ambiguous or rapidly changing environment.

- Describe a time when you had to sacrifice the quality, planning, or detail of your work in order to meet a deadline.

- Tell me about a time when you had to manage a large or complex project from beginning to end.

- Tell me about a time when you had to bring structure and organization to a chaotic work situation.

- Tell me about a work situation when you were concerned that you wouldn't achieve the results of a project.

- Tell me about a time when one of your projects failed.

- Tell me about a time when you did not follow through on a work commitment.

- Tell me about a time when you leveraged others to improve your performance at work.

- Tell me about a circumstance when you took the initiative to develop yourself in order to improve your performance.

- Tell me about a time when you were surprised about the indirect impact of a business decision you made.

- Tell me about a time when you created a new product, process, or service.

- Tell me about a time when you initiated a significant business redirection in response to changes in the external environment (e.g., due to competitor or industry changes).

- Tell me about a time when you challenged the status quo in order to implement a change you felt was necessary.

- Tell me about a time when you failed to meet a customer or internal client's requirements or let them down.

- Tell me about a time when you led a project team to an exceptionally high level of accomplishment.

- Tell me about a time when you had to form a team or work group from scratch.

- Tell me about a time when you had to terminate a top performer or someone you were particularly fond of.

- Describe a time when you had to significantly redirect the efforts of others because goals were not being met.

- Tell me about a time when solving a problem required input from a number of different departments or business functions.

Hypothetical Questions

While the basic and behavioral questions should prepare you for most questions you will be asked, some interviewers also favor injecting hypothetical scenarios as a way to better gauge an applicant's thought process and ability to think on his or her feet. As Director of Construction Training at Waypoint Homes, Steve Nellis will sometimes pose this hypothetical situation to graduating college students:

> *To delve into their problem-solving skills, I will present a hypothetical situation based on my actual experiences and ask them how they would solve the problem. My favorite scenario is what I call "Mrs. Smith's plumbing problem." It goes like this:*
>
> *"You are a field manager on a job. It is Friday afternoon at 5:00 p.m., and all of your trade contractors are gone. It is your significant other's birthday, and you have plans for dinner at 7:00 p.m. Yesterday, Mrs. Smith closed on her house, and she is so excited that tonight she has thirty people coming over for a housewarming party. You are about to leave the neighborhood when she catches you in your truck. She claims her new home's plumbing is all backed up and she can't use the toilets, sinks, or bathtubs. All of these people will be here in two hours! What do you do?"*
>
> *At this point, I will watch as the candidate begins to think through the problem and devise solutions. I will constantly challenge them in their thought process in an effort to determine their practical experience, industry knowledge, and the value they place on customer service. This exercise works well because things like this really do happen. We need people who, in a pressure situation with no outside assistance, can figure out a solution NOW![4]*

When interviewing food and beverage staff at the Commerce Club in Greenville, South Carolina, Service Director Kevin McPhee will sometimes cite an actual experience from earlier in his career:

"It was only my second day on the job when I witnessed a highly irate server wielding a chair over his head and chasing a guest throughout the restaurant. In front of the other astonished patrons, the server was threatening to kill the person. As the department manager, what do you do?"

This provides an opportunity for me to see how the applicant thinks and how he or she would respond in a very real situation with no advance warning and no time to consult others. I particularly want to find out if their immediate response would factor in all of the parties involved and what they would say to the guest being chased, the server doing the chasing, and the other guests and the employees in the vicinity.

As you can imagine, the challenge with hypothetical questions is that it's practically impossible to prepare for them in advance. Instead, you are required to articulate how you would react to situations that might not be similar to any of your past experiences. What's critical to remember is the interviewer is looking for insights into how you think and react, as well as for what's important to you. If you find yourself confronted with a hypothetical question, I recommend you avoid the tendency to race to an answer. Rather, you may want to ask some additional questions of the interviewer to ensure you fully understand any parameters, relevant factors, and resources available to you.

Whenever possible, think of a similar situation you have encountered in the past, and consider sharing it by responding with something like, "That sounds similar to an incident I had to deal with when I was working at . . . ." By answering the question with comparisons to a real example of your own, you expand the question from being solely hypothetical to being behavioral, and most interviewers will appreciate the factual content of your response.

As the interviewer is observing how you process information, thinking aloud is generally acceptable and sometimes preferred. Your research should have given you some clues as to what is important to the employer, so you may want to factor those insights into your response. For instance, knowing in advance that JetBlue

Airways places great emphasis on delivering a pleasant passenger experience whereas Spirit Airlines seems to care much more about maximizing revenue from fees would be helpful in formulating responses for either company. Regardless of your answer and the interviewer's reaction, you probably won't be very happy working for an employer that doesn't share some of your core values. Therefore, I strongly advise against giving insincere responses just because you think that's what the interviewer wants to hear.

Odd Questions

In addition to asking questions that focus on the past, present, and future, some interviewers get especially creative and even unorthodox. With objectives similar to those behind asking hypothetical questions, they are attempting to assess the candidate's cognitive capacity, thinking style, and strategies for handling stress. Sometimes it's also intended to get a peek into the creative side of a candidate's brain. Whatever the reasons, here are a few questions that have actually been asked of job candidates:

- If you were a car, what kind of car would you be? Why?
- Why are manholes round?[5]
- If you were an animal, what kind of animal would you be? Why?
- What company brand and culture most reflects your personality? Why?
- Other than a family member, who is your favorite hero? Why?
- Why shouldn't I hire you?
- If you could have a conversation with anyone, alive or dead, who would it be? Why?[6]

Trying to anticipate questions of this nature is pretty much pointless. But just spending some time conjuring up odd questions and then rehearsing how you would respond to them should serve to reduce the chances you will get rattled in the event you are ever asked one.

PLEASE REMEMBER THIS

Some of the key lessons in this chapter include:

- ✔ The three essential components of effective interviewing preparation are discipline, practice, and commitment.

- ✔ Recruiters desperately want to avoid making a "bad hire" and will sometimes look for any reason to reject a candidate.

- ✔ Regardless of the industry, most employers want candidates to be able to demonstrate basic skills, behaviors, and accomplishments such as quantifiable results, a positive attitude, the ability to handle change, and enthusiasm for the job.

- ✔ When telling an interviewer about yourself, make sure your response is concise, factual, and relevant to the job.

- ✔ Whereas basic, hypothetical, and odd interview questions often allow for subjective responses, behavioral questions require the recollection of actual experiences.

- ✔ Durfee's Laws combine to point out that effective interview preparation is essentially a learning process requiring considerable effort, research, attention to detail, and actual or simulated experience.

"The will to win is not nearly as important as the will to prepare to win."

JOHN WOODEN (1910–2010)
INDUCTEE, BASKETBALL HALL OF FAME
(COLLEGE COACH AND PLAYER)

CHAPTER 7

ACING THE INTERVIEW

"Dress shabbily and they remember the dress; dress impeccably and they remember the woman."

Coco Chanel (1883–1971)
Fashion Designer

The resume, the networking, and the search for job opportunities—all of these activities are intended to accomplish one goal: to get you an interview. And while it's certainly possible to land an interview without expending any effort in these endeavors, it's doubtful you will receive a job offer if you don't do well in the interview itself. The reason is the interview generally represents the most critical determinant of a mutual fit between the employer's needs and your needs. Invoking an old adage, the interview is "where the rubber meets the road."

In many ways, the interview is similar to a sales presentation. You are trying to determine what the employer needs (this is where your research pays off) so you can demonstrate why your "product" (that's you) meets those needs. If you are successful, the interview process may ultimately lead to an acceptable job offer. If you are not, it's likely because the product (that's you again) isn't right for the employer or you failed to make an effective sales pitch (a particularly frustrating third option is when the employer puts the position on hold or decides not to fill it at all). The objective of this chapter is to help ensure that if a "sale" isn't made, it's not because of the sales pitch.

As mentioned in the previous chapter, more employers are using formal and structured selection processes to assess fit and skills. These may include pre-employment screening, personality assessments, IQ testing, and behavioral interviewing. Combined with a greater appreciation for what is commonly referred to as human capital, the interviewing process overall is getting more rigorous, thorough, and demanding.

Technical Fit + Personal Fit + Cultural Fit = Job Fit

If you have diligently considered and rehearsed responses to possible interview questions and done your homework by thoroughly researching the employer, you should be in possession of the technical content necessary for a successful interview—or at least be able to demonstrate that you can develop the necessary technical skills. However, just because you may have the skills, experience, and certifications necessary for the job doesn't mean the employer will necessarily consider you a good match.

Optimally effective interviews determine whether the technical fit and the personal fit are sufficiently aligned with the requirements of the employer. In other words, you may be a very smart and talented person with an impressive resume, but that may not be enough if your personality doesn't match the organization's culture or, quite bluntly, if the hiring manager simply doesn't like you. So while the previous chapter largely addressed technical fit, this chapter is intended to help you develop the skills necessary to deliver your message in a manner that increases the likelihood that you will be extended a job offer.

Tim Arnst, Senior Vice President of Human Resources for Universal Parks & Resorts expressed the marriage of fit in these terms:

> *Of course you have the technical skills or you wouldn't be sitting in the interview. I want to know, are you a fit for our organization? Are you a match for our particular company DNA and culture? This is where you, as the applicant, must have the ability to read the organization quickly and be*

prepared to talk about how you will contribute to the overall
success of the organization by understanding the intricacies
of how the work gets done.

At the risk of repeating myself, I will reiterate that you should never forget the job search process is about much more than just getting a job. It's also important to find a job where you will be both happy and successful. If you pretend your personality is different from what it is or that your skills match the job more than they do, there's a good chance you'll soon find yourself either miserable or unemployed.

Garry Randall, Senior Vice President of Human Resources at Disney Consumer Products and Interactive Media in Burbank, California, cautioned, "Unless you're an Academy Award winner, don't attempt to be someone you're not in the interview as it will likely come across as inauthentic and seal your fate as the one who didn't get the job."

In short, devote just as much effort—if not more—toward assessing how well you would fit into the employer's organization, culture, and management practices, and stay true to your capabilities and behavioral style despite the allure of the job.

Before the Interview

Before you even arrive at the interview location, there are a number of things requiring your attention besides getting prepared to answer questions. The following are some of the most important.

Clear your schedule. Whenever possible, clear both your personal and professional schedule the day of the interview. Sometimes interviews run longer than anticipated, and you don't want to get preoccupied or stressed over matters such as picking up the kids from school or running late for a meeting at work.

Dave Gallagher, former Board Director of Boyden Global Executive Search, recounted an incident where a job candidate could have benefited from this advice:

Several years ago, a highly qualified executive was interviewing for a senior position with a well-known entertainment company. The executive arrived appropriately early for a

9:00 a.m. interview and indicated the need to make a pri-
vate phone call. The individual was then taken to an empty
office. A few minutes later, the Vice President of Human Re-
sources entered the office ready to start the interview, only
to find papers spread out all over the desk and the executive
involved in a seemingly important conference call. As the call
lasted for over forty-five minutes, it disrupted the entire in-
terview schedule. Furthermore, the company was not able to
expand the schedule because of the executive's return flight.
The result was this otherwise impressive candidate did not
get offered the position.

The moral of this story is if you accept the interview, you
really must put other matters out of your mind. If a major
conflict arises at work, it is better to reschedule the inter-
view than to try to juggle two things at once.

Get a good night's sleep. It sounds like common sense, but I know
of too many people who partied or engaged in other late-night activities the evening before an interview. Rest is very important as
you will need your energy, and you don't want to look haggard or
tired. You should look and feel healthy and energetic in an interview as that will help convey enthusiasm for the job.

Prepare your clothes the day before. The last things you want to
deal with on the morning of your interview are shining your shoes,
ironing your shirt, or searching for your lost belt. You'll also want
to avoid rushing out at the last minute to buy a new pair of shoes
or some other needed garment. To illustrate, I remember a rather
big-footed college roommate who owned only one pair of dress
shoes and when he couldn't find them before an early morning
interview, he arrived wearing his business suit and white tennis
shoes inside black rain galoshes in a desperate attempt at camou-
flage. His odd footwear was immediately detected, but fortunately,
the interviewer accepted his explanation that the missing shoes
were lost in a recent move and offered him the job anyway. To avoid
such last-minute drama, get your clothes ready the day before your

interview, and take extra care to ensure that they still fit and are in good condition (e.g., no missing buttons, no stains, etc.).

John Delpino, a staffing executive at Walmart, provided a very salient anecdote from when he ran the corporate staffing department for a Fortune 100 business earlier in his career:

> *Prior to casual attire, the company I worked for was quite formal—so much so that casual was interpreted as no cuff links! With that in mind, we were once interviewing an engineer from the McCormick spice company for a position at our headquarters. He was to begin his interview schedule over lunch with one of my staffing managers. When he walked into the office, I happened to notice that he must have bought a new blue suit for the interview because there was a stitched white X on the back of his jacket holding the vent at the bottom together. I quickly pulled my staffing manager aside and suggested they not wear their suit coats into the cafeteria. After they left the office, I took the liberty of cutting the stitching to prevent them from unnecessarily distracting others from the reason he was here—his relevant skills and experience.*

Groom and get groomed. Take a very critical and objective look at your physical appearance, and if necessary, get your hair cut, your nails manicured, and your teeth whitened. The day of the interview, make sure things such as perfume, cologne, make-up, etc., are applied conservatively so as not to serve as a distraction.

Dress as if you're serious about the job. While many employees enjoy dress codes allowing for casual or business casual attire, do not mistake yourself for an employee with the same privileges. As a general rule, dress above what the job requires, and the higher the job level, the more formal the attire. If the job is an hourly or non-management position and the employees typically wear blue jeans, I'd recommend a male applicant wear business casual attire such as khaki slacks and a conservative sport or dress shirt. Business casual for women would be slacks or a skirt and a conservative blouse.

If the job requires business casual dress, men should wear a jacket and tie or a suit. Should the employer not be particularly stuffy, a man may want to soften his attire by wearing a tan or blue shirt and a soft-toned complementing necktie versus the traditional power look of a white shirt and red necktie. If a tie is worn, John Faix, a sales associate for Macy's who personally assists with the selection of my attire, advised, "When wearing a necktie to an interview, select something conservative to reduce the risk of it being bolder than the hiring manager's."

I recommend that women wear a tan two-piece business suit and a white blouse. However, if a black, blue, or dark gray suit is worn, the blouse should be of a softer color and pattern.

With very few exceptions, a dark business suit should be worn for senior management or executive positions regardless of gender. With respect to footwear, women should wear conservative closed-toe pumps. If invited, you can always remove your suit coat if the environment is much more casual than anticipated. Remember your first impression should generally reflect someone who is professional, so lean toward conservative colors and styles. Don't confuse applying for a job with dressing for a party or nightclub. In addition, keep the sexy clothes and loud jewelry at home, and hide the tattoos.

8

CASE IN POINT FROM THE RELUCTANT EXPERT

Several years ago, I was scheduled to interview with the Chief Executive Officer of Hard Rock Cafe for the position of global head of Human Resources. It seemed like a great job in a really fun environment.

As I prepared for the interview, I was faced with a little bit of a dilemma regarding what to wear. For executive positions, I had always worn a business suit to interviews. In this case, however, I knew there was a very good chance the CEO would be wearing blue jeans and a T-shirt—fairly typical attire for all Hard Rock corporate office employees.

So what did I wear? I still wore a business suit, but instead of the outfit I wore when interviewing with more conservative companies, I toned down the look by wearing a dark tan dress shirt and a soft-colored burgundy tie. My goal was to avoid appearing too stuffy as I didn't want the CEO to think I wouldn't fit into the culture. At the same time, I wanted to give him the impression I was a professional who was serious about the job. I ended up accepting an offer, and within a short period of time, I, too, was wearing blue jeans and T-shirts to the office.

As someone who has conducted thousands of one-on-one interviews, I don't like it when someone dresses down for an interview. It gives me the impression they're arrogant and acting as if they're already on the payroll or that they really don't care about the job.

So while you may have to make some adjustments to your wardrobe depending on the job and the company you're interviewing with, dress as if you're serious about the job you want to get.

Valid exceptions to the above may include industries, professions, and organizational cultures that unequivocally embrace a much more liberal and carefree dress code than found in more traditional workplaces. For example, as the Chief Human Resources Officer for Viewpost, a start-up technology company at the time, I spent a great amount of my time recruiting software engineers, and some of our best hires wore T-shirts and blue jeans to their interviews. Just be certain in advance that the attire is acceptable for candidates by asking someone with insider knowledge of the recruiting process, such as employees or well-connected vendors.

Eat. Although you may be nervous and not very hungry the morning or afternoon of your interview, be sure to eat something light anyway. Not only don't you want the distraction or embarrassment of a growling stomach but you will also need the energy if you meet with multiple interviewers.

Know where to go and be early. Make sure you have clear directions to the location of the interview and take into account traffic patterns such as rush hour and weather delays. Also, plan to arrive at the work location at least thirty minutes early in order to be at the interviewer's office ten to fifteen minutes before you are scheduled. The extra time will allow for unanticipated delays and last-minute preparations.

Be aware, however, that finding the actual building is not always enough—another lesson I learned the hard way. David Polansky, a friend and the Chief Financial Officer for AAA, once arranged for me to interview with one of his colleagues at a previous employer for a General Manager position in another business unit. I arrived in the parking lot on schedule and entered the lobby only to realize it was a multi-tenant office building with no shared receptionist. While I knew the name of the individual who was scheduled to interview me, it was distressing to discover the tenant directory didn't list the business unit (I later found out the office was listed under the unfamiliar name of the parent company). Suddenly desperate and frazzled, I attempted to call David on my cell phone for more precise directions only to have the battery completely die as I was dialing.

After poking my head into a number of businesses and asking if the person I was to meet with happened to work there, I finally found the right office. By then, I was twenty minutes late. The interviewer did meet with me, but for all practical purposes, I had pretty much blown my opportunity, and no amount of explanation or apology was going to get me beyond such a fundamentally inexcusable faux pas.

Turn off your cell phone. Once you enter the employer's premises or the location of your interview, turn off your cell phone and keep it turned off. Period.

During the Interview

Don't forget—you only have one chance to make a good first impression. If you have adequately prepared, you should be ready to anticipate and effectively respond to many of the questions an employer will ask. Now you will need to demonstrate your personal fit. JoAnne Kruse, Chief Human Resources Officer for American Express Global Business Travel, described the importance of personal fit in these terms:

> The candidate that makes it to the next round with me is the one who can demonstrate experiences and personal choices that align with our values and objectives as a business.

As an example, I once spent two days interviewing at a top-tier college campus and walked away without identifying a single candidate who warranted further consideration. Frustrated at the loss of time and lack of results, I waited for my car at the valet station. The valet, a student at the school, struck up a discussion with me, and in a matter of just a few minutes demonstrated the level of savvy, humor, and intellect I had not seen in two days of formal interviews. I gave the student my card and told him to give me a call. By the time I was home, he had already sent me a follow-up note with his resume. I invited him for an interview, and he ended up getting hired.

IMPRESS AND SURVIVE

The remainder of this section should help you better understand the actual interviewing process, the basic dos and don'ts, and the opportunities to sell your personality, style, and accomplishments in a manner many employers will find appealing.

If offered water, take it. Oftentimes, you will be invited to have something to drink during an interview. Decline the coffee and soft drinks as they can be messy and cause you to awkwardly ask for a bathroom break. Instead, accept a bottle of water, and then only sip it.

Perhaps because of stress or so much talking, interviewing tends to dehydrate applicants. Having water available is not only for your own comfort, but I find it tremendously annoying and distracting when the person I'm interviewing starts coughing or making a smacking noise due to a dry mouth.

Smile and be nice to everyone. As unfamiliar and intimidating as the surroundings may be, make sure you are polite and smile at everyone you come in contact with from the moment you arrive at the employer's premises. This includes security guards, administrative assistants, receptionists, etc. While these individuals may not be part of the formal interviewing process, they could have informal but meaningful influence with the hiring manager. This doesn't mean being insincerely engaging or overly chatty, but it does mean conveying the same level of respect and friendliness you'd extend to the hiring manager.

9

CASE IN POINT FROM THE RELUCTANT EXPERT

Earlier in our careers, Dan Hahn and I were working together on the human resources staff of the Mayflower Hotel in Washington, D.C., when it was announced he had earned a promotion to another hotel. As we were interviewing possible replacements, my administrative assistant handed me a resume that immediately caught my attention. The individual possessed some of the service industry experience I needed, plus he knew the local labor market. Conveniently, he was delivering his resume in person, and it turned out I was immediately available to interview him. I quickly became impressed with his professional appearance, personality, and responses to my numerous questions. In short, we hit it off, and I was relieved to think Dan's position would be filled without a prolonged search.

While I was expressing my enthusiasm for the candidate, Dan slowly shook his head and pointedly advised, "I don't think he's the guy you want." When I asked why, he said the candidate had been rude to him and another member of the staff while in the waiting area. As I had witnessed nothing of the sort in my interview, I dismissed his objection and arranged for the candidate to meet with other members of the executive committee. Later on, I checked his references, and they came back fine.

I hired the candidate, but shortly afterward, I was kicking myself because the guy was an unmitigated disaster. While loaded with talent, he also seemed to have a propensity for self-destructive behavior and, very possibly, was a pathological liar. Time after time, his reckless and irresponsible behavior embarrassed me and my department. After several months of fruitless coaching, I fired him in what turned out to be a rather ugly episode. To make it worse, I was the Director of Human Resources, and, of all people, I should have done a better job of hiring my right-hand man.

Looking back, I remember Dan warning me not to hire someone who left such a poor impression on my staff. Not only was he right but this individual also turned out to be the worst hire of my entire career. From then on, I vowed I would never hire a candidate who was discourteous to employees, regardless of their position.

And to this day, I never have.

Senior human resources executive Mitch Parnell takes particular care to informally assess the personalities of candidates who travel to interview with him.

> *"Everything is an assessment opportunity when interacting with a potential employer," he said. "I have asked receptionists, hotel clerks, car service drivers, and travel agents to give me their impressions of candidates. It is a good indicator as to how they treat people and if they'd be suitable for our culture."*

Speak clearly. Speak and enunciate clearly, and try to keep terms like "uh" and "um" and "you know" to a minimum. Also, guard against talking too much or too quickly. It's better to be more thoughtful with the words you choose than to be quick and less articulate. If you adequately prepare for the interview by rehearsing in front of the mirror, on video, or with a friend, this shouldn't be an issue.

Listen actively. Effective interviewers will appropriate most of the time in the interviewing process for asking questions in an effort to assess your capabilities and overall fit for the job and the working environment. While this is to be expected, much can also be learned by carefully listening to the questions asked of you.

Mary Ellen Russell, Chief Human Resources Officer for Genesee & Wyoming in Darien, Connecticut, and former executive search recruiter, advises candidates not to miss the opportunity this provides:

> *"Important clues as to an organization's culture, priorities, and job expectations can be revealed by making a deliberate effort to understand the reasoning behind why an interviewer asks certain questions. As a candidate, you should also be assessing your fit for the job and employer's culture and generating questions based on what has been asked of you that may lead to deeper insights about what they value."*

Greet the interviewer. This is when basic sales techniques apply. Smile, establish good eye contact, and offer a friendly greeting and a firm, but not bone-crushing, handshake. If escorted into an office, do not sit down until invited. Also, be prepared to respond to small talk (e.g., "Did you have any trouble finding us?"), and find something in the office to compliment such as the view, a painting, a photo, or a personal item. So as not to make the interviewer uncomfortable, avoid complimenting things like an accent or physical appearance.

Energy and interest sell. Your energy and interest level can help project your enthusiasm for the position and your readiness to start delivering results. In contrast, an overly relaxed approach can give the impression you are bored, disinterested, or even lazy. Little things like leaning slightly forward in your chair, a bounce in your step, and a high level of attentiveness throughout the interview can go a long way in selling yourself as a candidate with a healthy dose of drive and determination as well as an appropriate level of excitement.

A somewhat bizarre example comes to mind in which years ago, I called in an applicant for an interview when I was the Human Resources Manager for Coca-Cola Enterprises in Jacksonville, Florida. I was looking forward to meeting with this candidate in person as he was very excited over the phone when we first talked. I even remember him exclaiming, "I'll be there with bells on!" Inexplicably, the person who showed up for the interview was so laid-back that at one point I actually think he fell asleep while I was talking to him. The contrast between the person I met and the one I talked to on the telephone was so great, I am convinced the initial applicant changed his mind about wanting the job and invited his very tired uncle or father to go in his place.

Eye contact. Good eye contact comes across as engaging and natural. This means you don't want to incessantly stare at the interviewer but you also don't want to look out the window. In more precise terms, it's perfectly okay to momentarily divert your eyes when thinking of a response to a question as long as you look directly at the interviewer when giving your answer. Eye contact is important because if you consistently look away for a prolonged period of time or appear to go into a statue-like trance while considering your response, the interviewer may think you lack confidence or that you're hiding something.

Body language. As mentioned above, energy sells. However, too much energy is not a good thing either, as it could distract from the point you are making. While some gesticulation is expected, avoid being too animated and expressive (e.g., don't wildly wave your arms or nod continuously). On the other hand, if you are too reserved and keep your arms crossed or don't ever move them, you could appear insecure, defensive, or even untruthful. Just as with eye contact, your body language should be natural yet confident.

Personality counts. While professional traits like staying sharp and attentive during the interview will help convey your capabilities and experience, most hiring managers want to work with people they like on a personal level too. As a search firm executive counseled me after my first interview with Dave Loeser, a Vice President of Human Resources at Frito-Lay International at the time, "He knows you can do the job; now he wants to know if he'd want to have a beer with you after work." The message was clear: I was so focused on demonstrating my technical fit that Dave couldn't get a glimpse of me as a person. During subsequent interviews, I made a point to loosen up, and we even shared a few laughs about non-work stuff like hobbies and personal anecdotes. Dave ended up hiring me, and we've now been friends for nearly twenty years. (Note: Take extra care to avoid comments or controversial subjects that would give the interviewer a reason to be offended.)

Act naturally. If you did a really outstanding job of practicing for possible interview questions, there's the risk interviewers may sense you have read this sort of book and that you're too prepared. Unfortunately, this could lead them to question the validity and authenticity of everything you have said.

To guard against the chance your preparedness could come across as mechanical, occasionally divert your eyes, pause, and say something like, "Hmmm, that's a good question. I'll have to think about that." After a momentary pause, share the response you had prepared all along. Not only will you have potentially played to the interviewer's ego by commending him or her on a good question but you will also appear more natural. While this advice may seem contrived to some people, you should not feel any more uncomfortable about knowing how to instantly respond to an interviewer's question as you would if you were a politician in a debate. The personal dynamics of interviewing, however, sometimes require a little more thoughtfulness concerning how you share your knowledge.

Balance the bragging. Think of how many braggarts you enjoy hanging out with. How about people who only talk about themselves and their seemingly single-handed accomplishments? Chances are you prefer being around people who are a little more secure and not afraid of admitting they aren't Superman. When showcasing your achievements, make sure you share some of the lessons you have learned and how others at work have contributed to your success. Of course, don't shy away entirely from taking credit for your individual contributions, especially considering behavioral interviewing responses are really about describing what you accomplished versus those around you.

Stay on course. The interview process can be particularly challenging if you are scheduled to meet with more than one interviewer. As a result, be prepared for some questions to be repeated and, in turn, repeat your answers. Regardless of the arrangement, leverage your training and preparation, and stay focused. Keep your responses informative and concise, and if you sense your answer was too broad or too lengthy, simply ask the interviewer, "Did I answer your question?"

Pace yourself. As employers frequently schedule candidates for multiple interviews on the same day, it can be an incredibly exhausting experience despite your abundance of enthusiasm and energy. To make matters worse, many selection processes have you interviewing with progressively higher levels of management as the day goes on, making it even more critical that you remain attentive. If you start feeling fatigued, engage in some self-coaching by repeatedly reminding yourself to stay focused.

CASE IN POINT FROM THE RELUCTANT EXPERT **10**

Someone who hasn't had to endure multiple interviews on the same day may not fully appreciate how mentally taxing it can be. The candidate must be focused and energized for every moment of the process.

Upon graduating from college, I traveled to Atlanta and interviewed with a company that is now Harland Clarke, one of the nation's largest bank check printers. It was the first time I had ever been scheduled for a full day of interviewing, and I entered the building both rested and excited.

Throughout much of the day, things went well. I had my answers ready, and I seemed to have hit it off with the main corporate recruiter. By the time of my last interview, however, I was mentally drained. Unfortunately, as is often the case, the person I interviewed with at the end of the day was also the most important. In this situation, it was the Vice President of Human Resources, and it was by far my worst interview of the day. I was so worn out that instead of giving intelligent and cohesive answers to her questions, I was doing little more than babbling. I'm sure she must have been wondering how such an inarticulate idiot had made it so far in the interviewing process.

I had a contrasting experience just a few months later when I was in the Washington, D.C., area interviewing at Marriott's worldwide headquarters. While the interviews also lasted all day and even resumed the following day, I maintained my stamina throughout the entire process by simply telling myself over and over again, "Stay focused, you can collapse afterward." And in the taxi on the way back to the airport, I did just that.

I have used this self-coaching technique successfully throughout the years, and I have found it not only improves my self-awareness but it also serves to cheer me on when I sense my stamina and concentration are starting to wane.

Sell yourself first. Since employers are the ones who decide if an offer will be extended, it only makes sense that you should devote most of your initial interview impressing them. Specifically, I recommend that 90 percent of the first interview should be devoted to this goal with the remaining 10 percent set aside for obtaining a basic understanding of the job, culture, expectations, and people you would be working with. If the interviewing process progresses, you can devote a greater percentage of time determining if the job is a fit for you. But never lose sight of the fact that you must sell yourself in every interview. Diane Maner, Director of Client Relations for Navigator Executive Advisors, summarized:

> *Interviewing has a strong sales component to the process. It is essential to establish a relationship with the interviewer, identify the employer's needs, and present how your skills and experience will address those needs. As with any sale, it's important that you finish with a strong close.*

Should an offer be extended before you are satisfied with your knowledge of the job or the employer, it's perfectly appropriate and advisable to ask for additional information, including a request to meet with others in the organization. Just make the request in a polite and professional manner, and don't forget you are still selling yourself.

CASE IN POINT FROM THE RELUCTANT EXPERT

While it's true that the interviewing process should be a two-way street—that is, a way for both you and the employer to find out enough about each other to determine whether or not there's a mutual fit—the manner in which that give-and-take unfolds can be critical to your success.

For instance, I was an executive at Pepsi when I got a call from a search firm regarding a bigger job at Pulte Homes, one of the country's largest homebuilders. While I wasn't initially excited about the thought of working in the homebuilding industry, I decided to interview at Pulte's corporate office in the Detroit area anyway.

Once I got there, I was very impressed with just about everything I heard. The head of human resources also came from Pepsi and he and his team were adding a lot of value to the business. Plus the company was rapidly expanding, and there was a lot of opportunity for career growth.

Upon my return, the headhunter asked me what I thought about the job. I told him I was pleasantly surprised to learn what a great company it was and that I was excited to continue with the interviewing process.

A short while later, he called back and told me Pulte was no longer interested in me. When I asked why, he said they didn't think I was sufficiently interested in and enthused about the opportunity. And then it hit me: I was so busy interviewing them and figuring out why I would want to work there that I forgot to sell myself.

If I had it to do all over, I would have made much more of an effort to get them to know me as a person and to understand what I could do for them. Had I done that, I may have had second and third interviews where I could have found out more about the company and the culture. But because I interviewed them too much and too soon, I never had the chance.

GROUP OR PANEL INTERVIEWS

Sometimes employers prefer to have more than one person interview an applicant at the same time. This could be as few as two people or it could be a large group. The most important thing to remember in a group interview is not to get rattled. While it can be intimidating, confusing, and stressful to be the center of an entire group's attention and asked questions by multiple people, staying calm is essential. Answer a question as you would if it were a one-on-one interview, and make initial eye contact with the person who asked it. Midway through your response, slowly make eye contact with each of the others in the room, and then finish with the same person. All of the other interviewing lessons apply, so rely on your preparation to get you through.

Kim Marshall, a Senior Vice President of Human Resources for Wyndham Vacation Ownership, once had a second interview for a job and found out in advance that it would be held in the company's large executive boardroom, where twenty or so members of the senior management team would conduct a panel interview. With all eyes upon her as she entered the room and took her seat, Kim broke the ice and set the tone for a very favorable group interview when she jokingly remarked, "Wow, this looks like a congressional hearing." By the end of the day, she was the top external candidate for the job.

TESTING AND PERSONALITY ASSESSMENTS

Per Durfee's Law #44 in the previous chapter, while studying is encouraged in advance of intelligence tests, no preparation is needed if the testing involves personality assessments. Barry Ogle, founder of the Business Momentum Group and an organizational and leadership consultant, pointed out, "People have ambivalence toward assessments. This need not be the case. Assessments serve as an invaluable asset for both employers and candidates as they allow the latter to validate who they say they really are. As for employers, they are always seeking authentic candidates."

There are no correct answers for these kinds of evaluations, so just respond as truthfully as possible, and don't worry about the consistency of your responses. Not only should you want to know if your personality represents a good match (after all, do you really want a job where you'd be unhappy?) but many tests also have a validity index that alerts the test administrator if someone appears to be trying to guess the right answers. This is particularly important to know because when I see a poor correlation between the validity index and the results, it causes me to question the candidate's integrity.

TARGETED QUESTIONS FOR THE INTERVIEWER

At the end of an interview, you will likely be asked if there is anything you would like to know about the job or the employer. I recommend you first ask a few insightful questions that pertain to the employer's competitive, regulatory, and marketplace landscape, as well as strategy. One approach for doing this is to follow the SWOT analysis process, in which you ask about the employer's strengths, weaknesses, opportunities, and threats.

Mike Grennier, Vice President for Global Solutions at KellyOCG, adds:

> I'm surprised at how poorly candidates, generally speaking, have prepared themselves for the interview. It's the little things, such as not researching the company and its strategies, customer base, and competitors and then developing a set of questions around how they might help the organization achieve its goals.

If something has recently transpired that has placed the organization in an unfavorable public spotlight, don't avoid asking about it out of fear that you may embarrass the interviewer, as that may suggest you haven't done any meaningful pre-interview research. However, be sure to ask subsequent questions of a more positive nature so the exchange of information doesn't come across as though you are only digging up dirt. The overriding message is to follow the principle of Durfee's Law #21 and go into the interview ready to ask as well as to tell.

GENERAL QUESTIONS FOR THE INTERVIEWER

In addition to questions relevant to the specific type of work, the people you will work with, the reporting relationships, and how performance will be measured, you should always ask these four questions:

1. Is there anything about my experience, skills, or interests that concerns you with respect to my fit for this job?

This question is critical. So much so that if you only have time to ask one question, this is it. Many times, interviewers are looking for reasons to reject a candidate, and this question is designed to bring those reasons to the surface. Otherwise, the interviewer may have drawn an unfavorable conclusion regarding your candidacy on incorrect or incomplete information. In contrast, if the interviewer is pleased with you, it would be nice to hear, "No, I think you are a very good candidate for this job."

Susan Chadick underscored the importance of this type of question by revealing what can happen if a candidate dismisses this advice:

> An example of how to blow an interview occurred recently. I had a candidate who was very flat, answered questions too briefly, and gave no illustrations of her points. There wasn't a lot of energy displayed, and when the opportunity was provided to ask questions, she had none. None! You should always have something you want to know more about. At the very least, make some statement. I even appreciate it when a candidate says, "From what I understand so far, I can tell you

*I am very enthusiastic about the opportunity. What do you
think about my candidacy, and where do you see my assets
and liabilities in regard to this role?" Asked sincerely, this
can be a very beneficial question for both the candidate and
the interviewer.*

Earlier in his career and before he became a schoolteacher,
my brother Steve had considerable success with a much more succinct and direct question at the conclusion of an interview when
he would bluntly ask, "Do I have the job?" True, it often put the
employer on the spot, but what's wrong with that? His inquiry inevitably invoked some clue as to the status of his candidacy since, at a
minimum, the interviewer felt compelled to offer a response about
his fit or the interviewing process.

**2. What do you really like about working here? Is there anything you
would change for the better?**

As this question solicits a mix of personal and professional perspectives, it can be particularly revealing. This is likely when you will get
the most candid and sincere insights. Be sure to listen closely for
anything warranting follow-up questions or clarification. For example, if the interviewer says his or her least favorite part of the job
is handling irate customers, you may want to respond with, "That's
interesting. Why do you suppose they are irate?"

**3. Would you mind telling me something about yourself and why you
have been successful at ABC Company?**

Flattery will get you everywhere . . . sometimes. Depending on the individual, you may get responses ranging from seemingly never-ending lists of self-congratulatory highlights to evasive answers suggesting the interviewer would rather not talk about him or herself.
Chances are, however, you will get the former. This question serves
two primary purposes. First, it can potentially give you a wealth of information about the individual's leadership style as well as the organization's culture, including values and competencies, business plan
imperatives, and much more. Second, it could make the interviewer
feel better about themselves, and in the process, you.

4. What are the next steps in the interviewing process?

It often drives people nuts when they believe they have nailed an interview only to be left in limbo without any follow-up from the employer. This question is intended to give you some sense of where you are in the process. For instance, if you are told you are the first applicant they have interviewed, then it may be a while before you hear anything. Conversely, if you are told they hope to make a decision within the next two weeks, you might find yourself racing to the phone every time it rings. Either way, it's helpful to know their process and time frame, particularly if you are concurrently interviewing for other jobs.

JOB DUTIES AND HIRING MANAGER FIT

Once you have progressed beyond the first or second interview, it's especially important to start gathering specific information about job content, responsibilities, and the compatibility level with your would-be boss. In short, this is when you shift from primarily selling yourself to devoting a greater percentage of your interactions to zeroing in on the particulars of the duties, systems, processes, budgets, staff support, management styles, etc. For an idea of what questions you should be asking, momentarily skip ahead to Chapter 10, and review the sections "Questions for Your New Boss" and "Questions for Your Peers." While developed for onboarding, these lists are also helpful for assessing your professional and personal fit during the interview process.

Doug Peddie, an HR Director for EthosEnergy Group, wished he had asked more probing questions before accepting a previous job:

> *Just at a time when I wanted to get out of the day-to-day operations and move into more strategic compensation and benefits projects, a position came open in a growing company. The job reported to someone held in high personal and professional regard in the regional human resources community, and he was looking to upgrade his organization and make it more strategic. The role sounded perfect, and I happily accepted an offer and started my new job.*

Unfortunately, it didn't take me long to realize the or-
ganization didn't have any need for either the skills I had to
offer or the ones I wanted to develop. Their definition of a
strategic compensation role was essentially a combination of
low-level salary and payroll administration and the main-
tenance of a very basic benefits plan supported by outdated
systems. What I could deliver versus what needed to get
done required two vastly different skill sets.

What happened? Very simply, neither I nor the organi-
zation did the appropriate homework. A closer look at the de-
partment's backroom operations, its current activities, and
my boss's background would have revealed that we defined
"strategic" in entirely different terms.

ODD OR RUDE INTERVIEWERS

In the last chapter, I covered how to respond to odd interview questions. As you may recall, those kinds of questions can be part of
a deliberate effort to gain insights into how you think and handle
something unexpected and unrehearsed. While odd questions are
asked by even the most effective and talented interviewers, sometimes the interviewers themselves are rude or behave oddly. In this
context, I'm defining an odd or rude interviewer as someone who
is evidently ill trained, impolite, unprofessional, and seemingly dis-
connected from the goal of the interviewing process.

Unsurprisingly, applicants can find it very unsettling to prepare
for a formal interview only to find themselves in front of someone
whose approach is atypical or inappropriate. In addition to being
distracted, disinterested, or curt, such interviewers might also ask
irrelevant questions or spend too much of the allotted time talking
about themselves instead of finding out about you.

When interviewing with such individuals, it is best to stay focused and try not to get rattled. Remain in a professional mode, and
wait for an opportunity to contribute a point that is favorable to
your candidacy. If after a while you sense a personal connection is
important to the interviewer (e.g., the interviewer places a premium
on working with people he or she likes), you may want to relax your

demeanor slightly and seek an opportunity to share some common beliefs or interests. While it's possible the interviewer is deliberately trying to evoke a reaction for reasons they think are pertinent to the selection process, it's almost always best to maintain your composure. It's possible he or she is just having an off day.[1]

In short, do your best to make a favorable impression despite the situation. If you later decide you don't want the job, then withdraw your candidacy. But always try to give yourself as many options as possible, even if it means having to deal with an unorthodox interviewing process.

ELECTRONIC INTERVIEWS

Before determining whether to incur the time and expense of in-person interviews, recruiters will sometimes arrange for telephone or video interviews with providers such as Skype and HireVue. While not having to contend with traffic or unfamiliar surroundings would seem desirable and less stressful to candidates, it is not uncommon for candidates to find the lessened human connection of electronic interviews awkward and disconcerting. Be that as it may, this is an interviewing trend that will continue to proliferate with advances in technology, and therefore it is incumbent upon candidates to master it.

For telephone interviews, it is vital to never schedule a call when you are unable to talk without distractions (e.g., driving down the highway while the kids are fighting in the backseat). One way to avoid being caught off guard and finding yourself speaking with a recruiter at a time or location that is less than optimal is to simply refrain from answering calls from telephone numbers that you do not recognize. Immediately check your voice mail for any messages, and return the call when the conditions are more suited to a professional exchange. If the circumstances happen to be conducive to picking up a call from someone who may be a recruiter, always answer your telephone in a pleasant and professional manner.

For scheduled telephone interviews, make sure that your cell phone is sufficiently charged. Unlike in-person interviews, the nice thing about phone interviews is you can spread out your preparation materials, such as interview question responses and other notes, on a table, desk, or even a bed and reference them as needed. Be careful the recruiter doesn't hear you shuffling the papers as that could be distracting and give reason to question your ability to think on your feet.

For video interviews, dress professionally as if you were meeting with the recruiter in person. Position the camera so there's a background connoting professionalism such as a home office, a large wall map, a bookshelf, or a setting commensurate with the position. While talking to someone on a screen may feel awkward at first, do your best to behave as if you were interviewing in person. If there's a delay in the transmission, momentarily pause after each exchange to ensure the entire message has been received and to minimize the chance you will inadvertently talk over one another.

Regardless of whether the interview is conducted over the telephone or via video, make every effort to ensure you won't be interrupted by a barking dog, screaming kids, or a jackhammer outside of your window.

After the Interview

While it may be tempting to take a long breather after your last interview, there is still more work to do. Upon the conclusion of each interview, thank the interviewers, and ask for their business cards. Once you get home, immediately prepare a follow-up note to thank them for meeting with you. While the note should be sent electronically, as speed matters, I also recommend sending a short follow-up letter in regular mail. Not only is this courteous but fewer applicants are using the postal service for this purpose, and it will help you get noticed.

THANK-YOU NOTE
Thank-you note or letter after an interview (mail or e-mail)

If e-mailed, the subject line should be: "Follow-up: Job Interview"

If mailed through the postal service, there is no subject, so begin the letter with a formal or informal salutation.

Dear Patsy,

Thank you for taking the time to meet with me yesterday afternoon regarding the Director of Business Analysis position at Kimberly Company. I am very impressed with everything you and your staff have accomplished since the merger with Maupin Enterprises, and I have no doubt you will soon deliver on your strategic plan objectives.

I also want to reiterate how excited I am about the possibility of joining your team. Given my background in financial analysis, purchase accounting, and systems integration, as well as my career interests, I really believe I offer both the technical talent and personal qualities you are looking for in this position. Additionally, the experience that I shared with you from my involvement in the acquisition of Newman's rental business seems to be particularly applicable to Kimberly's post-merger consolidation of support services.

Patsy, thank you again for your consideration, and please let me know if you would like any additional information regarding my skills, experience, and interest in a career with Kimberly.

Warm regards,

Gary Keene

Key Lessons

1. Reiterate your appreciation for being considered for the opportunity.

2. Let the interviewer know how impressed you are with their organization, product, service, people, etc.

3. Declare your interest in the position.

4. Summarize in specific terms why your skills and experience would be an asset, and provide an actual example relevant to the position.

5. Thank the interviewer again, and offer to provide additional information.

6. Keep it brief, and sign it using both your first and last names.

COACHING YOUR REFERENCES

As discussed in chapter 4, your references should already be identified and pre-qualified. If things have gone well thus far in the interviewing process, you may have to use them. If anyone within the employer's organization asks for your references, it usually means you are being seriously considered for the job (that's the only reason I ever check references). To ensure your well-intentioned references don't inadvertently knock you out of consideration, take the time to:

1.   Contact your references and let them know they may be contacted by the employer.

2.   Explain the job, tell them about the employer, and share why it's a good fit.

3.   Coach them on what to say and what not to say. For instance, if during your networking activities you told them you were looking for a job with a big corporation, they may tell someone checking your references, "Despite the size and complexity of operations, Jeff is very good at getting things done in big companies." But what if it's a small employer with little infrastructure and complexity? If that's the case, there's a chance your reference just scared off your prospective employer. To prevent this from happening, tell your references why you are interested in the job, and provide them with the specific attributes, experience, skills, etc. you would like them to convey to the employer.

As the Managing Director for the Avis Budget Group's Northern Europe region, Mark Servodidio recalled an incident when someone didn't follow this protocol:

> I believe references are a critical part of your profile. It speaks to who you are and how you deal with many situations. On the other hand, if you are a reference, it is a responsibility that should be taken very seriously. If you do not feel comfortable giving a reference, you must be honest and decline when you are asked.
>
> I was once surprised when I received a call from a colleague of years past. I was excited to hear from him and quickly called him back. After a few minutes of catching up, he asked, "So what can you tell me about Jeff Nichols?"[2] I replied, "Do you mean Jeff from the other business unit in our company?" After a slight pause, he responded that we were talking about the same person.
>
> Without my knowing it, Jeff had used my name as if to imply we had a close relationship. Unfortunately for Jeff, I

was honest and told my colleague I was surprised he had used me as a reference as I really did not know him very well. As you can imagine, the caller took issue with Jeff's judgment, and it sounded as though his candidacy had come to a grinding halt. Although I understand Jeff is a smart guy, he forgot a key lesson when invoking a name for a reference—cover the bases by making sure you have the person's permission.

REACTING TO "NOTHINGNESS"

Perhaps the cruelest part of the job search process is the "nothingness." Nothingness happens when you either have no job leads or when you have interviewed for a job and you don't get any kind of follow-up or response from the employer. In the latter case, the timing of what you do next is important.

Once you have mailed your thank-you note, wait about five days, and then e-mail the interviewer or hiring manager and reiterate your interest in the job. If you don't get a response, wait another five days and then call. If you still don't get a response, it's likely the job is on hold or another candidate is being pursued. So as not to be a pest and annoy the hiring manager to the point that he or she will lose interest in you altogether, wait another two weeks before reaching out via e-mail or telephone. If that doesn't get you a response, it is almost certain that the employer is no longer interested in you. Nonetheless, it may be worthwhile to reconnect after a few months just in case another position opened up.

Durfee's Laws for Interviewing

Here are some important things to know when interviewing:

DURFEE'S LAW #23: **Get your pitch in.** Even though an increasing number of employers are adopting more formal and structured approaches to interviewing, many are still fumbling through haphazard processes. Some interviewers are simply so inept they either do all the talking or don't know what to ask. While a situation like this might seem easy given that there are few questions for you to deal with, such one-sided interviews also deny you the opportunity to promote yourself as a great candidate. In these situations, look for an appropriate opportunity, such as a pause, for you to interject relevant skills, experiences, or attributes so the interviewer can better understand what you have to offer. Referring to your resume makes it easier to highlight your abilities, so bring extra copies just in case the interviewer doesn't have one readily available.

This actually happened to me when I went to North Carolina for an interview with the top executive of a national business unit. The executive was a really nice guy and very smart, but it seemed he was neither comfortable interviewing me nor very well prepared. Based on his questions about my background, it was clear to me he had not seen my resume (which is precisely why you want to bring a few with you). As I handed him one, I summarized my skills and experiences and how I could help him achieve the goals he had established for the business. Just in case he endorsed me for the position, I also wanted to make sure he could give the parent company's head of human resources some very specific and relevant reasons.

Even in situations where the interviewer is more capable, always look for an opportunity to add something of value. For instance, my oldest brother, Jer, once interviewed for a management position with a local auto service business. When the hiring manager mentioned he needed to increase sales, Jer volunteered that he had a large number of friends in the area who were business owners and potential new customers. He impressed the manager by offering to tap into his network and solicit their business.

DURFEE'S LAW #33: Deliver the "win/win" compensation response. Depending on your flexibility, you may decide to decline an interview or opt out of consideration if you are absolutely certain the compensation package would not be acceptable. If you choose to pursue the opportunity and don't want to be summarily rejected because your compensation requirements may seem too high, one way to respond to inquiries about your expectations is to say you are interested in something that is "fair and represents a win/win" for the employer and yourself. If pressed into giving more specifics, offer a range spanning from your bare minimum to what you really hope to get and add that it "really depends on the responsibilities and scope of the position."

If asked about your compensation history, share it! I have literally ended interviews on the spot when candidates refused to tell me what they were paid in current or previous jobs. Why? Because I simply wasn't going to waste my time or that of others in my company without knowing if we had a good chance of ultimately making an offer the candidate would accept.

Vic Benoit, a former corporate executive who has headed up the staffing functions for companies such as the Pepsi Bottling Group and Heineken USA, similarly advises job candidates to always be open and honest in matters of compensation.

> *If a search firm recruiter approaches you about a job opening, reveal your compensation requirements and history early on, and don't exaggerate. Be prepared to give details such as when you may be expecting a raise, what you think your bonus payout will be, and if you have any other benefits or perks such as a company car or stock options. Also, if the recruiter shared the total compensation range with you and it's not even in the ballpark of what you would accept, don't waste everyone's time by accepting an interview. Otherwise, you risk burning the bridges for future opportunities with both the employer and the search firm.*

DURFEE'S LAW #36: Put yourself in the position to say no. It's okay to interview for jobs that are in the realm of your career interests but don't immediately appeal to you. By going forward, you stand to benefit from the interviewing experience, plus you may later find you have a genuine interest. If you receive an offer but decide the job isn't right for you, you'll also have the satisfaction of knowing the decision to decline it was all yours.

DURFEE'S LAW #45: Answer all the questions. Despite all the fear human resources departments have quite convincingly instilled in employers throughout the United States, there are no illegal questions. Granted, it is illegal to discriminate in some cases, but even so, the questions themselves are not prohibited by law. So answer all of the questions you are asked, provided they are not so personally inappropriate or offensive as to cause you to change your mind about working for the employer. If you do not get hired and you believe it was the result of illegal discrimination (Note: Not all discrimination is illegal), then in the U.S. you have the option of filing a complaint with local, state, or federal authorities. For more information, visit www.EEOC.gov.

DURFEE'S LAW #59: Remember that meals are not about food and drink. If invited to breakfast, lunch, or dinner, don't forget you are still on an interview. Stay away from distracting food (e.g., sizzling fajitas), sloppy food (e.g., barbeque sandwiches and spaghetti), food that sticks to your teeth (e.g., spinach), and don't go wild with the employer's expense report by ordering a lobster or a twenty-four-ounce porterhouse steak. Also, never drink alcohol at lunch, and be very, very cautious at dinner. If your host orders a cocktail and encourages you to do the same and you decide to accept the invitation, forgo the hard liquor and limit yourself to one glass of beer or wine. Many recruiters, myself included, also observe how candidates treat the service staff at restaurants to get a sense of their character and how their personalities will fit in with an employer's culture. Rudeness always raises a huge red flag for me as, quite simply, I don't want to work with boorish people, and neither do my clients.

If you eat too lightly at breakfast or lunch, in subsequent interviews, there's a chance you could end up with the distraction of a growling stomach. As a precaution, pack a few snacks or energy bars in your briefcase or suit coat pocket, and, if necessary, excuse yourself for a bathroom break where you can eat them in privacy. Admittedly, it's a far cry from an ideal dining ambiance, but it's certainly better than losing out on a great career opportunity.

DURFEE'S LAW #61: Thank the interviewer. Upon the conclusion of each interview, shake the interviewer's hand and graciously thank him or her for meeting with you. If possible, get a business card (you will need this to mail a thank-you note).

PLEASE REMEMBER THIS

Some of the key lessons in this chapter include:

✔ The interview is not unlike a sales pitch where you are selling both your technical and personal fit.

✔ Before the interview, considerable attention should be devoted to important details such as personal grooming, selecting and preparing clothes, and planning to be at the employer's designated location early.

✔ During the interview, be friendly and treat everyone you encounter with politeness and respect. It is also critical to be energized and focused throughout the entire interviewing process.

✔ Ensure your body language and eye contact project the intended messages by rehearsing in front of a mirror, on video, or with a friend.

✔ Employers will generally expect you to ask questions. In addition to targeted questions about the job and industry, always attempt to ask the four main questions regarding (1) the status of your candidacy, (2) perceptions of the work environment, (3) the interviewer's background, and (4) the next steps in the selection process.

✔ After the interview, e-mail and mail a thank-you note reiterating your applicable skills and experiences.

✔ Only provide references after you've had the opportunity to coach them on why you are a fit for the position.

✔ Durfee's Laws provide coaching on how to optimally convey your strengths, effectively respond to questions about compensation, and succeed in different interviewing settings.

"**Americans are suckers for style.**"

RICHARD M. NIXON (1913–1994)
U.S. PRESIDENT

CHAPTER 8

NEGOTIATION SKILLS

"In business, you don't get what you deserve; you get what you negotiate."

Dr. Chester L. Karrass
Author and Negotiation Skills Trainer

Perhaps one of the most anxious times my clients experience is when they are anticipating an offer. Two questions generally run through their minds: (1) Am I going to receive an offer? and (2) Will it be a good offer? Receiving an offer is never a sure thing despite all the positive indications and even outright assurances. Many times, candidates get their hopes up only to be surprised and disappointed when an offer never comes. When an offer is extended, candidates have the opportunity to reject it, accept it, or try to negotiate a better deal. As at least 75 percent of the hiring managers in the companies where I have worked were prepared to enhance their initial offers to entice a candidate to accept, this chapter will primarily focus on the importance of negotiating skills.

Preparation

While thinking about the details of an offer before it is extended can seem premature and end up being a moot issue should an offer not be forthcoming, advance preparation allows you to consider what may be acceptable based on what you have already learned about the job through research and interviews. It also gives you ample time to determine what you really *need* (for instance, health benefits and enough money to cover your fixed living expenses) and what you may *want* (things like advancement opportunities, a fun environment, and a short commute). To get a sense of what the going rate may be for different jobs, visit online salary survey sites such as monster.salary.com, www.payscale.com, and coach.careerbuilder.com.

For a job with great allure due to the employer's reputation, location, type of work, hours, or perks, you may decide a lower compensation package than what you previously earned would be acceptable provided it meets your minimum needs. Conversely, if the job is stressful, especially demanding, or just not something you are very thrilled about, you may require more pay to make it worthwhile. Regardless, it will be to your advantage to think about what you would accept before the offer is extended—especially if the employer requires a quick response. Without a head start, you may find yourself further stressed by the combination of a compressed time frame and the magnitude of the decision.

What's Important to You?

People are attracted to particular jobs, professions, and employers for a wide variety of reasons. And while base pay is important, it certainly isn't everything (otherwise, employers wouldn't find it necessary to spend an amount equal to 20–40 percent of your total pay on benefits). As you identify what you would want or need in your next job, here are some things for you to consider:

Advancement opportunities	Commission rates	Educational benefits
Autonomy	Community involvement	Employment contract
Bonuses	Customer contact	Empowerment
Boss and coworkers	Discounts and perks	Environmental or green commitment
Clean environment	Diversity	

LIST CONTINUES

Financial stability

Flexibility of schedule

Fun work environment

Health benefits

Holidays

Hours

Job security

Location

Nature of work

Office accommodations

Outdoor/indoor work

Overtime

Personal satisfaction

Physical requirements

Prestige

Product or service

Professional environment

Public or private employer

Relocation

Reputation of employer

Reputation of industry

Respectful culture

Retirement plan

Rewards and recognition

Safety

Salary/pay

Shift schedule

Stock options

Stress

Teamwork

Training

Travel

Union shop

Vacation

Value of experience

Work at home

Work week

Negotiable Items

While it can be argued that everything is negotiable, here are some common concessions many employers will consider if requested by a candidate.

Association dues paid

Base pay increase

Bonus guarantee

Bonus target increase

Car allowance

Cell phone expenses

Change of control protection

COBRA reimbursement

Commuting expenses

Conference fees

Education reimbursement

Employment contract

Home office equipment

Job title

Parking

Prorated annual merit review

LIST CONTINUES

Prorated bonus payout	Six-month pay review	Travel policy
Relocation benefits	Stock options	Vacation allowance
Schedule flexibility	Temporary living	Vacation vesting
Severance guarantee	Training commitment	Work at home
Signing bonus		Work location

RELOCATION FOR HOMEOWNERS

Just a few years ago, homeowners in upper management were often extended relocation benefits including paid realtor commissions, closing costs, packing and transport of household items, temporary living, lump sum bonuses for incidentals, and even the purchase of their current home if it didn't sell within a reasonable time period. As relocation benefits are a taxable event, employers would routinely gross-up the benefit expense to pay the employee's income tax liability. As you can imagine, all of this was very costly (I regularly approved individual relocations exceeding $100,000, including some that exceeded that figure considerably).

With such generous benefits, employees had every reason to feel financially secure when signing purchasing agreements for new homes in new locations while For Sale signs dangled from their front lawns back home. While many homeowner relocation plans have since been drastically reeled in by cost-conscious employers, there is still a tendency among many recently hired employees to risk financial ruin by seemingly betting everything on the premise that their new jobs will work out.

But what happens if they don't? What if the new boss is a nightmare or the employer abruptly changes direction with respect to strategy or structure? The result is employees can find themselves trapped in a dire situation professionally, personally, and financially. Not only have I seen this happen many times throughout my career but I personally have had to grapple with the profound despair that accompanied a bad career move. Considering that the increasingly fragile and unpredictable work environment is making job security even more fleeting, a wiser alternative to immediately relocating may be a well-orchestrated stall.

To hedge against being stuck in a city or a job that you don't want to be in without an easy way to retrench, you may want to consider negotiating a delayed relocation. This is actually rather common for other personal reasons. For instance, many people whom I recruited told me they wouldn't be able to move until their kids graduated from high school or for other personal reasons. Provided they were willing to endure a long-distance commute, I would negotiate some kind of travel or temporary living allowance until they could relocate. Now, when I coach my clients on negotiating job offers requiring a move, I almost always encourage them to find a reason—any reason—to avoid starting the relocation process until they've had the chance to delve deeply into their jobs and determine whether they appear conducive to a long-term fit. While distance and personal circumstances can greatly influence the endurance for a prolonged commute (it's particularly difficult if family is involved), the longer you put off relocating, the better. At a minimum, however, I recommend trying to delay moving for six months.

Durfee's Laws for Negotiating

Here are some important things to know when negotiating a job offer:

DURFEE'S LAW #17: Have other irons in the fire. Remember this—you always have "other irons in the fire." And even if you aren't expecting an offer anytime soon, just the act of applying for or even inquiring about other opportunities permits you to make this statement. The value of this fear-of-loss sales technique is employers may be less inclined to toss out a low-ball job offer if they think you have other options. For the same reason, they may also expedite the interviewing process rather than allow it to drag on at their convenience.

DURFEE'S LAW #19: Be positive and respectful. As stated in the previous chapter, the employer has likely made you an offer partly because he or she likes you. The objective in negotiating a better deal is to keep the employer liking you and wanting you. To do this, stay positive, be excited, and reiterate your desire to work there. But don't think that just because an offer has been extended that you now have all the power. If you act arrogantly, unreasonably, or indignantly, the employer may very well determine you're not the person you seemed to be and revoke the offer.

This actually happened to one of my clients. The individual was unemployed due to a restructuring but was fortunate to land an interview with a competitor shortly afterward. His interviews went very well, and he impressed the prospective employer with his intellect, skills, and relevant experience. As the offer was not quite as attractive as he had hoped, he engaged in discussions with the senior executive in charge of the department in an effort to secure a better deal. Unfortunately, the negotiations slipped into a rather cold and impersonal debate, with exchanges so upsetting to the hiring executive that the offer was revoked. To make matters worse, the items being negotiated were really not deal breakers, and my client soon regretted not accepting the offer under the original terms.

DURFEE'S LAW #29: Think in terms of the entire package. While a job offer with a high salary may seem like a good deal, it's important to investigate the other components of the offer. For instance, higher health insurance or commuting costs may negate an offer's value. Conversely, a car allowance or higher bonus target may offset a lower salary. Before you accept an offer, make sure you understand the value of the entire package.

DURFEE'S LAW #32: Don't forget that they want you too. Usually an employer has interviewed a number of candidates before deciding to hire you. It may have been a very time-consuming process for everyone involved and one they hope will end once you accept their offer. While the easiest and safest option is to simply accept a job offer without attempting to negotiate, knowing they potentially want you as badly as you want them should give you some confidence to ask for enhancements. Plus, many employers anticipate the initial offer won't be unconditionally accepted and keep some goodies in reserve should the candidate ask for something more.

DURFEE'S LAW #34: Use the offer letter as a contract. Unless you're at the executive level, it can be almost impossible to negotiate an employment contract with an employer who does not already routinely provide them. Many will, however, agree to document a few key enhancements in your offer letter. While not a contract, it is nonetheless a written document that can be tremendously helpful should the terms of your job offer ever come into question.

As the former head of corporate compensation for a Nestlé company, Wendell Gustafson recalled:

> *I once met with a recently hired and well-regarded executive who had given notice he would be leaving the company. After cutting through the surface generalizations such as the job "just isn't a good fit," he rather casually mentioned he had been promised a six-month salary review but was informed it would not be forthcoming with the explanation that the person who extended the offer to him must have misspoken. Indignant and convinced he had been lied to, he considered this a matter of principle and confessed that was the real reason for his resignation. Regrettably, the matter could have been easily cleared up if he had only ensured the commitment was contained in his offer letter.*

Determined not to make the same mistake, Dave Spear was in charge of purchasing for a company in Fenton, Michigan, when it was acquired by a Chicago-based company. After he declined their offer to relocate to their headquarters, they proposed a temporary consulting arrangement while they integrated the purchasing function. Unfamiliar with the leadership and culture of the company, Dave asked for the terms of his assignment to be captured in a memorandum. When the person in charge of the deal asked why he felt it necessary to capture their agreement in written form, Dave responded:

> *"Please understand it's not a matter of trust or anything like that. But should something unexpected happen, I will feel a lot better knowing there won't be any confusion about what we have discussed."*

When pressed as to what I thought could happen, I ca-
sually responded, "I don't know, you could get hit by a bus,
and then there would be no way to verify our agreement."
After a short pause, the individual agreed and then
light-heartedly remarked, "I guess I better be careful when
crossing the street!"

DURFEE'S LAW #46: Quantify your previous package. If you had a position with great benefits and perks, be sure to quantify them in terms of dollar costs. Employers without such things may not understand how to accurately figure them into your offer. As a result, you may have to diplomatically educate them should their offer not take these items into account.

As an example, the executive travel privileges I enjoyed with one hotel company entitled me to complimentary rooms anywhere in the chain, as well as free food, beverages, dry cleaning, and a golf club membership at one of our resorts. When discussing my total compensation package with the search firm recruiter who was working on my offer for a job with Frito-Lay International, I made sure to tell him how much these benefits were worth in dollars because they weren't the type of benefits generally available outside of the hospitality industry, and reverting to paying for them out of my own pocket would have cost me a great deal of money.

DURFEE'S LAW #50: Use the headhunter as your agent. If a search firm is helping to orchestrate the employment process, leverage the firm's relationship with the employer to help you get what you want. Headhunters have a vested interest in brokering a deal between you and the employer, and candidates usually find it's easier to be candid with them.

Vic Benoit further suggested:

If the negotiations start getting complex, I would much
rather see the search firm recruiter as the bad guy versus the
job candidate. But if I make it clear to the recruiter or the
candidate that I've presented our best and final offer, it needs

to be understood that continued efforts to cut a better deal can negatively affect the perception of the candidate. Many times, fighting for a few extra dollars simply isn't worth losing the goodwill that can be sacrificed in the process.

DURFEE'S LAW #51: Leverage the signing bonus. A signing bonus is generally a one-time payment offered as an incentive to attract a candidate or offset a request for money that wasn't extended elsewhere in the compensation package. For example, if an employer is unwilling to increase the base pay in your offer because it would disrupt established pay ranges or create internal equity issues, you may want to suggest a signing bonus as an alternative solution. While executives frequently command big signing bonuses due to pending forfeitures of stock options and other forms of long-term equity, employers such as Disney have also been known to offer them in tight labor markets for entry-level positions such as cooks, housekeepers, and lifeguards.

DURFEE'S LAW #52: Use your research. Sometimes organizations simply do not know the prevailing rates for someone with your skills and experience. If you have done your homework and found a competitive compensation survey for your location and industry, it's okay to bring it up if you think it will aid the negotiation process. However, such data represent just one reference point that does not by itself prove an employer's offer is inadequate. Use the survey if necessary, but be respectful when doing so (see Durfee's Law #19).

DURFEE'S LAW #56: Delay for more pay. The best time to discuss your pay requirements, at least in any specific terms, is when you have determined the prospective employer is truly serious about preparing an offer. Otherwise, you simply may not have enough information about the scope and demands of the job to give an educated response. But if early in the interviewing process you are asked what you are hoping to earn, one delay tactic is to reverse the inquiry by asking, "Would you mind giving me an idea of the range for the position?" Unless it's significantly below what you would accept, you should tell them it seems fair given what you know so far about the job. If the attempt to reverse the question is unsuccessful, offer a range spanning from your bare minimum to what you really hope to get, and add, "It really depends on the responsibilities and scope of the position." However, as emphasized in Durfee's Law #33, never refuse to provide specific details of current or previous compensation. Doing so risks coming across as arrogant or combative, and it could result in the abrupt end of your candidacy.

DURFEE'S LAW #64: **Propose a six-month review.** With the exception of senior executives, for most jobs, the most important component of an offer is the base pay. Unsurprisingly then, it often represents a disproportionate share of the time spent in the negotiation process. If attempts to get more money through a higher base pay or signing bonus prove futile, a third option is to ask for a six-month review. This option is often more acceptable to employers as it reduces the risk of creating internal equity problems, and it gives the added comfort they will be able to assess your performance before paying you more. While there is usually no guarantee as to the value of the raise you'll get (or if you'll get one at all), it's still better than waiting for your annual review.

Responding to an Offer

The thrill of an offer can be wonderful—provided it's at least what you were hoping to get. Before accepting an offer, give it careful consideration. You don't want your immediate excitement, or disappointment, to cause you to forget to clarify or inquire about all of the terms. Regardless of how the offer may initially appeal to you, I recommend you respond with something like, "I really appreciate the offer and the confidence you have in me. Would it be all right if I review the offer further before I give you an answer—just in case I have any questions?"

Unless the employer is in a dire situation and needs to know immediately (which can happen, especially if there is fear of losing a backup candidate), the hiring manager should be willing to give you a little time to decide, even if it's just a few hours. You should use this time to fully consider the offer and to create a list of any outstanding items that were not addressed.

Negotiation Scripts

The extension of an offer positions you to contemplate asking for some enhancements or modifications to it. The following scripts are provided for your reference.

EXAMPLE 1
Phone call with hiring manager (or staffing manager)—request for more pay

> Hi, Angela,
>
> I wanted to follow up and let you know how excited I am about your offer to join you at The Steve Bayley Company. I'm really impressed with what you have accomplished, and I think my skills and experience represent a great fit for the kind of role we've discussed.
>
> Also, I want to thank you for the offer. Overall, it appears to be a nice package, and there's really only one area where I'm hoping there could be some flexibility. In particular, at my last job, I was earning $50,000 a year and I guess I was hoping the offer would be closer to that amount.
>
> Is there any chance that part of the offer could be enhanced so I won't have to take a step backward?
>
> *Signing Bonus Option: If they respond that they cannot accommodate your request because it would exceed the pay scale or be more than others in the same job, you may want to come back with:*
>
> Well, I certainly don't want to start off on the wrong foot by causing internal equity problems, so how about if we were to consider a one-time signing bonus of $_____? That way, my salary won't be an issue for you or the company, and I will be able to maintain my lifestyle without having to cut back or dip into my savings.
>
> Do you think that would be possible?

Key Lessons

1. Start the conversation in an upbeat, respectful, and personal manner (e.g., saying "you" vs. "the company") while briefly reiterating why you are a great fit for the job.

2. Thank the hiring manager for the offer.

3. Important: Do not be demanding or confrontational, and do not spar as if you are trying to win an argument. Rather, in a professional, personal, and congenial manner, specify the request you are "hoping" can be accommodated.

4. Explain the request in monetary terms that make sense.

5. Propose a solution.

6. If the hiring manager agrees, thank him or her warmly.

7. If he or she does not agree to your request or an alternative solution, then you need to make a personal decision as to whether to accept or reject the offer.

8. Once the final offer is verbally accepted, request that the terms be included in an offer letter.

EXAMPLE 2
Phone call with hiring manager (or staffing manager)—request for vacation allowance to be immediately vested

Hi, Autumn—

I wanted to follow up and let you know how excited I am about your offer to join you at Schatow & Sons. I'm really impressed with what you have accomplished, and I think my skills and experience represent a great fit for the kind of role we've discussed.

Also, I want to thank you for the offer. Overall, it appears to be a nice package, and there's really only one area where I'm hoping there could be some flexibility. In particular, I see from the benefits information that I won't be eligible to take any vacation time until I've been with the company for one year.

Option 1: While I don't plan to take any vacation time right away, I am kind of hoping I won't have to tell my kids we can't take a vacation together this year. Is there any chance my vacation allowance could be immediately vested so I won't have to be the bad guy?

Option 2: Since I have already planned a family vacation this summer, I am kind of hoping I won't have to tell my kids we'll have to cancel it. Is there any chance my vacation allowance could be immediately vested so I won't have to be the bad guy?

Option 3: Given that I've already committed to go on a trip to _____ this summer with a group of close friends, I'm kind of hoping I won't have to tell them we can't go.

Is there any chance my vacation allowance could be immediately vested so I won't have to be the bad guy?

Key Lessons

1. See Key Lessons 1–3 and 5–8 in Example 1 above.
2. Let the hiring manager know in real terms how others are impacted by the offer, and don't be afraid to pull at the heartstrings a little without being too dramatic or whiny.

EXAMPLE 3
Phone call with hiring manager (or staffing manager)—request for multiple enhancements to an offer

Hi, Alex—

I wanted to follow up and let you know how excited I am about your offer to join you at Remillard Corporation. I'm really impressed with what you have accomplished, and I think my skills and experience represent a great fit for the kind of role we've discussed.

Also, I want to thank you for the offer. Overall, it appears to be a nice package, and there's really only a couple of areas where I'm hoping there could be some flexibility. In particular, at my last job, I was earning $50,000 a year and I guess I was hoping the offer would be closer to that amount.

Is there any chance that part of the offer could be enhanced so I won't have to take a step backward?

Note: Refer to Example 1 for the remainder of the script. Unless suggested otherwise, resolve each item individually versus grouping them together in the beginning.

Also, I was wondering if it would be okay if my vacation allowance could be immediately vested. You see, I already have a family vacation planned for this summer, and I would appreciate it if I don't have to be the bad guy and tell my kids we'll have to cancel it.

Note: Attempt to resolve this issue before proceeding to next item.

Lastly, I understand many companies located downtown provide free parking for their employees. I didn't see that mentioned in the offer letter, so I just wanted to check to see if that's an expense I'd have to incur.

Note: If the answer is that parking is not included, ask how much parking costs. If it's a minimal amount, it may not be worth pursuing. If parking is expensive, inquire as to what other employees do and/ or ask:

Would it be possible for parking to be included or for the base salary to be adjusted by $1,200 a year to keep me whole?

Key Lessons

1. See Key Lessons 1-8 in Example 1 and Key Lesson 2 in Example 2.
2. Prioritize by beginning with the most important item first.

Rejecting an Offer

If you decide the offer is not for you or if you have accepted another job, be very gracious and appreciative in your explanation to the recruiter or hiring manager. If it was a difficult decision, say so. It is not uncommon for an employer whose offer has been rejected to hire the person in a different position or at a later time (this actually has happened to me twice). To keep this option open, you will need to leave a positive and lasting impression.

EXAMPLE 4
**E-mail or letter to hiring manager (or staffing manager)—
following up after rejecting an offer**

Hi, Kerry—

As a follow-up to our discussion earlier today, I wanted to thank you again for your generous offer to join Hauer Hospitality as a Senior Interior Designer. Given that it was a difficult decision to ultimately have to decline the opportunity, I also wanted to let you know how much I appreciate your understanding and support.

Kerry, I very much valued our discussions about the position's responsibilities as well as the career potential with your firm. In turn, I would be happy to offer my assistance in helping you find another candidate by referring to you any colleagues who I think would be a great fit.

Thank you again for the offer, and I wish you and Hauer Hospitality the best of luck and prosperity.

Sincerely,

Pete Andresen

Key Lessons

1. While an offer should be rejected in a discussion, a follow-up letter or e-mail is a nice addition that contributes to a more lasting and favorable impression.

2. Thank the hiring manager for the offer, and let him or her know if it was a difficult decision.

3. Offer to refer other potential candidates.

4. Thank him or her again for the offer.

Accepting a Lower Offer

Even the best negotiators often do not get what they want. So what happens if you are presented with a firm and final offer and it's less than what your last job paid or less than what you want? As stated at the beginning of this chapter, you can either reject the offer or accept it. If you decide upon the latter, be aware that the initial relief or excitement of landing a new job, particularly if you are unemployed, can wear off quickly should you feel you are not being fairly compensated. You will then either have to rationalize your predicament in an effort to achieve an acceptable level of job satisfaction or risk the possibility that encroaching resentment will negatively affect your attitude, motivation, and performance.

Jeff Schimberg, formerly a Senior Vice President of Human Resources with companies such as Marriott, Fidelity, and World Savings Bank, recommends a longer-term perspective when considering a job offer that falls short of your goals:

> *I have frequently advised new hires and employees wishing to climb the ladder to not be shy about accepting less in the short term in order to prove their worth. When doing so, I share how I once volunteered to take on more responsibility at the same amount of pay in an effort to demonstrate greater value to the organization. That approach successfully positioned me for a promotion with a commensurate increase in compensation. Whatever your situation, I have found if you are forward-thinking and if you believe you can add value to the business, you stand a good chance of achieving your career and financial goals.*

This is the same strategy I used when accepting a position at a level and pay structure below some of my previous jobs. As I wasn't willing to relocate, I knew it would be unlikely I would find another big corporate job without having to endure an extreme commute where I would only come home on the weekends. So I accepted a lower level job in the immediate vicinity that matched my skills, experience, and interests. After eighteen months of staying focused on delivering results and contributing wherever I could, my boss gave me stock options, a car allowance, and a $50,000 raise— essentially bringing me up to the same level as some of my former employers but with lesser responsibilities.

PLEASE REMEMBER THIS

Some of the key lessons in this chapter include:

- ✔ When presented with a job offer, you essentially have three options: accept it, reject it, or try to negotiate a better deal.

- ✔ Advance preparation will help you distinguish wants from needs and help you determine what's most important to you.

- ✔ The list of things you can try to negotiate is long and includes pay, benefits, and non-financial perks.

- ✔ When responding to an offer, always ask for some time before making a decision.

- ✔ Negotiating for more pay and benefits should always be done in an amicable and respectful manner without ever appearing demanding, confrontational, or indignant.

- ✔ When negotiating things like vacation time, explain how others are impacted by your decision.

- ✔ If you reject an offer, be appreciative and cognizant that you may end up applying with the same employer in the future.

- ✔ When accepting an offer below your expectations, consider your willingness and capacity to sacrifice short-term goals for long-term opportunities.

- ✔ Durfee's Laws in this chapter share tactics for enhancing job offers such as appealing to an employer's fear of loss, requesting signing bonuses, leveraging the role of the headhunter, and considering the overall value of the offer.

"I know God won't give me anything I can't handle. I just wish He didn't trust me so much."
MOTHER TERESA (1910–1997)
NUN AND HUMANITARIAN

CHAPTER 9

ONBOARDING

**"If I had eight hours to chop down a tree,
I'd spend the first four sharpening my axe."**

ABRAHAM LINCOLN (1809–1865)
U.S. PRESIDENT

F inding a new job requires considerable stamina and tenacity—efforts that must be kept up not only during the job-finding process but also throughout the entire career transition as a whole. After all, even when your job search has been successfully concluded, you must still adapt to a new job with new people in a new environment. And chances are a lot of what you will experience will be vastly different from your last job. In order for your career transition to be complete, you must successfully assimilate into your new surroundings and figure out the expectations of your new employer. This process is commonly referred to as onboarding.

The Importance of Onboarding

Let's be very clear about the importance of assuming personal ownership for your onboarding—if you fail to do this well, you may quickly find yourself launching a new job search. As a human resources executive, I always made sure offer letters and handbooks included a declaration of a ninety-day probationary period for the sole purpose of allowing my employer to quickly and easily terminate new hires who failed to measure up to our expectations. Not only did I invoke this policy on occasion but, regrettably, many of the new employees we fired never even knew they were performing at an unsatisfactory level until it was too late. Too often, their conflict-avoidant supervisors didn't want to confront them about why they weren't meeting expectations and used the probationary period as a safe and convenient way to simply make them go away.

While most employers do provide new hires with some kind of orientation, these tend to be canned one-time events designed for the masses. While it is important to understand things like the benefits plan, company policies, and where to park, this generic type of information is unlikely to help you begin the process of figuring out your boss or the personalities of your coworkers. Even when orientations do involve scheduled meet-and-greet sessions with key people, the interactions are usually unstructured and more about pleasantries than substance.

For your career transition to be successful, it is critical you understand the dynamics of your new organization, including:

- The nuances of the culture and how they affect your area of responsibility
- What you are expected to accomplish in your job
- How you are expected to achieve results
- How to identify priorities
- The critical dos and don'ts of the employer
- Most importantly: how to make your boss happy

Given these topics generally are not adequately spelled out in company materials or formal orientation programs, it is incumbent upon you to take charge of finding out about them.

GETTING A HEAD START

One way to help achieve an effective onboarding is to begin the process before you are even scheduled to show up for work. Typically, this means finding out what you can about the people, organization, processes, operations, business strategy, and anything else that will assist with your assimilation. While there are many exceptions, most employers will not automatically send you a stack of really great information unless you request it. (I rarely sent materials such as organizational charts, financial reports, performance reviews for direct reports, presentations on strategy, operations information, etc., to new hires—except for those in senior executive positions—without being asked).

Corey Heller, Chief Human Resources Officer for Intermountain Healthcare in Salt Lake City, requested a very extensive and specific list of materials before starting his job.

> *Before my first day as the Chief Human Resources Officer at Intermountain, I used the same approach I've followed for my last few jobs. It has proven to be a very effective way for me to shorten my learning curve and entails collecting information on the organization as soon as I sign my offer letter. In particular, I want to know what success looks like for all of the primary stakeholders, including their objectives, goals, milestones, and metrics. I also ask for the organizational charts for any area considered mission critical. For my department, I request just about everything you could think of, such as performance histories of the staff, employee survey results, the talent management review process and succession planning model, employer of choice initiatives, compensation and benefit document plans, training and development programs, and copies of any line and HR presentations for the last twelve months. I also schedule meetings with key members of the HR staff and the executive team before my first day on the job.*
>
> *Not only does this accelerate my understanding of the business but it also lets the organization know I take my role seriously and that I have a sense of urgency.*

As the current CEO of Participant Media in Beverly Hills and the former CEO of Hard Rock Cafe International, Jim Berk has established a specific strategy to quickly understand the business and establish a clear leadership role when he takes the helm of a new enterprise.

I always ask for as many materials as possible about both the current and past performance of the company and staff. Nothing is too small: formal materials, external coverage, training manuals, employee evaluation forms, and customer-facing materials and analysis. This information allows me to immerse myself in the company's operations and provides the chance to quietly and thoughtfully review what's going on before I take charge of the day-to-day responsibilities.

Within the first week, I meet with the executive team as a group to establish the formal decision-making structure and process. To address any anxiety the rest of the organization may have about what their new boss plans to do, I call for functional area meetings to introduce myself, share my reasons for joining the company, and talk a little bit about our collective short- and long-term goals.

Within my first thirty days, I then schedule meetings at least two levels down in the organization so that I get to know the less visible but often highly influential decision makers. In addition, I schedule small group meetings with representatives from all customer-facing groups in order to understand firsthand how the frontline employees view the company's capabilities to deliver a quality customer experience.

The bottom line is I get in front of my executives, establish a visible presence, and communicate a positive vision quickly so that I can create a positive and productive transitional environment.

You shouldn't be shy about requesting staff meetings shortly after starting a new job and information prior to the first day even if you are not a senior executive. Employers have a vested interest in getting their newly hired employees, regardless of level, up to speed as quickly as possible, and many will oblige anyone, including rank-and-file employees, who proactively offers to contribute to those efforts. I recommend going straight to your future boss and asking something along the lines of, "To better enable me to hit the ground running when I start my new job, would it be possible for me to get a copy of the operations manual and customer satisfaction reports now so that I can get a head start on learning your processes?" Should your new job entail supervisory responsibilities, consider asking your boss if someone could schedule a meeting with you and your team for immediately after you start. Even if your new employer chooses not to accommodate your request, you stand to benefit from having demonstrated your initiative.

THE ENLIGHTENED ORGANIZATION

While definitely in the minority, there are some leaders and organizations who really understand that the added expense of an effective onboarding process pales in comparison to the cost of failure. When considering the tens of thousands of dollars employers typically spend on search firm fees, relocation expenses, and costs related to training new hires, I am at a loss as to why so many employers drop the ball when it comes to helping their newly acquired talent succeed. It seems they have the unrealistic expectation that new employees will somehow be effective from day one. And while I'm guessing that does happen on occasion, I'm much more certain it usually doesn't.[1]

Chris Knipp, now a partner with Acertitude, once joined a new company where he was fortunate to have a boss who was not going to take any unnecessary risks with his new head of human resources.

> My new boss and I sat down together and established a clear orientation schedule. He insisted I agree to follow it completely and not get distracted by the myriad of other priorities awaiting me. His overriding demand: "Your only deliverable for the next thirty days is to learn as much about the business and our people as you can." This turned out to be a true gift as in the past, I typically got immersed in the immediate demands of the new job, which made it much more difficult to complete the initial learning necessary to be successful later. His insistence that I "go slowly now to go fast later" continues to serve as a mantra as I move through my career.

Designing Your Onboarding Plan

The approach I have personally used for designing an onboarding plan is based on a rather simple four-step process: Diagnose, Design, Develop, and Deliver.

STEP 1: DIAGNOSE

Diagnosing the work environment and your boss's leadership style is essentially a fact-finding mission. It is your job to find out what others may already know and to learn as much as possible as quickly as possible. This is not always easy to do because (1) the people you need to get this information from (your boss, peers, subordinates, etc.) are busy doing their own jobs and (2) they may be so accustomed to the working environment it may be difficult for them to objectively identify what may be interesting or illuminating to a new employee. In other words, they may be blind to individual and cultural idiosyncrasies simply because they are so familiar with them. In such an established and accepted environment, how do you go about diagnosing the landscape?

In his bestselling book, *The 7 Habits of Highly Effective People*,[2] Stephen Covey identified the need to "seek first to understand, then to be understood" as a core principle for obtaining interdependence. As interdependence can be defined in terms such as teamwork and collaboration, it will likely be important to your career success. In the context of onboarding, you'll need to identify the things that will help you to become effective in your job. Without sufficient research, you could be in for a tough and unproductive start to your new job.

Human Resources Executive J. Robert Gould provided a very personal account of how he learned the value of making a real effort to understand his new organization:

> Back in 2001, I was very fortunate to be hired as the Vice President of Human Resources for a division of one of the world's largest corporate travel companies. While it was initially exhilarating to come onboard with such a fine organization, at my first meeting, I was made to feel like an outsider with the entire divisional executive team that consisted

of thirteen vice presidents. Regardless, I had been in this position before and I was certain they would soon warm up to me. Wrong! It was not but forty-five days into the job when I was brought into the president's office and told I was not seen as a team player and that some on the team thought I was not willing to work with them. Needless to say, I was stunned and immediately began defensive posturing with sound justification—at least from my perspective.

There are times when lightbulbs flash in your mind and times when you simply hear your inner voice talking. This was the moment I heard my inner voice telling me in no uncertain words to shut up! It was an epiphany that took too long to come, but I am glad it finally did. What hit me is it wasn't the executive team's fault—it was mine. In the simplest terms, it wasn't their responsibility to understand me; it was my responsibility to understand them, and to do that, I needed to listen. I spent the next forty-five days meeting with each and every vice president, listening to their concerns, and saying absolutely nothing in return. Did it work? You bet. In that period of time, my adversaries became my advocates.

Here's the moral of the story: When you join the organization, listen to what is going on and, whenever possible, say nothing. You'll be amazed at what you actually hear. (Are you listening?!)

To help make sure you are working on the right things at the right time and in the right way, you need to approach your new job in the same way that a detective approaches a crime scene. That is, you need to act quickly and ask the right questions of the right people and be diligent in your desire to get the facts.

CASE IN POINT FROM THE RELUCTANT EXPERT

As thrilling as it is to receive and accept a job offer, actually starting the new job can be a very awkward and stressful experience. After all, you are trying to make a good first impression while dealing with such uncertainties as the management styles and behaviors of your new boss and coworkers.

A few years ago, I accepted the position of Vice President of Human Resources for a national business unit of Centex Homes. And while it turned out to be a great job with great people, it took me longer than expected to get traction with both my boss and his other direct reports, partly because this was a newly created job for a new and innovative business. As there was no established way of doing things like recruiting, fostering a collaborative culture, onboarding talent, assessing talent, developing leaders, etc., I had to figure out my immediate priorities from a long list of pressing needs.

In order to get an understanding of what was important to my boss, I would listen very carefully to what he said in the executive staff meetings. I figured that by understanding his priorities, I could then establish and align my priorities. Before long, I was very busy working on numerous initiatives that, based on his remarks, I believed to be important. As it turned out, most of them weren't.

What everyone else who had worked with him already knew was that as a highly creative leader with a tendency to brainstorm, he didn't always mean what he said. For instance, the others on the team were conditioned to simply ignore his requests until he made them three times! Looking back on it, I now understand what they meant when they would say to each other, "Okay, that's two times," or "That's number three, let's get started."

Not knowing that he was probably just thinking aloud had resulted in my wasting time and effort on things that just didn't matter. From then on, I decided I would not leave my onboarding to chance. I was going to take personal control of it, and to make sure that I didn't miss anything, I developed the formal process and tactics contained in this chapter. I also trained the HR team on how to facilitate new leader transition sessions so all our new leaders would benefit from more effective onboarding experiences.

To take charge of your onboarding, prepare a list of questions to help you understand how things are done and how to get things done. You should plan to ask these questions of your boss, your peers, and any others who may be able to provide you with valuable and accurate insight. The following lists offer some suggestions.

Questions for Your New Boss

- What are your top three priorities?
- How can I help make you more successful?
- What are your expectations of me and for this job?
- What are my specific deliverables in my first thirty days? Ninety days? First year?
- How will I know what to prioritize and when something is particularly important?
- How would you describe your management style?
- What would others say are your idiosyncrasies?
- How should I make you aware of a problem?
- How do you prefer me to communicate with you: e-mail, phone, walk-in, etc.?
- What are some of the things that, as your direct report, I should avoid doing because they would really tick you off?
- How will I know if I'm doing something wrong? Right?
- How often should we meet?
- What hours do you want me working?

Questions for Your Peers

- What are your top three priorities?
- What do think should be my top three priorities?
- How would you describe the boss's management style?
- What are the boss's idiosyncrasies?
- What really ticks off the boss?
- How will I know if the boss is happy?
- How will I know if the boss is displeased?
- Whom does the boss seem to work with really well? Why?
- Whom doesn't the boss seem to work with very well? Why?
- What do you like about working here?
- What don't you like about working here?
- What are some of the things that I should avoid doing because they would really tick you off?

- How can I help make your job easier?
- What do you think we do really well here?
- What do you think we can improve upon?
- How does everyone prefer to do their work (e.g., as a team, individually, etc.)?

As you start becoming more familiar with your job, you should think of additional questions relevant to your role, employer, and industry. Also, while the above questions are work related, it is okay to ask safe personal questions regarding hobbies, interests, sports, children, etc. However, stay away from unsafe questions, such as religion, sexual orientation, political affiliation, etc.

Find Your Agent
When you start a new job, it's advantageous to identify someone to help you understand its critical components, as well as the nuances of the organization. In some organizations, newly hired managers are assigned a mentor who is responsible for providing career guidance, encouragement, and insights into workplace politics, culture, people, and how things get done. In non-management positions where there is a greater focus on operational training and technical skills, it is not uncommon for a lead trainer or "work buddy" to be charged with helping new employees become expeditiously productive.

If there are no formal mentoring programs—which is often the case—you may have to find someone on your own to help you succeed and maybe even serve as your role model. The first step is to identify someone who is honest, candid, communicative, and held in high regard by colleagues and bosses alike (responses to the questions contained above in "Questions for Your Peers" should help you identify these individuals). To find out if this person would be willing to assist with your onboarding and professional development, ask if he or she would be willing to share personal perspectives on what is required to become a valuable member of the organization. If he or she conveys a willingness to help, seize that opportunity and cultivate the relationship by regularly scheduling meetings to tap into this bank of knowledge.

Rick Larson has witnessed the importance of finding helpful colleagues during his twenty-plus years in the corporate environment and refers to them as "agents":

> *Successful people all have "agents." That is, they have found someone along the way who believes in them and will sponsor their career. It may be a recruiter in HR who sees the potential in unpolished talent or a senior executive who sees rising stars.*
>
> *These are the people who will go to bat for the individual and make an extra effort to help them succeed. Just like it's dangerous to scuba dive or hike a rugged mountain trail alone, it's also unwise to venture into the unknown territory of a new organization without quickly identifying someone to be there for you and to show you the ropes.*

STEP 2: DESIGN

Once you understand what is most important to your new boss and others, it's time to begin thinking about how you can design your job for success. By this, I mean how to plan your onboarding so your efforts, skills, and attention deliver the most value. The objective of your onboarding plan should be to:

- Focus on priorities
- Accomplish critical tasks and deliver results
- Make your boss happy
- Create a plan

Focus on Priorities

Through your diagnosis, you should have an understanding of the most critical priorities for your boss and the organization. Therefore, you should think about where you can directly make a meaningful impact—right now.

If all of the priorities you have identified are long-term objectives, you may want to expand your scope and think in terms of where you might be able to achieve a few quick wins elsewhere within your boss's area of responsibility. If others are already working on those priorities, avoid stepping on anyone's toes by offering a helping hand. For example, you may say to a peer, "I understand from our meeting that one of your priorities is to shorten customer wait times. I'm still working with my boss to identify my priorities, but is there anything I can do to help you?" If the answer is yes, explain that you will talk to your boss and get back to him or her—then do it.

Accomplish Critical Tasks and Deliver Results

While there may be some important priorities you have to address, make sure you don't ignore all of your other responsibilities. Rarely are people given the luxury to focus on just one or two important tasks at a time. Normally, they must tend to other tasks as well (sometimes referred to as one's "day job"). This holds true regardless of your level.

For example, a boss may tell her new administrative assistant that a top priority is to create a new tracking system for charitable activities. If that's all the administrative assistant works on, however, chances are the boss will be pretty upset if she rushes out the door for the airport only to find out her travel itinerary was never finalized. What makes onboarding so challenging is the process of identifying and prioritizing tasks with limited firsthand experience with that particular organization and that particular boss. This often results in a tendency to assign a high level of importance and urgency to multiple tasks when only a few items may really matter.

While it is always preferable to ask your boss directly for guidance in any areas where clarity is needed, that may not always be possible if the boss is unavailable or busy with things like supervising other direct reports, dealing with customers, or traveling. The value of finding an agent is that this individual's experience and familiarity with your boss, the organization, and the culture can help you prioritize your responsibilities in the boss's absence.

Suppose your boss is tied up in all-day meetings and cannot be interrupted. In front of you are notes from an earlier discussion that capture six items, in no particular order, that you've been asked to accomplish. A computer outage has impeded your productivity and you now realize you will only have time to finish three of them. Rather than guess which three warrant your immediate attention, tell your agent (and others), "I'm still learning how things work around here, including prioritizing my boss's directives. Given that you have worked here awhile, would you mind if I asked you for some help in identifying the most pressing tasks so that I don't end up wasting time on the less important ones?" Whether you are the CEO or working in the mailroom, an educated guess derived from tapping into the institutional knowledge of others is usually better than blindly guessing.

Make Your Boss Happy

This is rule number one. So much so that I would argue in many cases nothing else really matters. Sure, you may hear all kinds of rhetoric about doing what's right for the business and the shareholders and the customers and to think like an owner and . . . blah, blah, blah. The reality is you must devote your attention to the things important to your boss, which, as stated above, requires finding out what those are and prioritizing them. Otherwise, you may lose your boss's support, and, if that happens, you're at risk of also losing your job.[3]

Create a Plan

Although some employers do a nice job of providing newly hired employees with an onboarding plan and calendar, be prepared to create one on your own should one not be prepared for you. The plan does not need to be complex or, for that matter, even pretty. It does, however, need to include a calendar and timelines for when you are expected to learn processes, reach certain milestones, and complete specific tasks.

A simple tool I developed for my own use when onboarding consisted of my job duties and priorities for my first ninety days. In addition to a calendar and timelines for completing objectives, I included the resources I'd need and whomever I would rely on to help me during my onboarding (e.g., IT support, guided tours of operations, etc.). The plan kept me on track to accomplish my onboarding goals, and I would also give a copy to my boss to review whenever we got together. This gave me an opportunity to share the status of my onboarding and discuss any changes to the plan.

The overriding premise is to assume a high level of ownership for assimilating into a new role, and a written plan, whether it's given to you or created by you, will help keep you focused and disciplined.

STEP 3: DEVELOP

By now, your onboarding plan should have given you key insights into how your boss and the organization work, what your priorities are, and what to do versus what not do. The Develop step is intended to help you confirm you have the support and resources to implement the plan you have designed.

The Right Things

If you have been thorough in your efforts, you should be able to meet with your boss, as well as any others important to your success, and confirm that you have identified your immediate work priorities and tasks. The value of this meeting is to ensure nothing has changed and you and your boss remain aligned. Make every effort to secure your boss's commitment to meet with you on a frequent basis during your onboarding period.

The Right Times

In addition to working on the right things, you need to confirm the applicable timelines. While core job responsibilities may be an everyday task, one-time projects may need to be accomplished within certain time frames, and your boss should help you identify milestones and due dates. Since you are new to your job, be careful that you don't overcommit, as you may not know enough to anticipate any upcoming events that could interfere with your plans.

The Resources

Your boss may have a lot of things he or she wants you to do in your first ninety days, but have the necessary resources and money been made available to you? If not, you want to know this from the outset just in case you need to modify your priorities, tasks, and timelines.

STEP 4: DELIVER

You now know what's important to your boss and what he or she wants you to do and by when. So go do it!

Get the Results—Quickly

You have done your research and figured out what needs to get done. It is now imperative you deliver on your onboarding plan commitments. If you're still in your probationary period, remember it is particularly important that you do not fail.

Updates

From the feedback you got from your boss in step 3 (Develop), you should know how and with what frequency he or she wants to meet with you. Even if your boss isn't available to meet with you in person, at a minimum, try to communicate via e-mail or telephone no fewer than once every week to start. This is important because you want to:

1. Update your boss on the progress you are making on your onboarding plan.
2. Find out if there are any changes in your tasks or priorities.
3. Share any unanticipated obstacles that may interfere with your plan.

Report Back

Upon the completion of your onboarding plan, share what you have learned with your boss. Your boss may be interested in not only how much you have learned but also how your observations and recommendations could benefit future new hires.

Durfee's Laws for Onboarding

As mentioned in the chapter on interviewing, you only have one chance to make a good first impression. If your job requires working or interacting with others, the following laws are intended to help you navigate through the awkward period when you are trying to get to know them.

DURFEE'S LAW #5: Onboard for yourself. While it would be nice if all employers provided structured and effective onboarding plans and processes, the reality is many do not. Regardless of your position and level, employers want new employees to start contributing to the objectives of their organizations as quickly as possible. Take ownership of your onboarding by diligently executing an assimilation plan prepared for you or by creating one on your own that will accelerate your ability to become proficient at your job, understand the nuances of the culture, and deliver upon the expectations of your boss and the organization.

DURFEE'S LAW #14: Get there early and stay late. How soon some people forget how badly they wanted their new job. Once eager to do whatever it takes to get hired, they soon start strolling in a little late or disappearing a little early. The first impression you make doesn't end on your first day, your first week, or even your first month. If applicable, tell your spouse and kids that for at least the first ninety days, the traditional probationary period, you will need to work extra hours to learn your new job. Not only is that likely to be true but your dedication—or lack of—may be noticed by your boss and coworkers.

Whenever I mention this law to my clients, I share the story of a salesperson who left her job at one of my former employer's hotels in Crystal City, outside of Washington, D.C., and found another sales position nearby with a uniform supply company. She had only been in her new job a handful of weeks when one Friday afternoon, she found herself all alone in the office. Thinking no one would notice, she decided to leave early only to have her boss call to check on things shortly before 5:00 p.m. Upon discovering her new employee was not there, she concluded the salesperson had a poor work ethic and promptly fired her on Monday morning. Kevin Larabee, Vice President of Human Resources for Westwood Professional Services, believes:

> *Getting a jumpstart on a new job means establishing your personal brand and quickly building that brand's equity. One way to do that is to establish yourself as someone who*

is reliable and ready to do whatever it takes. As trite as it sounds, that means matching and exceeding the organizational norms for hours worked. Get in early, stay late, and your brand grows in value.

DURFEE'S LAW #26: Be interested in them. It's normal for a newly hired employee to be asked a lot of questions regarding previous jobs, family, hobbies, etc. Show some interest in return by asking your new coworkers about their backgrounds, experiences, and interests. Not only may you learn something valuable but it also will serve to give you a break from the spotlight.

DURFEE'S LAW #27: Remember names. In his book, *How to Win Friends & Influence People*[4], Dale Carnegie wrote, "Remember that a person's name is to that person the sweetest and most important sound in any language." If you're not very good at remembering names, try repeating them back when you are first introduced or think of someone he or she resembles with the same name (e.g., a friend, relative, celebrity, etc.). As soon as you are alone, write the name down on a seating chart or work station schematic.

DURFEE'S LAW #43: Reel it in. New employees sometimes feel compelled to talk too much about the impressive things they have accomplished, seemingly in an effort to validate why they got hired. While there may be relevant opportunities to share your credentials in the context of providing valuable perspectives and experiences, a little humility the rest of the time can go a long way.

DURFEE'S LAW #48: Smile. You smiled during the interviewing process, and that helped you get the job—so don't stop now. Although you are now an employee, in some respects, you are still being interviewed—this time by the other employees who are curious as to why you were hired and who you are as a person. Continue to make a good first impression with a warm and sincere smile for whomever you come into contact with.[5]

DURFEE'S LAW #58: Hide the frustration. It is easy to get frustrated in a new job given everything and everyone is so unfamiliar. Plus there's likely to be a lot to learn—which means you may find yourself in a virtual fog of technical ignorance. While your frustration is understandable, letting it get the best of you isn't. Don't forget that you were hired because the employer believes you can learn the job, and, by all means, don't give anyone reason to have second thoughts by having an emotional meltdown or an ugly outburst. Stay calm, cool, and collected, and seek help in a manner that reinforces your standing as the best person for the job.

DURFEE'S LAW #60: Hold the comparisons. Want to annoy your new employer? Just tell everyone in glowing terms how great your last job was compared to where you now work. If you do it enough times, it may not take long for them to suggest that you go back. Should the situation be just the opposite, it's okay to talk about how happy you are now, provided you don't bad-mouth your old employer and sound like a complainer.

DURFEE'S LAW #62: Apologize. Because you are new, you are likely to make mistakes and forget things. Demonstrate you are a conscientious employee by apologizing for your mistakes and offering reassurances that you are catching on.

DURFEE'S LAW #65: Avoid the prima donna label. If you are accustomed to certain perks or considerations that your new employer doesn't currently offer, temper your dissatisfaction. If people are talking about your excessive or self-centered demands, then they're probably not talking about more positive things like your capabilities and potential. Wait until after the probationary period to ask for something that might raise eyebrows. When the time is right, be diplomatic and explain the reasons for your request in a business context.

DURFEE'S LAW #66: Be thankful. Undoubtedly, the newness of the surroundings and the operational processes will require you to call upon others for assistance. At times, you may even sense your reliance on their help is becoming bothersome. No matter what, always extend a sincere thank you in return.

PLEASE REMEMBER THIS

Some of the key lessons in this chapter include:

✔ Your career transition does not end with finding a job. It continues through the onboarding process, and it's imperative you take ownership of your development.

✔ If you don't make your new boss happy within your first ninety days, you risk being fired during the probationary period.

✔ Many successful executives get a head start on their onboarding by requesting information such as organizational charts, performance reviews, financial reports, and strategy plans before their first day of work. Employers will often give relevant information to non-executive employees, too, provided it is requested with the intent of getting a head start on their training and assimilation.

✔ A structured onboarding plan should include these four steps: Diagnose, Design, Develop, and Deliver.

✔ Your onboarding plan includes asking the right questions to understand the organization's people, creating a plan personalized for you and your role, working on the right things at the right time, and getting the results you promised.

✔ Durfee's Laws stress the importance of making a good first impression and avoiding the pitfalls that could send the wrong messages to your boss and peers.

> **"We have such a tendency to rush in, to fix things up with good advice. But we often fail to take the time to diagnose, to really, deeply understand the problem first."**
> STEPHEN R. COVEY
> AUTHOR, THE 7 HABITS OF HIGHLY EFFECTIVE PEOPLE

CHAPTER 10

RUDE AWAKENING

"Life doesn't give you all the practice races you need."

JESSE OWENS (1913–1980)
U.S. OLYMPIC CHAMPION

Now that you know what is required to conduct a successful job search and transition, it would be wise to embrace, retain, and develop this knowledge for the remainder of your career. Unless you are lucky enough to find yourself among an increasingly shrinking workforce population that embarks upon or concludes careers free of involuntary disruptions and detours, you may very well need to draw upon these skills again. Regardless of location or vocation, the turbulence brought on by global socio-economic forces will most assuredly continue to have a ruinous effect on job security, pensions, and lifetime employment. For many in the workforce, the realization that they must now be in a near-continual and agile state of career transition is a rude awakening. For all, it is the new reality.

In fact, career success today is largely dependent not on performance, work ethic, union membership, or loyalty but on the ability to adapt to and master the profound and sometimes insidious forces of change. Where careers were once charted on a well-defined continuum with neatly marked milestones for measuring progress, career planning is now more akin to a maze where considerable skill and resolve are required to navigate around unexpected dead ends and sometimes bitter disappointments. Sherri Merbach, a career coach and organizational development specialist, frequently advises her clients to "no longer look at your career path in terms of climbing straight up a ladder but rather as a lattice where you may have to occasionally climb sideways, diagonally, or even down to achieve your ultimate career objectives." Increasingly, this applies not only to traditional movement within the same organization but also to job changes among different employers.

The trend of hostile takeovers of publicly traded enterprises also continues unabated and with little consideration for the wants and needs of the employees in the targeted corporations. Add brutal competitive factors, perpetual cost reduction mandates, and insatiable shareholder expectations to the mix and it's no surprise that the once implied long-term social contract between an employee and employer is being replaced by a much more transitory and temporary association. In a broader sense, a laser-like focus on bottom-line performance is being played out every day in less conspicuous ways by employers big and small, public and private. While this new reality may not be welcome and it may not be pleasant, particularly in light of the devastating impact it has on individuals and local communities alike, it is pervasive and it is real. For most people, effective preparedness for this increasingly prevalent approach to business begins with a willingness to overcome the reluctance to truly accept it.

Silver and Gold

To understand the dramatic shift that is taking place in today's career climate, it's first essential to understand where we came from. In decades past, it was common for companies to offer their employees irresistible benefits and financial perks that often kept individuals at a single company for an entire career. (Have you ever seen one of those old black-and-white movies where some gray-haired executive is chasing his secretary around the desk? There must have been some pretty good reasons employers were able to get away with such offensive conduct without a massive exodus of staff, and as difficult as it may be to appreciate in today's enlightened work environments, I believe such reasons did exist.)

Whereas much of today's media spotlight around compensation shines on generous pay plans for captains of industry, proportionately little has focused on the diminishing financial security of the rank and file—people like the production worker, administrative assistant, and mid-level accountant. With the exception of relatively few companies, mostly in the emerging technology sector, few non-executive employees can expect to get wealthy from stock options. Up until several years ago, however, a large percentage of the non-government working population enjoyed what I refer to as "silver handcuffs" in the form of pension plans.

Pension plans were once viewed by employers and employees alike as a standard workplace offering. As with health insurance, it was simply expected that employers would extend this particular type of retirement benefit to their throngs of loyal employees. As the formulas for calculating the amount of retirement income factored in years of service, pension plans made it financially prohibitive for employees to quit their jobs. The result was it could be tremendously costly to leave one job for another if the long-term impact on the retirement plan was not fully factored into the overall equation (that is, lost pension benefits from one job were not always recouped in the next job). In such cases, enduring even the most bullying, bureaucratic, and insensitive bosses was more tolerable than giving up a cushy retirement.

Often lost in the widely publicized reports of big Wall Street bonuses and lucrative executive stock options is the fact that compensation plans for key talent are at least partially designed to discourage people from jumping ship for even higher-paying jobs. While many in the general public bemoan such lucrative arrangements, it's hard to argue with their effectiveness as a retention tool.

In the case of executives whose stock options are in the money (i.e., the market rate for their allocated shares exceeds the grant price) but not yet obtainable due to vesting restrictions, "golden" handcuffs still remain.[1] It's the silver kind that are rapidly disappearing. Even where pension plans are still provided, they're essentially a moot point as the odds are very remote that someone entering the workforce in today's dynamic labor market will actually work long enough for the same employer in order to collect the benefit. Instead, many pension plans have been replaced, and more will be, by 401(k) plans that allow employees to contribute tax-deferred portions of their pay into individual retirement accounts. While employers typically match some of their employees' contributions, they are considerably less financially burdensome for the employer than pension plans. Unlike pensions, they are also very portable, so employees can easily quit their jobs and take most, if not all, of their retirement account balances with them. Compared to pension plans, this is an immensely beneficial feature as it reduces the negative financial impact of switching employers.

What all this means is that new entrants to the workforce are drifting away from any reasonable expectation that a paternalistic company will cradle them in a blanket of lifetime job security. It doesn't take a crystal ball to foresee how this revelation will further alter the landscape of the employee-employer relationship. As pension plans continue to disappear, so does a huge reason to hang around if you don't like your job or your boss. Furthermore, I believe there's a much lower tolerance on the part of post-baby boomer generations[2] to work in autocratic and uncaring environments. This combined with the fact there are now few incentives to stay committed to an employer means that job search skills will increasingly become an essential requirement for achieving long-term career goals.

When Job-Hopping Was a Bad Thing

Shortly after starting my new job as Human Resources Manager at a Coca-Cola bottling operation in Jacksonville, Florida, the regional head of finance paid a visit to our facility. When I mentioned I had recently left Marriott's headquarters after three years, he proudly proclaimed Coca-Cola has been his only employer and, in obvious reference to me, stated he wasn't a job-hopper. Even though I didn't really hold the guy in high regard, I nonetheless admit I felt the sting of his remark. After all, it was 1986 and leaving one job for another was often a sign of disloyalty as in, "How could you be so self-centered as to put your needs ahead of the company's?" Fast forward thirty years and I get some measure of satisfaction from the realization that in some ways, I was simply ahead of the curve!

Of course, many employees have never had to look for another job for reasons entirely unrelated to their performance or career choices. Perhaps they happened upon employers who were doing the acquiring versus being acquired. Or maybe the technological whiz kids in Palo Alto have yet to figure out how to replace their jobs with a bundle of powerful microchips. It's also possible they have thus far been spared job eliminations simply because their employers have not yet found reliable and economical vendors for outsourcing their jobs. As for those charmed souls, God bless them. Maybe their loyalty has paid off after all. Or maybe they have just been lucky.

While I have occasionally referred to myself as a corporate mercenary (partly because it just sounds cooler than job-hopper), the reality is that I worked for ten major corporations primarily because many of my jobs had been eliminated and I had no choice. Paradoxically, several of those job losses were with the very same companies that grilled me incessantly in interviews about my loyalty quotient and then demonstrated none to me in return.

Tommie Kennedy, Vice President of Human Resources for Rain for Rent in Bakersfield, California, accepts that job changes may be outside of the candidate's control: "The U.S. marketplace is so volatile with companies rightsizing, downsizing, and reorganizing and mergers and acquisitions happening that many employees who would love to stay in a position for years end up switching jobs multiple times. If the candidate can explain that there were layoffs, reorganizing, a change in management or ownership of the company, or that the company folded, then I am comfortable with moving on with that candidate."

GENERATION X AND MILLENNIALS

Were you born between the mid-1960s and the new millennium? Then as a member of either generation X (born in the early 1960s to early 1980s) or the millennials (born somewhere between the mid-1980s and the early 2000s), you probably already know about the realities of job insecurity through your own experiences or those of family and friends. In her book, *Generation Me: Why Today's Young*

Americans Are More Confident, Assertive, Entitled—and More Miserable Than Ever Before,[3] Dr. Jean Twenge describes millennials as narcissistic, confident, cynical, and, among other things, anxious and depressed. Given what they've already experienced in the short time they've been in the workforce, I'm not surprised.

Millennials (also commonly referred to as generation Y) have witnessed or endured enough havoc in the labor market to figure out the trend among countless employers to outsource work to Mexico, India, China, Thailand, Bangladesh, Vietnam, or other places with comparatively cheap labor costs. For them to achieve anything remotely resembling career continuity means planning, adapting, pursuing, and orchestrating their individual career paths among a myriad of employers who are tempted to shift jobs to countries with vastly lower cost structures.

Among many in the millennial crowd, there are also grave doubts the once stalwart Social Security system will be waiting for them at the end of their proverbial career rainbows. Even more cynically, some dismiss the program as nothing more than a public Ponzi scheme that is propagated and protected by the generations before them and is on track to leave them empty-handed when their eligibility dates arrive.[4] And pensions? Highly unlikely even in what was once the safe haven of the public sector. So is it any wonder that they're anxious and depressed? Perhaps a heavy dose of self-confidence is exactly the counterbalance they need just to get out of bed every morning.

Many older gen Xers have experienced the same uncertainty but with greater frequency. In their prime and feeling invincible during the technology dot-com era of the 1990s, they were engulfed in the sector's ugly implosion in 2000 and 2001. To make things worse, they were hit with the double whammy of massive unemployment and the disappearance of billions of dollars in technology stock valuation. Countless gen Xers went from being multimillionaires on paper to moving back home with their parents when once enamored Wall Street analysts and investors finally wised up and could no longer rationalize severely flawed financial models.

With an economy subsequently pounded by the terrorist attacks of September 11, 2001; the accounting scandals of companies such as Enron, WorldCom, Adelphia, Tyco International, and Sunbeam; and the Great Recession that began in December 2007, both gen Xers and millennials have either witnessed or learned firsthand that job security is little more than nostalgia from their parents' era. For them, frequent job changes are not something they expect to have much control over.

Preparing for Change

So what does all this mean to you? With relatively few exceptions, it means that before your career is over, there is a very good chance you will repeatedly have to confront the changes brought on by a job loss or career transformation. As a result, learning how to deal with change should not be a one-time event but rather a continual process. In this regard, there are a few things worth considering.

Speed matters. Unlike in Scandinavia and many western European countries, displaced employees in the United States do not enjoy lucrative social safety nets that can turn unemployment into a prolonged holiday. Rather, most Americans have to move quite fast to find gainful employment before the financial toll wreaks havoc on their savings and lifestyle. If you fall into this category, begin developing your job search skills so you will be ready to deal with any unexpected periods of unemployment without delay.[5] Even if you have a very secure job at present, you don't want to be unprepared for an interview should the career opportunity of a lifetime suddenly present itself.

Embrace self-development. To avoid professional obsolescence, it's vital that you continually learn and obtain relevant and substantive skills. Even if not required in your current role, expanding your capabilities can make you more marketable should you suddenly find yourself back on the job market. This is particularly true with respect to developing and maintaining a high level of prowess with technology and software programs. A singular expertise or skill may have once been sufficient to underpin an entire career, but Nancy Geraghty, Vice President of Capstone Logistics in Atlanta, cautions,

"In today's world, adaptability, mastery of change, and resiliency are increasingly the attributes that will define career sustainability and success."

Hire a financial adviser. Now that pensions and long-term job security are largely things of the past, hiring a professional financial adviser can help with your retirement planning, 401(k) rollovers, and short-term budgeting. An adviser can also help identify benefit plans such as life insurance (which I recommend you purchase separately from your employer's plan so that you don't lose coverage during periods of transition).

When I was considering my career options after a job loss in 2004, for example, I met with my Ameriprise financial adviser, Paul Prewitt, and he was able to offer some valuable perspectives regarding the risks and rewards of pursuing the entrepreneurial route. In addition to the practical matter of assessing how my financial resources would factor into the decision, one thing he said that really resonated with me was, "One of the really nice things about working for yourself is you'll never have to worry again about someone eliminating your job." Although I did accept a corporate job a few months later, from that moment on I knew the appeal of career self-determination was too great for me to ever entirely dismiss it.

Keep your options open—always. Too often people will not even consider other opportunities because of contentment with their current job and employer. Unfortunately, when they do lose their jobs, they scramble to develop a network, and their lack of readiness contributes to blown opportunities. By always being willing to at least consider other jobs, you sharpen your interviewing skills and your network becomes more robust.

Offer assistance. We covered this topic in Chapter 4, but it's worth mentioning again: should you be in a position to help others network for a job with your employer or where you have contacts, I highly recommend doing so. They will likely be appreciative of the help and more inclined to return the favor should you ever find yourself in their situation. A word of caution, though—don't refer people who wouldn't be a good fit for a job. Not only will you lose credibility regarding your ability to identify talent but you also never want to risk compromising your most valuable relationships for the sake of pleasing others.

Believe the new reality. Every day, in boardrooms and offices across the country, chief financial officers and their staffs are trying to maximize earnings and reduce expenses. It is what they do; that's their job. Unsurprisingly, outsourcing, automation, and technology are regularly explored as labor-saving options. In their defense, if the top executives don't find a way to please investors and Wall Street analysts practically every quarter, they may soon find themselves unemployed. Given that so much of their performance is measured by their ability to deliver favorable financial results through whatever legal means are at their disposal, reducing payroll and benefit expenses represent very tempting options.

It would, however, be unfair to point fingers only at the finance department. As a human resources executive, and with strong encouragement from our employment attorneys, I always went to great lengths to ensure our employee handbook and offer letters clearly stated employees were "at will" and could be terminated at "any time, for any reason, and without notice." I often got the sense that neither long-term employees nor new hires ever really believed me until those sad occasions when I had to give them the news that their jobs were being eliminated.

In short, I don't believe you can fully embrace the new reality until you come to terms with the basic premise that loyalty must be a two-way street. So unless your employer provides you with a solid and lucrative employment contract (which you shouldn't expect below the executive level), never forget that you remain vulnerable to being fired at any time, for any reason, and without notice.

Anticipating Change

While learning how to get a new job is immensely valuable in its own right, job search experts know *when* to start looking as well—and that's well before their jobs have actually gone away. In this section, I provide some insights on the timing of looking for a new job rather than the skills involved.

Dr. Nick Horney, Principal and Founder of Agility Consulting & Training, specializes in helping individuals and organizations effectively anticipate and manage change. Based on an underlying assumption that the business environment will only continue to be turbulent, Nick maintains that a fundamental capability for success and survival in this turbulent environment is to become more agile.

THE CASE OF SAM

To help illustrate how to adapt to a rapidly changing world, Nick combines the five critical behaviors of his firm's The Agile Model® with the fictional account of Sam, a vice president of a Fortune 500 company who was shocked to find his job had just been eliminated. While on his way home to break the news to his wife and kids, Sam started questioning what he could have done differently to have prevented the decision or at least to not been surprised by it.

1. **Anticipate Change.** Sam could have been more alert to the changing business conditions beyond his own department and company and identified macro-level risks that might occur during the year. This would have given him the advance notice he needed to prepare for the most likely or least pleasant outcomes. But since Sam did not anticipate his job loss, how does he focus on anticipating change to help him manage it now that it's upon him? He could begin by studying the marketplace and avoiding industries likely to be more challenged in the immediate future. For instance, when the homebuilding industry started to crash in 2006, it didn't take long for the furniture and appliance industries to follow suit. In light of the domino effect among interdependent economic sectors, Sam will be more able to focus his job search in more resilient industry sectors if he increases his awareness of what's transpiring in the economy both nationally and globally.

2. **Generate Confidence.** Sam should focus on building his self-confidence by doing things like getting active in networking groups and, as covered in Chapter 1, increasing his exercise regimen to reduce stress and improve his psychological disposition. He will also generate confidence with his family by communicating his plan of action and keeping them updated on activities and results.

THE AGILE MODEL®

3. **Initiate Action.** A so-called "bias for action" also serves to generate confidence for Sam, and his demonstrated skill at making things happen at work will serve him well during his job search. However, as he will be the one primarily responsible for getting things done, he must understand his ability to delegate tasks is severely limited.

4. **Liberate Thinking.** Sam should analyze how he searched for a job in the past and realize there are new resources at his disposal such as LinkedIn and Facebook. To enhance his skills, Sam needs to study the recommendations from those in the business of finding jobs and improve his overall job search skills through online coaching resources such as the Navigator Institute.

5. **Evaluate Results.** Sam needs to monitor his plan to determine what's working and what isn't. He should set a reasonable but aggressive time schedule and celebrate any progress to sustain his momentum. Importantly, Sam needs to keep track of the actions yielding the most success.

What Doesn't Kill You Can Make You Stronger

For generations X and Y, resiliency has become the key to career progress—if not outright survival. They must learn to adapt and change if they are to avoid professional irrelevance. A failure to roll with the punches, including complete career changes if necessary, can quickly lead to financial ruin as they generally lack the total net worth and rainy-day savings that older generations have accumulated in their lifetimes.

While certainly stressful and unsettling, working for a number of different employers can be quite beneficial. For one, you can gain insights into a great number of processes, best practices, and experiences that can make you tremendously valuable to your next employer. For example, when Hard Rock was staffing up to expand its hotel brand, my extensive experience in those industries was particularly helpful to an organization dominated by restaurateurs. Likewise, when Centex Homes entered the vacation home market, I was able to actively contribute to strategy sessions for both resort operations and branding initiatives because I generally knew more about the topics than my colleagues whose backgrounds were predominately limited to building houses.

And while this may be unsettling for the "I'm not a job-hopper" crowd, consider this: I am very reluctant to hire senior talent who have only worked for one employer for more than twenty years. Whether as a recruiter or hiring manager, I am concerned they only know one way of doing things. It also makes me wonder if they fear change or are overly risk-avoidant. So while loyalty to only one employer was once regarded as highly desirable and admirable, it now raises questions about a candidate's ability to adapt and contribute in a different workplace and culture.

TANGIBLE REWARDS

An interesting and potentially encouraging twist to losing your job is that you may find out it was all for the best—although you may not realize it until years later. While this may sound like the kind of cliché your mother may have used after a heartrending breakup with the love of your life ("It's all for the best, dear"), I've seen countless situations when the first employees who were laid off felt they were getting the short end of the stick only to have the timing work out in their favor. For example, less generous severances and the loss of outplacement support often accompany subsequent staff reductions as financially strapped employers look for additional ways to save money. Additionally, the first employees out the door often enjoy a head start in landing jobs that may no longer be available after subsequently terminated employees with similar skills and experiences enter the labor market.

I recall how despondent I once was when my job was eliminated at what I thought was precisely the wrong time. With around 200,000 shares of vested stock options in my account, I received advanced notice that a restructuring would require me to either relocate or leave the company. As relocation was out of the question due to family reasons, I had no choice but to sell my shares, as they would expire shortly after my pending termination. To make matters worse, several Wall Street analysts were predicting the stock, which was trading for around $22 per share, would top $30 by the end of the year. If they were right, I would miss out on a huge payout.

Without any viable options, I started cashing in my options, with my last trade commanding $25 per share. A few days after I sold all of my shares, an unexpected thing happened: the price of the stock started to drop and eventually bottomed out at around $15. It took a couple of years for me to fully appreciate that had my job not been eliminated precisely when it was, I would have almost certainly held on to my stock in anticipation of a turnaround. Through sheer luck (admittedly, a rather odd term for describing the loss of a job), I was forced to cash in at what turned out to be the stock's high point for several years.

INTANGIBLE REWARDS

Over time, I have come to appreciate how fortunate I am for all the voluntary and involuntary job changes I have experienced because along the way, I have made more friends than I ever imagined possible. When my former executive assistant Julie Erlenmeyer told me, "You are the most networked person I have ever known," I didn't quite know what to make of it, as I don't think I ever really made a deliberate effort to create a vast network of contacts. Rather, I valued the friendships forged in the workplaces of previous employers, and I simply didn't want to see those relationships fade away just because I went to work somewhere else. So while numerous job losses are not something one would normally celebrate, I also cannot ignore the fact I have been rewarded with more than my fair share of friends as a direct result of those circumstances.

How about you? If your job has gone away, did anything unexpectedly pleasant or fortuitous come of it? Perhaps you learned a skill or gained some experience in one job that helped you secure an even better job later in your career. What about personal relationships that would never have been established had you not been forced to leave your last employer? A change in routine, even if unpleasant, generally leads to new adventures and new people.

While it may not always be evident at the time it's happening, there can be significant personal and professional upsides to change. I encourage you to spend a few moments now to clear your thoughts and consider how you may have unexpectedly benefited from an unwanted job transition.

What's Ahead

It would be nice to think we will someday go back to the days of job security, lifetime employment, and a smooth career track. But, while it is entirely understandable to long for those days, it is inconceivable that they will ever return, especially in the private sector. Doing so would somehow require the unfathomable—forgoing the never-ending advances in communications and technology. Plus, the political and socioeconomic developments that have so transformed the world are so formidable and relentless (the industrial rise of China, for instance) that there's simply no turning back the clock.

Jeff Carroll, Director of Leadership Development at Northern Illinois University and a career strategist who specializes in helping professionals reinvent their careers, advocates a bold new approach to thinking about careers:

*You see, careers as we know them, along with so-called per-
manent jobs, are over, done, kaput—really! In fact, here's
a suggestion: maybe we should just remove the word "job"
from the workplace to rescue us from the frustration of being
forever stuck between hoping for what was and accepting
what is. Instead, we need to build a mindset and a lifestyle
around the new reality of multiple careers and multiple organizations or, as some authors call it, a "portfolio career."*

So what do these changes in the employment landscape mean for
you? The following provides a few thoughts.

LESS BAGGAGE

With the stigma of losing one's job quickly waning, less time will be
spent recovering from a blow to one's self-esteem and coming up
with overly elaborate explanations for being in transition. In contrast to some of my older clients who struggle to earnestly accept
my ceaseless assertions that losing your job does not make you a
loser, gen X and millennials will have the luxury of being able to
more expeditiously brush off this type of emotional baggage and
move forward with less angst and greater focus.

FAST, FASTER, FASTEST

Americans love speed. Whether it's food, banking, traveling, or
whatever, we want it fast. And when it's already fast, we want it
faster. When McDonald's first opened units around the country,
customers marveled at how quickly they got their orders. But soon,
even that wasn't fast enough, and drive-through windows were
added to save customers the time of parking and walking to the
indoor counter. Since those days, it seems nearly every provider of
a product or service is looking for new ways to reduce wait times,
including those for online ordering and payment.

Unsurprisingly, the need for speed is also becoming critical for
job searches. To illustrate, a while back, I read a newspaper article
about a young lady who had just been informed her job had been
eliminated.[6] Upon leaving her employer's office on the way to her
car, she texted her name followed by "needs a job" from her cell

phone. By way of Twitter and Facebook, her three-word message was instantly sent to two thousand of her friends and family members, who responded with a mix of moral support and job leads. Within two weeks, she had two firm job offers and thirteen solid leads. This example serves as a powerful testament to not only her proficiency with social media and technology but also to the value of having a large network while employed just in case such unforeseen circumstances arise.

Contrast her action with others who launch their job search networking activities only after considerable delay and through the more traditional channels and it's obvious her utilization of online social networking venues has the capability of delivering much faster results. While generations X and Y are particularly adept with the latest communication technology, older generations are finding themselves at a distinct disadvantage. Catching up will not only require a greater comfort level with new gadgets and websites but they'll also have to rely on their similar-aged contacts to do the same. The advantages of having Facebook, LinkedIn, and Twitter accounts are greatly diminished if few friends, colleagues, and family members have them too.

MORE DIVERSITY

Population trends in the United States and virtually all industrial nations suggest there will be more diversity in the workplace from every conceivable angle, including race, sexual orientation, gender, and religious affiliation. While much of this will be the result of demographic changes, employer diversity initiatives will also continue to boost the representation of minorities and women in the workplace. With respect to the latter, white males will find it increasingly difficult to be considered for employment opportunities in those organizations striving for a more diverse workforce.[7]

As the life expectancy continues to rise in developed countries, older workers will also become more prevalent in the workplace. Led by the millions of healthy and active baby boomers, more people will remain employed beyond the traditional retirement ages of sixty-two to sixty-five, even if they are just doing part-time work. In fact, a projected labor shortage of younger workers is already causing the service industry to consider how it will be able to recruit and accommodate an older employee population. And many people will welcome this effort when faced with the realization that they simply cannot afford to retire due to insufficient or non-existent pensions, unpredictable investment account returns, skyrocketing medical costs (prescription drugs, in particular), and longer life expectancies.[8]

FEWER LAYOFFS

Don't allow this section's heading to fool you—a job market with fewer layoffs is not a good thing. Once widely used to define a temporary interruption of work until business picked up, layoffs are rapidly losing favor to outright job terminations where reemployment cannot be expected. Layoffs were quite frequent in the factory towns of my youth, and, while not usually a pleasant experience, few workers believed their jobs were lost for good. They figured that once the economy picked up, they'd be called back to work, and they were usually right. Automation, however, has in recent years contributed to the loss of millions of manufacturing jobs, and the financial appeal of cheaper labor elsewhere is only expected to grow. Accordingly, employers today and in the future will be less inclined to think in terms of layoffs because in most cases, the employees impacted by job cuts won't ever be coming back.

When employees do return to their former employers, it's generally the exception to the rule and not due to a formal call-back process. Take the case of Dion Kiernan, who was a national director of business development for a major international hotel company when his job was eliminated during a company-wide downsizing. Dion applied to other employers and regularly checked his former company's employment website as well. He also leveraged the internal relationships and network he had established over his seventeen-year career with the company to find out about any job openings. Nine months later, he was back at the same company, but it was far from a warm homecoming:

> Perhaps the biggest thing I learned from this experience is you have to take complete ownership for working your way back into a company. After my position was eliminated, nobody

from human resources called me about other job openings, so I was pretty much on my own. When I did find a job of interest, I realized that for all practical purposes the company had cut all ties to me, and I was given no more consideration than someone without my many years of service. The offer I initially received to return was $30,000 below what they had been paying me less than a year earlier, and I was treated as a new employee, meaning I wasn't given credit for past service for things like vacation vesting. I was even placed on the same ninety-day probationary period as new hires.

Although I expect there to be fewer layoffs in the future, I don't expect the term "layoff" to go away anytime soon. Why? Because for many supervisors, it just sounds so much nicer than coming right out and telling someone that he or she is fired. Beware of this popular misnomer, and guard against its tendency to inspire false hope. Instead, make sure you really understand what happened to your job and why so that you can plan your career transition smartly.

YOU WORKED FOR WHOM?

As I pointed out in Chapter 1, brand recognition and self-identity are often deeply connected. Living in Orlando, my friends and neighbors take a great measure of pride in saying, "I work for Disney," or "I work for Universal Studios." For all the reasons that marketing gurus and psychologists can articulate better than I, strong brand recognition influences people's initial assessment of you. For example, if you work for an oil company like Exxon at a time when gasoline hits $4 a gallon, you may be asked, "How come you are charging so much for gas?" even though you have absolutely no influence over pricing. Or if you tell someone you work for Ritz-Carlton, it may evoke a favorable first impression even if they don't know anything else about you.

But what happens when the big name-brand company you devoted so much of your life to goes away? For a lot of people, a part of their identity goes away with it. Of the companies where I have worked, six of them no longer exist. Candidly, I miss the immediate connotations I once enjoyed before brands such as Stouffer Hotels and First USA were discontinued. Many of my friends back in Michigan feel the same way about the passing of such automotive icons as Pontiac and Oldsmobile.

Looking ahead, the already rapid pace of change is only expected to accelerate, and a great number of established brands across all industries will fall to the competitive pressures of the global marketplace or get gobbled up in mergers and acquisitions. For anyone who has enjoyed the shorthand of conjuring up at least a partial picture of who he or she is simply by dropping the name of a previous employer, be prepared to do some explaining if the brand goes away. In many cases, your introduction may also need to change from who you work for ("I work for Bank One") to your professional occupation ("I work in finance").

JOBS FOR TOMORROW

In order to serve an aging population headed up by retiring baby boomers, the health care sector will most certainly have to expand beyond its current capacity. In addition to companies that staff doctors, nurses, home care providers, pharmacists, and medical office support staff, soon-to-be burgeoning retirement residences and assisted-living communities will also require an influx of employees.

While a great number of information technology, computer systems design, software development, and engineering jobs have been outsourced to India and other countries, there will still be a steady overall demand in the U.S., including for skilled designers and technicians to service local enterprises and consumers. With no reason to believe the threat of terrorism will dissipate anytime soon, job demand in the military and in the defense and private security sectors should also remain strong.

A heightened interest in protecting the environment from the effects of global warming will also lead to the creation of a potentially high number of "green" jobs as the search for affordable alternative energy sources grows. In order to train and develop the minds needed for growth industries, more help will be needed in public and private educational institutions. And while our trillions of dollars in federal government debt might logically suggest less overall job growth in the public sector, the likely outcome is actually unknown. After all, logic often takes a backseat to the interests of politicians seeking to gain the immediate favor of voters by creating new programs and services.

Across all industries, I expect an accelerated shift from core employees (i.e., those on the employer's payroll) to independent contractors, consulting firms, and outsourced vendors as mandated health insurance coverage makes it prohibitive for many businesses to absorb the added costs. As a result, more people than ever will find themselves working on an employer's premises without actually being an employee. For many others, the proliferation of telecommuting technology and home offices will continue to make it easier to find work as external contractors without the hassles of commuting.

Lastly, there will be a huge demand for employees in industries not yet invented. Periods of explosive growth in employment spurred by the development of now-commonplace products and services such as e-commerce, smartphones, computer tablets, and endless online services cannot help but to offer some encouragement for job seekers as none of those things existed to any meaningful degree just twenty years ago. What innovations will excite tomorrow's consumers and create the demand for millions of new employees? Stay tuned.

What to Do

Through countless career wins, losses, and multidimensional experiences, I became an expert on job searches because I was better prepared and more motivated than other candidates. Amazingly, I regularly encounter many otherwise intelligent people who choose not to spend the time or relatively nominal money to learn how to get their careers back on track. If you are truly serious about getting another job, then be prepared to devote the time, effort, and necessary resources to position yourself as the top candidate.

Fortunately, by reading this book, you have already demonstrated a level of understanding and commitment that will give you an advantage over most others as you pursue your career aspirations. In light of the new reality, these are skills you should continually strive to maintain and develop, as there is a very good chance you will be calling upon them repeatedly throughout your career. Few things in life worth having come easily, and effective job skills are among them.

RETOOL

Whatever opportunities arise on the horizon, it's safe to say the overall labor pool will be expected to have a higher collective level of education and technical skills. The days are quickly passing where an unskilled workforce can earn a good living and secure a place in the middle class with little else than a strong back and a good work ethic. Workers at all levels of the organization will increasingly be required to use advanced technology and operate sophisticated equipment. Just like manufacturing plants have had to invest and retool to be competitive, so, too, will human capital.

Ryan Franse, a lifelong friend who retired from GM as a production worker and lives in Michigan's Lake Fenton area just outside of Flint, foresaw the threat to the domestic auto industry years ago and decided to be proactive. Taking advantage of the company's educational reimbursement benefits, Ryan went to college part time and between shifts to earn his associate degree in science in the 1990s. When I asked what motivated him when so many of his coworkers had no interest in continuing their education, he replied:

> I started out in the auto industry just before the economy was hit with a couple of recessions, and I ended up getting laid off twice in my first few years. Those experiences served as a wake-up call, and I wanted something to fall back on in case they ever decided to close my plant for good. If it ever became necessary, I figured a degree in science would serve as a solid foundation for me to pursue an entirely different career in medical technology or as a physical therapist.

The soundness of Ryan's career-planning strategy is supported by statistical evidence that people with an associate degree have an unemployment rate of less than half that of workers without a high school diploma. When compared to workers with at least a bachelor's degree, those without a diploma are nearly three times more likely to be unemployed.[9]

OUTPERFORM THE COMPETITION

In tough economic times when the unemployment rate is particularly high, clients sometimes ask me, "What's the point of even looking for a job in this job market?" In response, I make sure they understand that in all probability, there is an employer looking to hire someone with their skills, experience, and interests. Sure, we may not know who these employers are, where they are, or maybe even why they may be interested in hiring him or her, but that's why it's called a job search. Plus there are jobs—plenty of jobs—out there! Even when the unemployment rate hovered around 10 percent nationally in 2009 and 2010, there were still 2.4 million job postings with nearly 100,000 new jobs being created each month.[10]

In contrast to economic boom times when people seemingly get hired simply because they have sufficient breath to fog a mirror, in a recession, you may have to compete with fifty or five hundred or even five thousand other candidates for a job. And to no one's surprise, the better the job, the tougher the competition.

I once heard a U.S. soldier fighting in Afghanistan say, "We don't want a fair fight." I routinely share this very quote and concept with clients when helping them to develop their job search and interviewing skills. In particular, I urge them to leverage their superior training, coaching, and the interactive technology of the Navigator Institute to beat out all the less prepared candidates vying for the jobs they want. This includes embracing all of the seventy Durfee's Laws and the three essentials set forth in Chapter 6: discipline, practice, and commitment. And as in a military campaign, superior intelligence—in this case, knowledge based on research of prospective employers and their interviewers—can be an invaluable asset for helping clients achieve their objectives.

PLAN TO PLAY GLOBALLY

As protectionist laws and trade barriers continue to fall to the wayside and foreign businesses set up offices and factories in other countries (including in the U.S.), a competitive advantage exists for those willing to develop international skill sets. In particular, learning another language, another culture, and basic foreign trade and labor laws can greatly enhance one's value to an organization with international owners or partners.

Ron Vaerewyck, a retired human resources executive from Dow Corning Corporation, lived overseas as an expatriate for thirty-two of his thirty-five years of employment. His experiences from having been based in the United Kingdom, Belgium, Germany, France, Australia, and Hong Kong equipped him with some insights that were particularly valuable to the son of a colleague:

> *Jarrod was in his senior year of high school, from which he subsequently graduated as valedictorian. After a short time in our discussion, Jarrod began to share with me his career aspirations. What evolved was a direction that matched not only a personal interest but also encompassed an exposure to global business needs, as he was dead set on learning Japanese and enrolling in courses that would focus on the Japanese market. After many discussions, I encouraged Jarrod to not just focus on this one platform but rather look at where the global dynamics of business were headed. I explained that one of the major markets of today and the future is China. To Jarrod's credit, he undertook extensive research on where the economic action was headed.*
>
> *What eventually evolved is that he enrolled at the Wharton School of Business, where he pursued his education with the eventual linkage to a law degree. And guess what? He headed up the Chinese club and has become fluent in Mandarin. He also spent a summer in Beijing honing his language skills as well as enrolling in courses at universities in both Beijing and Taipei.*

ALWAYS STAY SHARP

While this book offers job search advice for those with an immediate need, it is also important to guard against the complacency that often comes once a seemingly steady job is secured. Keeping your job search skills sharp is especially difficult if you have the good fortune of working for a generous and caring boss in a generous and caring organization. Even in the best-case scenario, however, you should always nurture and grow your network, as you never know when unforeseen events will suddenly show you to the door. More bluntly, it's foolish to think one's status quo is immune from severe disruption in light of the startling economic and industrial transformations already taking place in the new millennium.

From brand-name mega-retailers and once cutting-edge technology companies to manufacturing giants that have helped to change the world, even the most iconic organizations are not immune to the absolute carnage manifested in the forms of mergers, hostile acquisitions, poor management, global competition, and shifting consumer preferences. Those who tenaciously clutch their lunch boxes or company-issued smartphones and rationalize why their jobs are perpetually safe will be the least prepared to launch an effective job search should they someday be proven wrong. Those who make a conscious effort to learn from life's many lessons—their own and others'—will have devoted the time and effort necessary to develop and maintain strong career transition skills. In return, their preparation and motivation will make them effective job finders and attractive job candidates. As a result, they will maneuver the career path maze with much less stress and much greater success.

As for me, I never intended to be an expert in the job search process, yet here I am.

PLEASE REMEMBER THIS

Some of the key lessons in this chapter include:

- ✔ The new reality is that job security, pensions, and lifetime employment are now mostly vestiges of the past, a fact that represents a rude awakening for those longing for more stable and predictable career paths.

- ✔ Once a disparaging term, "job-hopping" is no longer applicable or relevant as the frequency of job eliminations have made numerous job changes increasingly unavoidable.

✔ The Agile Model® places a heavy emphasis on anticipating change by staying alert for changing business conditions, marketplace trends, and national and international events.

✔ While it may take time—even years—to realize it, there can be significant personal and professional upsides to an unwanted job change.

✔ Online social networking sites and smartphones allow job seekers to instantly solicit leads and assistance from thousands of contacts.

✔ More diversity, outsourcing, globalization, and emerging jobs in health care, education, and technology are in store for the future.

✔ A continual commitment to education, training, and job search skills is essential for anyone wishing to compete for employment opportunities in the highly dynamic and rapidly changing macro work environments of today and tomorrow.

"Live in each season as it passes; breathe the air, drink the drink, taste the fruit, and resign yourself to the influences of each."

HENRY DAVID THOREAU (1817–1862)
AUTHOR AND PHILOSOPHER

ACKNOWLEDGMENTS

Writing a book is a daunting task in its own right. Finding an agent and publisher who believe it belongs on the shelves of bookstores is nearly as challenging. Accordingly, I extend my sincerest appreciation to Linda Konner, my literary agent, who had confidence in me as a first-time author and both coached me and represented me to the publishing community. I would also like to recognize for their support and guidance the very talented and kind staff at Agate Publishing, including, but not limited to, Doug Seibold, Rachel Hinton, Jessica Easto, Marta Evans, Morgan Krehbiel, Susan Vandagriff, and Eileen Johnson. In addition, I would like to thank Ann Trovillion, my high school English teacher, whose unwavering expectation for perfection instilled in me the confidence to become a writer.

Although I have vast and multidimensional experience with career transitions, I never intended this book to be just about me. I am fortunate, therefore, to have an abundance of friends and family whose contributions have made this book richer and more valuable. For their assistance, I would like to thank Barbara Wilcox, Barry Ogle, Bert Garcia, Bill Cooke, Bill Dehart, Bill Horn, Bob Ravener, Brad Simmons, Brandon Widman, Catherine Mrowiec, Cecelia Gonzalez, Cherie Rivett, Chris Knipp, Chuck Snearly, Corey Heller, Dan Barr, Dan Carricato, Dan Hahn, Dave Gallagher, Dave Loeser, Dave Rowe, Dave Spear, David Polansky, Diane Maner, Dick Koch, Dion Kiernan, Doug Peddie, Duane Jones, Franz Hanning, Gabe Lazzaro, Garry Randall, Gary Mescher, Irma Moreno, J. Robert Gould, Jan Cannon, Jeff Carroll, Jeff Reeves, Jeff Schimberg, Jerry Durfee, Jr., Jerry Durfee, Sr., Jerry McGrath, Jim Berk, Jim Durfee,

Jim Lynde, Jim Whitaker, JoAnne Kruse, Joe Davis, Joe Filimon, Joe Gonzalez, John Delpino, John Faix, John Hill, John Sprouls, Jon Knotts, Julie Erlenmeyer, Kent Keoppel, Kevin Anderson, Kevin Larabee, Kevin McPhee, Kim Marshall, Laura Durfee, Laurie Weitz, Leon Lachance, Mark Servodidio, Mary Ellen Russell, Mike Bloomfield, Mike Grennier, Mitch Parnell, Nancy Geraghty, Nick Horney, Nick McLaren, Noel Ferguson, Pat Deering, Pat Walker, Paul Prewitt, Ray Stitle, Rick Larson, Roe Sie, Roger Green, Ron Vaerewyck, Ron Wilensky, Ryan Franse, Sarah King, Scott Cline, Scott Steiger, Scott Westerman, Steve Durfee, Steve Mitchell, Steve Nellis, Steve Steury, Sue Gladstone, Susan Chadick, Tami Mann, Tim Arnst, Toby Unwin, Tom Damewood, Tom DeLuca, Tom Jones, Tommie Kennedy, Tressa Lamm, Vern Horstman, Vic Benoit, and Wendell Gustafson.

And to all of my former employers who eliminated my jobs—all is forgiven.

NOTES

CHAPTER 1

1. Elisabeth Kübler-Ross, M.D., *On Death and Dying*, (New York: Simon & Schuster/Touchstone, 1969).

2. Mental Health America, Mental Health America attitudinal survey, Part 1: Findings on stress in America, 2006 (Alexandria, VA).

3. Your local Small Business Administration office or government employment office should also be able to provide you with information on free or subsidized training programs (visit www.sba.gov).

CHAPTER 2

1. Mika Kivimaki, PhD; Jane E. Ferrie, PhD; Eric Brunner, PhD; Jenny Head, MS; Martin J. Shipley, MS; Jussi Vahtera, MD, PhD; Michael G. Marmot, FRCP, "Justice at Work and Reduced Risk of Coronary Heart Disease Among Employees: The Whitehall II Study," *Archives of Internal Medicine* 165, no. 19 (October 24, 2005)

CHAPTER 3

1. What makes the inaccuracies in George O'Leary's resume all the more unsettling is those claims were not germane to the decision to offer him the position at Notre Dame. Personifying redemption, accountability, and perseverance, however, O'Leary accepted full responsibility for his actions and upon being hired a few years later as the head football coach at the University of Central Florida, transformed the program to national prominence both on the field and in terms of student-athlete academic performance.

CHAPTER 3 (CONT.)

2.   A bond is essentially an insurance policy to protect employers from the actions of their employees.

3.   This approach does not always work with online applications, including on-site employment kiosks.

4.   I used to get so annoyed by my staffing departments' carelessness with paper applications that I required them to circle key responses like this with red ink to ensure they had been thoroughly reviewed.

CHAPTER 6

1.   A formal interview differs from an informal interview in that the intention of a formal interview is clearly and openly communicated up front as being a significant part of the overall selection process. Informal interviews are casual and usually conversational in approach, and candidates may lose sight of the fact that they are actually being evaluated.

2.   Many recruiters will tell you that their employers or clients, in the case of headhunters, only consider them as good as their last hire.

3.   Roger hired me in 1986 when he was the Senior Vice President of Human Resources for the Stouffer Hotels & Resorts Company and left shortly after Nestlé sold the business to Renaissance Hotels in 1993. He took me under his wing, kicked me in the ass when I needed it (which was quite often), and immersed me in the international labor arena. He even arranged for my temporary duty with the U.S. State Department to serve as the U.S. delegate for a United Nations/International Labor Organization conference in Geneva, Switzerland, in 1990 and 1991. He also sent me to Mexico for an integration project for several months in 1991 and 1992 when we acquired seven El Presidente hotels and resorts.

4.   Successful candidates typically said they would have Mrs. Smith call a 24-hour plumbing service with the assurance that the homebuilder would reimburse her for the service call.

5.   The answer is that a round cover is the only shape that cannot fall into a manhole of the same shape. Questions such as this and others can be found in the book, *How Would You Move Mount Fuji?* by William Poundstone (New York: Little, Brown and Company, 2003).

6.   There is a joke that a not-so-bright candidate responded to this question with, "Gee, I guess I'd prefer to talk to the live one."

CHAPTER 7

1. I admit there have been times when my imperfections as an interviewer were evident. Catherine Mrowiec, currently the General Manager of the JW Marriott hotel in downtown Chicago, reminded me over breakfast a few years ago about the time when I first interviewed her for a job with the company. Sometime during the interview, I allegedly started playing with a rubber cockroach that I kept in my desk and sometimes used to help change the atmosphere in the office whenever the stress level got too high. I can't recall what would have possessed me to do that during our interview, but Catherine kept her composure and didn't bring it up again until that breakfast—more than twenty-five years later.

2. Jeff Nichols is not his real name.

CHAPTER 9

1. Given the widespread lack of internal resources and expertise necessary to effectively support the assimilation of new leaders, Navigator Executive Advisors offers a proven service that shortens the typical ramp-up time by as much as six months. For more information on how to greatly improve the odds a new leader will succeed in his or her new role, please visit the Navigator Executive Advisors website at www.navexec.com and click on New Leadership Transition.

2. Stephen R. Covey, *The 7 Habits of Highly Effective People*, (New York: Free Press, 1989), 237.

3. With the exception of those who come to us because of large downsizings, most of the clients in outplacement with my firm are with us not because of poor performance or misconduct but because they did not have their immediate boss's sponsorship.

4. Dale Carnegie, *How to Win Friends & Influence People*, (New York: Simon & Schuster, 1981), 113.

5. As the character Major Frank Burns on the iconic television show *M*A*S*H* once blurted out, "It's nice to be nice to the nice."

CHAPTER 10

1. As a member of the senior executive team, I regularly received calls from headhunters for some really attractive jobs that I declined precisely because there was no way I could afford to walk away from millions of dollars in unvested stock options. The same held true for my colleagues.

2. While it varies depending on the reference, the baby boom generation is generally referred to anyone born in the U.S. from 1946 to 1964.

CHAPTER 10 (CONT.)

3.   Dr. Jean Twenge, *Generation Me: Why Today's Young Americans Are More Confident, Assertive, Entitled—and More Miserable Than Ever Before*, (New York: Free Press, 2006).

4.   There's plenty of evidence to suggest their fears are well founded. *Parade* magazine (November 22, 2009) cited several sources, including the Heritage Foundation and Urban Institute, in a report that pointed out in 1960 there were 5.1 workers supporting every retiree, and in 2030, that number will drop to 2.2 workers. Combined with the recessionary impact that is forcing older unemployed workers into early retirement, *Parade* reported Social Security is predicted to "reach insolvency in 30 years"—which is when generation Xers and millennials will become eligible to for the benefit. A report by Theodore J. Sarenski posted on the American Institute of CPAs website states the federal government is projecting that the Social Security Trust Fund could run out of cash by 2033.

5.   One of the reasons for the Navigator Institute's success with individuals (www.navinstitute.com) and corporate clients (www.navexec.com) is the interactive online learning system enables terminated employees to effectively launch their job searches immediately after notification. In contrast, it is not uncommon for the old national outplacement firms to make recently terminated employees wait several days or even weeks before their traditional office-based approach begins rendering job search assistance.

6.   Etan Horowitz, "Lose your job? Tell your Facebook, Twitter friends," *Orlando Sentinel*, (April 21, 2009).

7.   I personally experienced this for the first of many times in my career in December 1996 when the headhunter seeking to fill the position of Director of Human Resources for the Philadelphia Coca-Cola Bottling Company told me I could not be considered for the job because I'm white.

8.   This point hit home, literally, when my parents once told me they would have been financially set for retirement except for the fact that they were living longer than they had expected.

9.   U.S. Bureau of Labor Statistics, Earnings and unemployment rates by educational attainment, Current Population Survey (March 24, 2014).

10. Philip Elliott, "W.H. report: 95,000 jobs monthly," Associated Press, (February 11, 2010).

INDEX OF DURFEE'S LAWS

51. Leverage the signing bonus, page 193

52. Use your research, page 193

53. Google yourself, page 144

54. Know your resume, page 145

55. Identify references early, page 90

56. Delay for more pay, page 193

57. Establish lots of references, page 91

58. Hide the frustration, page 220

59. Remember that meals are not about food and drink, page 182

60. Hold the comparisons, page 220

61. Thank the interviewer, page 182

62. Apologize, page 220

63. Add a Linkedin profile badge, page 75

64. Propose a six-month review, page 194

65. Avoid the prima donna label, page 220

66. Be thankful, page 220

67. Help headhunters (search firms) before you need help, page 91

68. Omit and protect, page 75

69. If it's not your fault, it's not your fault, page 28

70. Have a backup plan, page 41

INDEX

ABOUT THE AUTHOR AND CONTRIBUTOR

MATT DURFEE is the founder and president of Navigator Executive Advisors, Inc. and the Navigator Institute, two career services firms providing outplacement, executive search, and leadership development support to global employers and individual clients. Prior to launching the firms in 2006, Matt held chief human resources officer, senior vice president, vice president, and human resources management positions in a number of the world's most admired companies including Pepsi, Hard Rock Cafe, Frito-Lay International, Bank One, Nestlé, Coca-Cola Enterprises, and Marriott International. He earned his master's degree in human resources and labor relations from Michigan State University. His national newspaper columns for American City Business Journals, Navigating Your Job Search and Coach's Corner, appeared in 40 major US markets. He lives in Orlando, Florida.

WILLIAM N. COOKE, PhD, is a professor at and director of Michigan State University's School of Human Resources and Labor Relations. He received his PhD from the University of Illinois in 1977 and has served on the faculty at the University of Michigan, Purdue University, and Wayne State University. He also held visiting faculty positions at Cornell University and the University of California–Berkeley. He currently serves as Chair of the University Council of IR and HR Programs, LERA. He is the author of numerous articles and several books about multinational companies and their global HR/LR strategies. He lives in East Lansing, Michigan.